The Metacognitive Student

How to Teach
Academic, Social, and
Emotional Intelligence
in Every Content Area

Richard K. Cohen   Deanne Kildare Opatosky   James Savage
Susan Olsen Stevens   Edward P. Darrah

Foreword by Maurice J. Elias

Solution Tree | Press

a division of
Solution Tree

555 North Morton Street
Bloomington, IN 47404
800.733.6786 (toll free) / 812.336.7700
FAX: 812.336.7790

email: info@SolutionTree.com

SolutionTree.com

Visit **go.SolutionTree.com/instruction** to download the free reproducibles in this book.

Printed in the United States of America

Library of Congress Cataloging-in-Publication Data

Names: Cohen, Richard K., author.
Title: The metacognitive student : how to teach academic, social, and
    emotional intelligence in every content area / Richard K. Cohen, Deanne
    Kildare Opatosky, James Savage, Susan Olsen Stevens, Edward P. Darrah.
Description: Bloomington, Indiana : Solution Tree Press, [2021] | Includes
    bibliographical references and index.
Identifiers: LCCN 2021001749 (print) | LCCN 2021001750 (ebook) | ISBN
    9781951075033 (Paperback) | ISBN 9781951075040 (eBook)
Subjects: LCSH: Metacognition in children. | Affective education. | Social
    intelligence. | Emotional intelligence. | Academic achievement. |
    Mathematics--Study and teaching. | Reading comprehension--Study and
    teaching. | Social sciences--Study and teaching. | Science--Study and
    teaching.
Classification: LCC LB1050.2 .C644 2021 (print) | LCC LB1050.2 (ebook) |
    DDC 370.15/34--dc23
LC record available at https://lccn.loc.gov/2021001749
LC ebook record available at https://lccn.loc.gov/2021001750

Solution Tree
Jeffrey C. Jones, CEO
Edmund M. Ackerman, President

Solution Tree Press
President and Publisher: Douglas M. Rife
Associate Publisher: Sarah Payne-Mills
Art Director: Rian Anderson
Managing Production Editor: Kendra Slayton
Copy Chief: Jessi Finn
Senior Production Editor: Todd Brakke
Content Development Specialist: Amy Rubenstein
Copy Editor: Mark Hain
Proofreader: Kate St. Ives
Text and Cover Designer: Laura Cox
Editorial Assistants: Sarah Ludwig and Elijah Oates

Acknowledgments

This book stems from the incredible work of Dr. Maurice J. Elias and his colleagues. Thank you, Dr. Elias, for serving as an incredible role model of academic, social, and emotional intelligence and character and for being so generous with your expertise, guidance, and support. I also wish to acknowledge the Metuchen School District for being such a caring and inclusive community, and I give thanks to those who lead it: the Metuchen Board of Education and superintendent Dr. Vincent Caputo, who is an exceptional champion of whole child education and district leadership. Thank you to the Metuchen School District staff, especially Moss School, for their tireless work to support every student through everything this world throws at them. Thank you, Dr. Robin Fogarty and Brian Pete for all your mentorship. I also wish to acknowledge my SWATT students for teaching so many kids how to make good decisions; a special shout out to Josh Sanchez and Dominic Quema for all they taught me.

To the dream teamers, James, Sue, Deanne, and Eddie, thank you for being such an inspiring group of educators, leaders, and colleagues. We would all like to express our gratitude to Douglas Rife, Amy Rubenstein, Todd Brakke, and everyone at Solution Tree for their exceptional insights and professionalism.

Finally, I would like to thank my parents for giving me everything; my sister, Lonni, for always being there to help guide me; my wife, Camila; and children, Sarah, Benny, and Sofia for helping make the "Ricky process" real.

—Rick

I wish to thank all stakeholders at Metuchen School District, especially superintendent Dr. Vincent Caputo and assistant superintendent and coauthor Rick Cohen. Rick invited me on this amazing once-in-a-lifetime journey, which has proven to be the most rewarding professional and personal experience. I offer a special thank you to the Metuchen teachers who opened their classroom doors and welcomed me into their educational communities to experiment with SELf-questioning lessons.

My sincerest gratitude to Dr. Joseph Corriero and Dr. Lourdes Zaragoza Mitchel, who have always pushed me to step outside of my comfort zone and encouraged me to reach a larger audience beyond the classroom walls. As mentors, both made an everlasting impact on my understanding and commitment to collaboration, reflection, and lifelong learning.

Finally, none of this would have been possible without the support of my entire family, especially my loving parents and my devoted husband, Brian, who listened to every struggle and shared every success. I am forever indebted to you for your patience and understanding of my commitment to this journey, which included picking up many of our parenting responsibilities on your own. And to my children, Aiden, Liam, Colin, and Aubrey, who were and always will be my first and most important students. While this book teaches the importance of utilizing SELf-questioning, know you never need to question, nor could you possibly understand the depths of how much I love and appreciate you.

—Deanne

I'd like to thank my colleagues and coteachers at George Mason University and INTO Mason for their teamwork, tireless dedication to excellence in education, and their wonderful ideas and lessons. Our work together is the inspiration behind many of my contributions to this book. In particular, I'd like to thank Anna Habib for her mentorship and guidance both in teaching and scholarship and Esther Namubiru for helping to pilot structured SELf-questioning with university students. I'd also like to thank two former science teachers at Sheridan School, Adrienne van den Beemt and Kate Grinberg, for inspiring the K–2 science lesson in this book and my cousin Mark Kemler for his contributions to the science chapter as well as his kindness and friendship.

Another big thank you to the team: to Rick for bringing me on board and to Deanne, Sue, and Eddie for your collaborative spirit and openness. It's been wonderful working together.

Finally, thank you to my whole family, especially my wife, Simone, for supporting all my endeavors, big and small, and for helping me find the time. And to our children, Lili, Angie, and Julia. I love you.

—James

My thanks to Rick Cohen. We bonded during a job interview over SELf-questioning to solve reading problems, which led to him bringing me on the team. I'm so appreciative of our team of authors. We spurred each other on to better thinking and better writing. It's been a pleasure. Who would think that five authors could actually cheerfully collaborate with each other?

I'm grateful to Colegio Americano in Quito, Ecuador. The administrators and staff at CAQ taught me the value and purpose of good professional development and lifelong learning as a teacher. InterAmerican Academy in Guayaquil, Ecuador, and Country Day School in Costa Rica helped me develop and practice those skills—I'm so grateful. A special shout out to Rakitia Delk, who pushed my thinking and helped me develop structured SELf-questioning to help with reading decoding and comprehension. And to my students in those schools and others in the United States, you have taught me so much over the years.

Of course, I need to thank my sweet husband, Mike, who supports me in my writing in every possible way.

—Sue

Thank you to my family for your unconditional support and love. A very special thank you to Fr. Philip Lowe for your ongoing mentorship and guidance.

—Eddie

All of us would like to thank the following Metuchen School District teachers for sharing their model lessons: Danielle Movsessian, Robert Ulmer, Alexa Baird, Rachel DiVanno, Lauren Butler, Ann Lezama, Sarah Anderson, Danielle Mauro, Alyssa Polesky, Franchesca Hunt, Brooke Kirschner, Andrea Elton, Sofia Lopes, Stephanie Kandel, Candace Evans, Emily Peluso, and Kathleen Henn. You are all an inspiration!

Solution Tree Press would like to thank the following reviewers:

Kelley Capper
Instructional Coach
Shawnee Mission West High School
Overland Park, Kansas

Joe Cuddemi
Solution Tree Associate
Fort Collins, Colorado

Kristin Ellis
Principal
Wilmeth Elementary School
McKinney, Texas

Teri Gough
Sixth-Grade Teacher
Sundance Elementary School
Los Lunas, New Mexico

Dusti Larsen
Fourth-Grade Teacher
Gravette Upper Elementary
Gravette, Arkansas

Theresa Stager
Assistant Principal
Saline High School
Saline, Michigan

Ringnolda Jofee' Tremain
Assistant Principal
Medlin Middle School
Trophy Club, Texas

Esther Wu
Language Arts Teacher
Mountain View High School
Mountain View, California

Visit **go.SolutionTree.com/instruction** to download the free reproducibles in this book.

Table of Contents

Reproducibles are in italics

About the Authors

Richard K. Cohen is assistant superintendent of Metuchen School District in New Jersey and serves as co-adjunct faculty for Rutgers University in New Brunswick, New Jersey. He is former principal of Red Bank Primary School in Red Bank, New Jersey, a Title I school with a majority English learner–student population, where he led collaborative school improvement efforts resulting in dramatic increases in student proficiencies. Prior to Red Bank, Rick was the founding director of a new bilingual school, Colegio Americano, in San Salvador, El Salvador. Rick began his teaching career as a Teach for America corps member in 1996 in Phoenix, Arizona. Rick's first formal teaching assignment was in juvenile detention centers in Washtenaw County, Michigan, as a University of Michigan Project Community service-learning student facilitator. His professional experiences as an educator range from working in predominantly low-income schools as a middle and high school teacher, to vice-principal and principal for predominantly under-resourced traditional public and charter schools, to a teacher, director, and assistant superintendent of some of the most affluent and high-performing public schools in New Jersey and private schools in El Salvador.

Rick has served as a leader of social-emotional learning (SEL) at the district, county, state, and national levels. His work infusing academic state standards and SEL skills together along with evidence-based character education has won national and state of New Jersey School of Character Awards and a National Promising Practice Award from Character.org. In 2015, Rick also served on the New Jersey State Standards Revision Committee, helping add self-reflection and metacognition into academic state standards. Rick's work has been published in Character.org's *11 Principles Framework for Schools*, Edutopia, and *NJEA Review*'s Great Ideas column. He has provided training on embedding SEL into state standards–aligned curricula throughout the United States as well as served as a presenter on SEL for numerous professional organizations and universities throughout New Jersey.

Rick Cohen received a bachelor's degree in political science from the University of Michigan and a master's degree in educational administration from Rutgers University.

Deanne Kildare Opatosky has worked in the field of education for over twenty years. Since 2010, as president of BDO Consulting Services, she facilitates extensive professional development for both novice and experienced teachers in urban and suburban settings throughout New Jersey. Through the sustained, targeted, differentiated, and job-embedded support she provides, many districts confirm that her work directly impacts student achievement, often yielding high, data-backed growth.

Deanne began her career as a classroom teacher in Valhalla, New York, in 1997 and taught literacy courses at the graduate level shortly thereafter at the College of New Rochelle. Later, as a literacy coach for Cranford School District in New Jersey, Deanne worked closely with Seton Hall University's Professional Development School to simultaneously support both district K–5 teachers and undergraduate students by teaching on-site literacy courses that focused on how to implement research-based best practices. She also developed the school's literacy curriculum and taught coursework for the Alternate Route Teacher Program at the Morris-Union Jointure Commission. Deanne has provided staff development to diverse populations, including underperforming low-income public school districts through her work with Seton Hall University's Academy for Urban School Transformation, as well as affluent private schools such as The American School in Switzerland and in Puerto Rico.

Deanne has presented at local, state, and national levels, including her annual workshop at the Regional Professional Development Academy in New Jersey. Deanne presented at the National Association for Professional Development Schools in Las Vegas, Nevada and Orlando, Florida. She co-presented with Rick Cohen at the New Jersey Principals and Supervisors Association Empower Conference on integrating social-emotional learning (SEL) and standards-based curricula using structured SELf-questioning. She also provided extensive training on how to effectively and efficiently integrate SEL into literacy instruction in Metuchen, New Jersey. The successful impact of her collaborative work was published in *PDS Partners Magazine* and referenced in *NJEA Review*'s Great Ideas column.

Deanne graduated magna cum laude from the honors program at Pace University in Pleasantville, New York, with a bachelor of science in education. She also graduated summa cum laude with a master of science in teaching reading from The College of New Rochelle in New Rochelle, New York.

James Savage is a term assistant professor of English at George Mason University in Fairfax, Virginia. He teaches writing courses while pursuing a PhD in writing and rhetoric, and his research interests include metacognition and transfer, language justice, and the rhetoric of memory. James has taught academic writing to undergraduate and graduate international students as part of a joint venture between INTO University Partnerships and George Mason. He also served as the course liaison between the English department and INTO Mason, where he helped to develop curricula, onboard new faculty, and co-coordinate various undergraduate courses. James has over twenty years experience as an educator in various contexts, including as a seventh-grade English teacher in Phoenix, Arizona, and as a high school English teacher in Silver Spring, Maryland.

James's belief in developing problem-solving skills across academic, social, and emotional contexts, as well as his pursuit of language justice for all students, has led him to present several workshops to faculty at George Mason on topics ranging from self-questioning to linguistic noticing. He also helped develop curricula for several discipline-specific graduate-level writing courses.

James received a bachelor's degree in English from the University of Michigan, a master of fine arts in fiction from George Mason University, and a master of arts in liberal arts from St. John's College in Annapolis, Maryland.

Susan Olsen Stevens is an educational consultant in Saint Augustine, Florida. Her teaching experience spans private, public, and international schools, as well as homeschool. Susan's thirty-one years of teaching are roughly divided into halves: she spent one half teaching grades preK–12 art, including AP levels, and the other half teaching grades 3–12 English language arts. Susan served as curriculum coordinator for early childhood through middle school at Country Day School in Costa Rica and was a language arts curriculum team leader at both Country Day School and International American Academy in Guayaquil, Ecuador. Her mission as a teacher is to inspire a joyous exuberance in learning—especially in reading conjoined with writing as a way to learn and communicate important ideas.

Susan has written two educational books: *Dr. Goodreader: Teach Readers How to Diagnose and Cure Reading "Clunks" Through Metacognition* and *The Little Golden Book of Metacognition.* Susan has also given popular professional development workshops and classes on problem solving in reading and writing, metacognition and reading, literacy across the disciplines, and storytelling in the classroom using *Dr. Goodreader.*

Susan graduated from the University of Toledo in Ohio with a bachelor's in education, received a masters in Christian education from Logos University in Jacksonville, Florida, and a masters in literacy from University of New England. She passionately pursues professional learning through her continued reading and the courses she takes.

Edward Darrah is a licensed and certified professional counselor in the state of Pennsylvania and is triple board-certified in counseling, school counseling, and telemental health. He is currently a full-time staff member at Temple University in Philadelphia, Pennsylvania, and serves as a mental health and performance counselor with Temple University athletics. In 2015, Edward founded Edward Darrah Counseling & Athlete Wellness Consulting, LLC, a private practice in Lower Merion, Pennsylvania.

Edward's career in education started in 2010 in Lower Merion School District in Ardmore, Pennsylvania. His extensive training in mental health provided him the opportunity to work within diverse educational settings and a range of student populations. Prior to Temple University, he was employed as a school counselor at Catapult Learning, LLC, working within private and Catholic schools including The Philadelphia School, Visitation BVM Catholic School, and the Waldorf School of Philadelphia.

Edward's professional memberships include the American Counseling Association, Association for Applied Sport Psychology, and American Psychological Association Division 47. He is an advocate for advancing mental health and helping bring awareness to the student-athlete population. In 2018, he was invited to participate as a panelist at the Northeast Atlantic Sport Psychology Conference to discuss athlete wellness. In addition to his clinical work, Edward is a member of the Academic and Student Life Board Committee at Neumann University in Aston Township, Pennsylvania. He is also a Disaster Mental Health volunteer with the Red Cross.

Edward received a bachelor's degree in psychology from Neumann University, a masters in clinical counseling psychology from La Salle University, and a post-masters certificate in school counseling from Immaculata University.

Foreword

by Maurice J. Elias

What do students need to be prepared for their future years in school and their time after graduation? What do they need so they will be properly prepared for college, careers, and civic participation? Answer: they need to become metacognitive students. They need to become adept at sizing up situations, setting goals, making plans, responding effectively to obstacles, and learning from their experiences. In other words, they need to be terrific problem solvers who are guided by good character.

Being metacognitive involves students asking themselves questions about their own thought processes. Some of the most long-standing, evidence-based social-emotional learning programs you will find, such as *I Can Problem Solve* (Shure, 2001) and *Social Decision Making/Social Problem Solving* (Butler, Romasz-McDonald, & Elias, 2011), recognize the need for students to develop problem-solving skills to improve their coping abilities and mental health. But Richard K. Cohen, Deanne Kildare Opatosky, James Savage, Susan Olsen Stevens, and Edward P. Darrah, the authors of *The Metacognitive Student*, understand that this must be a pervasive approach that also embraces academic achievement and character development.

To accomplish this, Rick, Deanne, James, Sue, and Edward offer a simple metacognitive strategy students can learn to engage themselves in self-talk when confronted with a challenging academic, social, or emotional problem. With simple steps that have students *select a focus* (What is the problem?), *gather information* (What do I know?), *brainstorm* (What are possible solutions?), *evaluate* (Does this solution make sense?), *plan and act* (What do I do first, second, and so on?), and *reflect* (Did it work?), they teach students how the simple act of engaging in self-questioning can guide students to success in all of life's challenges.

Step back for a moment and consider the implication of self-questions: they are drivers of science, exploration, public policy, literary accomplishments, arts creativity and performance, and getting along with friends, family, and coworkers. Why have we never before systematically helped students to ask and answer these questions, individually and collaboratively, across academic and life disciplines? Well, that wait is over—*The Metacognitive Student* provides the way forward.

The attraction of this theory- and research-informed book is that it derives from thorough, long-term practice. Anyone setting foot into the schools of Metuchen School District in

New Jersey is treated to creative, thoughtful, and caring students and staff engaged together in the learning enterprise. In every classroom, from kindergarten through high school, you will hear them all ask and appropriately answer metacognitive self-questions. You also will hear these questions used in the counseling room, the hallway, and the lunchroom. The authors have trained numerous other educators in their methods, and, as you will see, they are intuitive and adaptable. Through this book, you and your students will reap the benefits of an accessible metacognitive strategy for self-questioning.

Using this strategy across all of these environments and content areas does more than create synergy. It builds among students the capacity to apply metacognitive thinking and self-questioning to new and unforeseen areas. Think about it. Recent years have guaranteed that the unexpected will occur, events for which a curriculum framework is not available, such as the COVID-19 pandemic and the antiracism marches for social equality and justice. The ability to respond with innovation and resilience must become the norm for students, and this book provides a range of examples that will allow you to develop a strategy for developing metacognitive students.

I return to the questions I asked at the start of this foreword, which summarize best as, How can educators equip students to be prepared for the definite uncertainties of the future? Students need to know how to be emotionally intelligent, academically organized, and confident in themselves and what they can do. They can be all of these things if guided by developmentally sophisticated and systematic self-questioning. Regardless of your role in education or mental health, read this marvelous book to learn how you can give the young people under your influence and care the strategies they will need for success in every aspect of their lives.

Onward!

Maurice J. Elias, PhD, is a professor of psychology at Rutgers University and coauthor of *Boost Emotional Intelligence in Students: 30 Flexible, Research-Based Activities to Build EQ Skills* and *Nurturing Students' Character: Everyday Teaching Activities for Social-Emotional Learning*.

Introduction

The work of promoting the social-emotional and
character development [SECD] of children is an inherent part of an
appropriate education. It is also vital for society. And we know a great
deal about how to accomplish this goal.

—Linda B. Butler, Maurice J. Elias, and Tanya Romasz-McDonald

Imagine for one minute students in every classroom independently coping with their emotions and dealing independently with the emotional and social stressors they come across in daily life. Also imagine that, in the face of difficulty and uncertainty, all students have developed the habit of mind of taking a step back, identifying their feelings, calming themselves down, thinking clearly, and resolving the problems and challenges they encounter in life.

Now, imagine all students transferring those same wonderful habits of mind and social and emotional skill sets to the classroom. Imagine every student—in the face of any academically stressful or overwhelming assignments, projects, tasks, or tests—taking a step back, identifying and calming their emotions, thinking clearly, and solving a wide range of academic problems. Since this takes perseverance, imagine that as well.

Sounds delightful, doesn't it? The question is, How might this even be possible?

Fortunately, as the epigraph for this introduction states, we know a great deal about how to accomplish this seemingly impossible dream. There already exist multiple evidence-based curricula that explicitly and successfully teach all students the social and emotional learning (SEL) competencies envisioned here. These evidence-based SEL curricula teach students how to identify and calm their emotions, self-monitor performance, make responsible decisions, and resolve conflicts.

Data further show that when teachers embed evidence-based SEL curricula and instruction into core curriculum, the benefits are astounding. According to a meta-analysis by education scholars Joseph A. Durlak, Roger P. Weissberg, Allison B. Dymnicki, Rebecca D. Taylor, and Kriston B. Schellinger (2011), teaching SEL competencies has the following benefits for student populations.

- Reduces aggression and emotional distress among students
- Increases helping behaviors at school
- Improves positive attitudes toward self and others
- Increases students' academic performance by 11 percentile points

Another meta-analysis, *Promoting Positive Youth Development Through School-Based Social and Emotional Learning Interventions* (Taylor, Oberle, Durlak, Weissberg, 2017), not only confirms these benefits but also finds the following additional benefits lasted years after programming.

- Increases SEL skill competency and academic performance
- Reduces conduct problems and emotional distress
- Reduces drug use

Perhaps most importantly, the report found that increased SEL competencies were the best predictor of long-term benefits and that these benefits were experienced equally regardless of students' socioeconomic status, race, or zip code (Taylor et al., 2017).

Even though teachers fully understand the benefits of and need for SEL, the challenges they encounter trying to develop their students' SEL skills have been two-fold. The first challenge has been teaching students the habit of mind of taking a step back and independently guiding their own thinking through multi-step problem solving. This involves teaching students to be metacognitive, which is an area very few teachers have learned how to teach. Second, and perhaps the toughest challenge for all teachers, has been finding time. We've worked with many educators who've struggled to balance teaching SEL and academic content, never mind adding metacognition. They've given up hope of finding additional time to embed SEL into core curriculum and instruction. As a result, there exists an SEL curriculum and instruction gap.

Fortunately, in this book, we explain how to teach both SEL and academic core curriculum at the same time using one simple, practical, and evidence-based metacognitive strategy that is applicable to any K–12 classroom and curriculum. In doing so, we demonstrate how easy it is for teachers to embed SEL competencies inherent in coping skills into any state standards–aligned curriculum through one strategy that prompts and guides students' metacognition. This strategy empowers them to take a step back and do a lot of great thinking about their own thinking in any situation. We also provide abundant examples across all subject areas and grade levels of teachers teaching students to use this one metacognitive strategy to solve all kinds of problems with greater confidence, flexibility, and perseverance. Whether at the district, school, or classroom level, you and your colleagues can put this one universal strategy to immediate use.

To get you started, this introduction establishes the concept of core SEL competencies inherent in coping skills, and it introduces you to our metacognitive strategy for SELf-questioning, which is built upon one common framework for problem solving that helps all students be more successful in academic, social, and emotional problem solving. Once you have an initial grounding in this one strategy and framework for all problem solving, along with a detailed explanation for why it's effective, we'll show how we've organized this book's chapters to make teaching students our metacognitive strategy for academics and SEL possible, practical, and effective.

Core SEL Competencies

The Collaborative for Academic, Social, and Emotional Learning (CASEL, n.d.) has a framework built around five core social and emotional learning (SEL) competencies that all teachers can teach and model in a variety of settings so all students can reap the benefits of SEL and live healthier, more successful lives in school and outside of school.

1. **Self-awareness:** The ability to accurately recognize one's own emotions, thoughts, and values; this includes traits such as integrating personal and social identities; identifying personal, cultural, and linguistic assets; and linking feelings, values, and thoughts.

2. **Self-management:** The ability to successfully self-regulate one's emotions, thoughts, and behaviors; this includes traits such as identifying and using stress-management strategies, exhibiting self-discipline and self-motivation, and setting personal and collective goals.

3. **Social awareness:** The ability to take the perspective of others and empathize with them; this includes traits such as showing concern for others' feelings and recognizing situational demands and opportunities.

4. **Responsible decision making:** The ability to make constructive choices about personal behavior and social interactions; this includes traits such as demonstrating curiosity and open-mindedness, recognizing how critical thinking skills are useful both inside and outside of school, identifying solutions for personal and social problems, and anticipating and evaluating the consequences of one's actions.

5. **Relationship skills:** The ability to establish, navigate, and maintain healthy social relationships; this includes traits such as communicating effectively, demonstrating cultural competency, and resolving conflicts constructively.

About SEL competencies, CASEL CEO Karen Niemi (2020) writes:

> When SEL is woven into the daily life of school—from academic instruction to discipline practices—it is more likely to produce the many benefits that research has documented, including the promotion of students' skills and attitudes, improved school climate and long-term academic achievement.

This book focuses on embedding into academic instruction the first four of the core SEL competencies and skills. These are the competencies all students need to be able to independently calm their emotions, think clearly, make responsible decisions, and successfully cope with the challenges and stressors of daily life inside and outside of school.

The Structured SELf-Questioning Framework

Now that we've established the concept of core SEL competencies and acknowledged the SEL curriculum and instruction gap, we'll show that educators can teach these competencies and close this gap through the use of one simple metacognitive framework and strategy, which we call *structured SELf-questioning*. To do so, let's consider what we know so far about the problem between the importance of SEL and the challenge of implementing it alongside academic instruction.

If we, as educators, have the evidence-based SEL curricula and instructional programs that empower students to develop core SEL competencies and skills, and we know how incredible the benefits are for students academically, socially, and emotionally, why aren't all students learning these SEL skills? To explain how we answered this question, let's put our framework for structured SELf-questioning to work by illustrating how it facilitates taking a step back and engaging in complex multi-step problem solving. In this example, you'll see how it guides our collective self-talk through a multi-step, real-world academic, social, and emotional issue. Here's how it works.

- **Select a focus:** What is the problem? What is the question? What is the task?
- **Gather information:** What do we know? What do we need to know? What is similar, and what is different?
- **Brainstorm:** How can we solve this problem? What are possible solutions? What can we do?
- **Evaluate:** What is the best way to solve this problem? Does this make sense?
- **Plan and act:** What do we do first, second, and so on? Does this work? Is this working?
- **Reflect:** Did it work? How do we know? Do we need to go back and try again.

This simple process reflects our strategy for structured SELf-questioning, and it's adaptable to any content or context, which you will learn more and more about as you read this book.

Select a Focus

This step asks the questions: *What is the problem? What is the question? What is the task?*

Even before the 2020 global pandemic, mental health concerns among students were at an all-time high. Research and polling support the conclusion that more and more students come to school with increasing levels of stress and anxiety. A Pew survey finds 70 percent of teens consider anxiety and depression a major problem among their peers (Horowitz & Graf, 2019). According to another poll of tens of thousands of high school students conducted by the social media app After School, "Today's teenagers view stress as a major component of their lives" (Collins, 2018). The poll further indicates another troubling statistic: "over one-third of teens (34.53%) responded that they do 'nothing' to try to manage their stress" (Collins, 2018). This is likely because adolescents don't yet have the tools they need to manage such stress.

Stress left unchecked or ineffectively addressed can lead to serious health concerns, including mental health disorders, and the rate of mental health disorders for students is at an all-time high. According to the National Alliance on Mental Health (n.d.), "Approximately 1 in 5 youth aged 13–18 (21.4%) experiences a severe mental disorder at some point during their life." Stress, especially stress left unaddressed, also has numerous negative impacts on student learning. In an interview for *EdWeek*, Anthony Cody (2011) talks to education researcher Catharine Warner about the effects of stress on learning; Warner states:

> Our findings indicate that stress in the classroom environment affects children's likelihood of exhibiting learning problems (difficulties with attentiveness, task persistence, and flexibility), externalizing problems (frequency with which the child argues, fights, disturbs ongoing activities, and acts impulsively), problems interacting with peers (difficulties in forming friendships, dealing with other children, expressing feelings, and showing sensitivity, or internalizing problems (presence of anxiety, loneliness, low self-esteem, and sadness in the child). These findings suggest that stress—in the form of negative classroom conditions—negatively affects the way children pay attention in class, stay on task, and are able to move from one activity to another.

Data, research, and polling all show that student stress leads to a downward spiral for students' academic, social, and emotional well-being. We also know that interventions have been very successful in prevention and recovery.

Students are not the only ones who are experiencing high stress levels. Talk to educators, and they'll tell you that with each year that passes, they feel as if they have to do and give more than ever before. And this was before the stressors of global pandemic, social unrest, and remote learning. According to a Gallup (2014) poll, 46 percent of teachers "report high daily stress during the school year" (p. 24). That's tied with nurses for the highest stress rate among all occupational groups in the report. One of the top reasons for teacher stress identified in the issue brief *Teacher Stress and Health* is "job demands" (Greenberg, Brown, & Abenavoli, 2016, p. 2). Therefore, the unfortunate catch with asking teachers to teach SEL competencies is that tasking teachers with adding evidence-based SEL curriculum and instruction to their already overwhelming daily demands often creates more stress and anxiety than it reduces.

In 2011, CASEL orchestrated a national survey, *The Missing Piece*, which finds "nearly all teachers (93 percent) believe SEL is very or fairly important for the in-school student experience . . . and nearly all teachers (95 percent) believe social and emotional skills are teachable" (Bridgeland, Bruce, & Hariharan, n.d., p. 5). Although these are very encouraging numbers, the survey results also show "a majority of teachers (81 percent) rank time as the biggest challenge to implementing SEL" (Bridgeland et al., n.d., p. 8). A more recent national survey finds that nearly two-thirds of teachers surveyed say they "need more time than they currently have to teach SEL skills" (McGraw-Hill Education, 2018, p. 6). Social worker, psychotherapist, and psychology instructor Amy Morin (2017) accurately states the scope of this issue: "We emphasize academic preparation and put little effort into teaching kids the emotional skills they need to succeed. . . . Without healthy coping skills, it's no wonder teens are feeling anxious over everyday hassles."

As a result, a nationwide gap in SEL curriculum and instruction prevents schools and teachers from utilizing one of the most effective solutions available to address one of the biggest challenges facing teachers, students, and families.

So, there's our problem (our focus), and it's *complicated*. But we've managed to boil it down to relatively simple concepts in rising student and teacher stress levels and a lack of instructional time needed to help both groups cope while improving academic achievement.

Gather Information

This step asks the questions: *What do we know? What do we need to know? What is similar, and what is different?*

As you are about to read, there are strong similarities between SEL and academic learning, especially in the area of teaching flexibility and persistence in problem solving. Teaching students coping skills and flexibility means teaching self-awareness and self-management of one's own emotions and abilities to manage them. For students to have coping flexibility, they need to be aware of the coping strategies they have at their disposal and the ability to use them strategically. They also need to manage how they apply these coping strategies and how well the strategies are working. The same is true in academic success. Teaching cognitive flexibility means teaching self-awareness and self-management of one's own cognitive (or critical-thinking) and problem-solving skills and managing the application of these skills.

Therefore, let's first gather some information about the importance of teaching persistent social and emotional problem solving skills, coping strategies, and academic learning strategies.

Teaching Persistent Social and Emotional Problem Solving

According to John T. Brentar (2018), executive director of the Morrissey-Compton Educational Center, one strategy to teaching coping skills is to teach students positive *self-talk* (literally talking oneself through something). In *Student Stress and Anxiety: Is the American Educational System at Fault?*, Brentar (n.d.) reports:

> A study done at Yale University found that 25% of teens between the ages of 13 and 17 met the criteria for an anxiety disorder as compared to 7% of Australian teens in this same age range. Another study funded by the Robert Wood Johnson Foundation found that 40% of parents report that their high schooler is experiencing significant levels of stress. Similarly, a survey by the American Psychological Association found that 45% of the teens they surveyed felt stressed by school pressures. The Chicago Tribune reported earlier this year that at one high-achieving suburban Chicago high school, the number of students participating in individual or group counseling rose from 35% in 2010 to 75% in 2017. (p. 1)

It's unlikely the 2020 global pandemic did anything to alleviate these grim numbers. One thing that has not changed during the pandemic or after it ends is what we know we can do about it. Brentar (2018) concludes by saying, "It is important for students to develop good coping strategies through a variety of techniques including positive self-talk" (p. 4), and we believe this remains true.

We've seen several teachers react with skepticism to the idea of teaching positive self-talk. While teaching positive self-talk may sound complex, even unrealistic, psychologists have already designed and tested curricula that successfully teach students how to guide their self-talk through the core SEL competencies inherent in coping skills and in developing as persistent social problem solvers. Prominent psychology researchers Linda B. Butler, Tanya Romasz-McDonald, and Maurice J. Elias (2011) write in their evidence-based SEL resource *Social Decision Making / Social Problem Solving, Grades K–1* that teaching early childhood students how to be persistent social and emotional problem solvers and decision makers can be accomplished by arming them with a single overall strategy for guided self-talk. Elias, who encouraged us to write this book, has seen firsthand what amazing things students can do when they receive opportunities to practice a strategy for guided self-talk "in the context of a variety of hypothetical, age-appropriate, and open-ended choice and conflict situations" (Butler et al., 2011, p. 4).

This book expands on the considerable research base we've written about throughout these sections to show how effectively any teacher can teach any K–12 student how to guide their self-talk through social, emotional, and academic problem solving in any context. Further, this book shows how teachers can do this without the need for additional instructional time.

Teaching Coping Strategies

According to the Anxiety and Depression Association of America (ADAA, n.d.), anyone can learn to reduce the impact of stress. One intervention teachers can provide students to help reduce stress is to teach the SEL competencies and skills inherent in coping skills. *Coping skills* are the strategies people use to manage stressful situations and take action, as well as be flexible and persistent in solving problems (National Cancer Institute, n.d.).

Many students learn at school a variety of coping strategies to help calm themselves down in times of stress. In 2020, schools across North America and around the world taught students in their classrooms or remotely in their homes coping strategies like deep breathing, mindfulness practices, counting to five or ten, and physical exercises like yoga. However, many students still struggle to cope independently with the emotional and social stressors they face in their daily lives. In other words, students often lack the ability to independently identify and apply an appropriate coping strategy to help them stay calm, think clearly, and resolve conflicts without help from an adult.

Teaching all students the coping skills they need to live healthy, well-adjusted lives in school and outside of school means teaching them more than just coping strategies for self-calming. For more students to be capable of independently coping with a wide range of situations, they need an additional ability—*coping flexibility*. This is the ability to discontinue an ineffective coping strategy and select, produce, and implement an alternative coping strategy, one better suited to the unique issue or situation (Kato, 2012). Without coping flexibility, students often struggle to apply their coping skills and strategies independently and effectively over time. With coping flexibility, students are empowered to maximize the coping skills and strategies they have learned and apply them with independence anywhere, any time. Teaching students our structured SELf-questioning framework helps them develop coping flexibility.

Teaching Academic Learning Strategies

We know from experience that, as with coping strategies, teachers are teaching their students a wide range of academic strategies and that students also struggle to use their academic strategies with flexibility and independence. For example, many teachers teach students numerous reading strategies for decoding and comprehension. But too often, when reading text independently, many students struggle to make the best use of their learned strategies. Or, when approaching a mathematics word problem, students have learned a variety of mental mathematics strategies but still struggle to apply the best one for the word problem in front of them without prompting from the teacher. Sometimes students simply lack the confidence to apply their strategies. Although teaching students a variety of reading decoding strategies, reading comprehension strategies, or mental mathematics strategies is valuable, when students only learn these strategies in individual, siloed academic disciplines, they don't develop the cognitive flexibility they need to make optimal use of their academic strategies.

One way to define *cognitive flexibility* is one's ability to switch between different mental sets and strategies (Archambeau & Gevers, 2018). Without cognitive flexibility, students often don't know which of their various learned academic strategies to apply. With cognitive flexibility, students can self-monitor and self-reflect to independently determine if a particular reading strategy, such as looking at picture clues, is really helping them understand the text. Or, as time goes on and the books students read at school include fewer and fewer pictures, students with cognitive flexibility can self-monitor and self-reflect to determine if it is time for them to apply a different reading strategy, like making inferences by using what they know from the text and their own background knowledge.

Students need coping flexibility to maximize their coping strategies and to independently deal with and cope with emotional and social stressors. Students also need cognitive flexibility to maximize their academic strategy-based curricula and instruction and apply strategies with greater independence and accuracy. Teaching students our approach to structured SELf-questioning helps them develop both coping and cognitive flexibility by teaching all students how to be strategic about their strategies.

Brainstorming

This step asks the questions: *How can we solve this problem? What are possible solutions? What can we do?*

With plenty of information about our problem, the next step is to brainstorm solutions. One nuance to teaching students flexibility and persistence within this vital problem-solving skill is to stress the importance of coming up with more than one possible solution to any problem or decision. This isn't always possible, but in this case, the evidence-based SEL gap is complex, so we came up with three possible solutions for how teachers can teach all students how to be flexible thinkers and persistent problem solvers within the confines of existing curricula: (1) teach all students metacognition, (2) link thinking skills, and (3) achieve transfer. The following sections explore each of these.

Teach All Students Metacognition

As you will learn more about in chapter 1, *metacognition* is really about self-awareness and self-management of one's own thinking. If awareness and management make up three of the four SEL competencies we focus on in this book (self- and social awareness and self-management), then teaching metacognition is a perfect fit for developing flexible, strategic, and autonomous thinkers.

We've seen several teachers react with skepticism to the idea of embedding and teaching metacognition as well as competencies such as self-awareness and self-management. For many teachers, it sounds overly complex and unrealistic, especially without extensive training. However, consider the following factors, derived from what we've written so far.

- Metacognition goes hand in hand with SEL and academics.

- Metacognitive strategies can be taught and learned (Lai, 2011; Wilson & Conyers, 2016).

- Metacognition improves "the application of knowledge, skills, and character qualities in realms beyond the immediate context in which they were learned" (Fidel, Bialik, & Trilling, 2015, p. 146).

As educators and future authors, all five of us were excited about the potential of teaching metacognition as a strategy to close the gap between the teaching of self-awareness and teaching social awareness and self-management, while simultaneously and dramatically improving student academic achievement.

Link Thinking Skills

Butler and colleagues (2011) recommend embedding their evidence-based SEL curricula into academics by linking social-emotional cognitive skills to academic cognitive skills. Since teachers perceive they do not have the time to teach evidence-based SEL curricula, we propose the reverse. Our approach is for teachers to teach the cognitive skills within academic state standards and curricula, and then link those academic cognitive skills to social-emotional cognitive skills. This linking of cognitive skills and processes is an evidence-based practice that we find closes the gap between best instructional practices for academic state and provincial standards and evidence-based SEL. With permission and encouragement from Maurice Elias, one of the authors of Butler and colleagues (2011), we came up with a way to embed their evidence-based SEL curriculum into core academic instruction that no longer requires additional time to teach the evidence-based SEL curriculum.

The evidence-based SEL curricula that successfully teaches students to be persistent, responsible decision-makers is built on social-emotional, problem-solving, and decision-making processes. These involve a long laundry list of higher-order cognitive skills (such as identifying, analyzing, evaluating, reflecting, and so on). Consider the core SEL competency of responsible decision-making, which uses the exact same higher-order cognitive skills familiar to any educator to challenge students to make responsible decisions: *identifying, recognizing, analyzing, evaluating, and reflecting* (CASEL, n.d.). Review any state or provincial standards across content areas, and you'll see the exact same or very similar terms. Through this alignment, or linking, of thinking skills, it is possible to bridge the gap between evidence-based SEL curriculum and academic thinking and decision making without the need for additional instructional time.

To give just a few examples of how the thinking skills within academic state or provincial standards naturally link with the thinking skills of social and emotional processes, here is an example from kindergarten. Students in kindergarten are almost always learning and applying in some form or another the cognitive verb (thinking skill) of *identifying*. In reading, teachers frequently ask kindergarten students about "*identifying* the sounds of the letters" (from the CCSS standard RF.K.3.D; National Governors Association [NGA] & Council of Chief State School Officers [CCSSO], 2010a) and to "*identify* characters, settings, and major events in a story" (RL.K.3; NGA & CCSSO, 2010a). In mathematics, those same kindergarteners learn to "*identify* whether the number of objects in one group is greater than, less than, or equal" (K.CC.C.6; NGA & CCSSO, 2010b). In Butler and colleagues (2011), Elias's social and emotional problem-solving processes also entail the cognitive verb of identifying: *identifying* (or *recognizing*) feelings and *identifying* the problem.

Although the thinking skill of identifying varies slightly between English language arts (ELA) and mathematics, students use the same cognitive process to achieve learning standards in both subjects. Thus, linking thinking skills like *identify* across academic, social, and emotional tasks empowers teachers to save time by teaching students one way to identify characters in reading and amounts in mathematics and then challenging students to transfer their ability to identify toward identifying feelings and social-emotional problems as they occur in the classroom, on the playground, or at home. In so doing, teachers teach essential skills in ELA and mathematics and SEL without extra steps, extra time, extra lesson plans, or feeling like they are introducing a skill that is completely new in each subject or situation. (See the "Linking Cognitive Verbs in CCSS and SELf-Questions" reproducible on page 222 for a list of connected cognitive verbs and their connection to SELf-questions.)

Achieve Transfer

Through teaching metacognition and linking thinking skills, Rick Cohen and coauthor Deanne Opatosky found an approach to embedding SEL and academic instruction that did not require more instructional time, but our work wasn't done. We needed a more structured approach to this strategy that could support students who struggle with multistep, multi-cognitive processes, as well as help students achieve transfer across all learning disciplines and grade levels. Rick and Deanne were left to ask, "How do you get students to transfer skills from one context to another?" They posed this question to Elias and the late Grant Wiggins, former president of Authentic Education. Elias said, "The main goal is self-questioning" (personal communication, September 12, 2019), and Wiggins said the key to transfer is metacognition (personal communication, August 28, 2012).

At this same time, Rick and a dear friend and colleague, coauthor James Savage, read *Pedagogy of Confidence*, by the CEO of National Urban Alliance Yvette Jackson (2011), which summarizes developmental and clinical psychologist Reuven Feuerstein's pedagogy for adaptive thinking as follows: "Such intervention includes introspective questioning that specifically elicits cognitive functions or mental tools that help individuals" (p. 59). Rick also came across a wonderful book, *Dr. Goodreader* by Susan O. Stevens (2012), which encourages teachers of reading comprehension to utilize a structured set of introspective questions (self-questions) to guide students' self-talk through difficulties with comprehension of text. With Elias's and Wiggins's help, Deanne, Susan (Sue), James, and Rick began to imagine a new metacognitive strategy involving SELf-questioning—self-questions students can apply not just in academic learning but also in SEL without the need to modify or change the questions—to assist in the transfer of skills and processes from academic content to social conflict resolution and from academic classrooms to emotional contexts without the need for additional instruction.

By establishing one common structure (one common set of steps and aligned SELf-questions) for all academic, social, and emotional problem solving, teachers no longer have to take additional time to teach one set of steps to solve problems in mathematics, then a different set of steps for the scientific method, still another set for resolving social conflicts, and so on and so forth. Establishing one set of steps and aligned SELf-questions for any problem makes transfer between subjects and contexts much easier for students.

Evaluate

This step asks the questions: *What is the best way to solve this problem? Does this make sense?*

Through our brainstorming efforts, we had arrived at three potential solutions to our problem: (1) teach metacognition, (2) link thinking skills, and (3) achieve transfer. But which was the best solution? In our case, we found the best option was to combine all three possible solutions together into one strategy, *structured SELf-questioning*. This strategy infuses all three of our brainstorms into one practical, evidence-based solution for teachers of all content areas and grade levels. Consider the following.

- Structured SELf-questioning incorporates the possible solution of teaching metacognition because the structure and SELf-questions guide students' self-talk through awareness and management as well as the multiple steps of complex academic, social, and emotional problem solving and decision-making.

- Structured SELf-questioning incorporates linking thinking skills and achieves transfer because each SELf-question prompts the explicit, targeted critical thinking skill students need each step of the way in all three contexts (social, emotional, and academic).

- Structured SELf-questioning is evidence-based. Butler and colleagues (2011) state that by asking open-ended, structured questions (verbally and in written formats) that offer cognitive choices, students enhance their social and emotional problem-solving skills, intellect, and character.

A critical outcome of our evaluation came from the realization that the difference between the evidence-based approach of psychologists (which recommends teachers ask open-ended questions first) and our intended approach to structured SELf-questioning is that the latter takes the onus off teachers to guide students' self-talk and places that onus on the students themselves. This approach works best because it provides evidence-based supports students can learn to use and practice in academic instruction with complete independence to guide their self-talk through stressors, low-level anxieties, and problems of everyday life before they become chronic or severe.

With the help of Edward (Eddie) Darrah, a school counselor confronting similar challenges teaching students coping skills in his office (over and over again), we collectively developed two separate but almost identical structured SELf-question sets. You will learn about these and how to apply them with students in chapter 1 and throughout this book.

To make the infusion of these two structured SELf-question sets into your classrooms even easier for teachers and to save even more time, we have developed a website (https://selfq.org), and a SELf-Q app, which put these interactive SELf-questioning sets and adaptive technology at everyone's fingertips. These tech tools empower teachers to place any complex, multi-step academic problem at the top of a teacher-selected SELf-question set and link that assignment to any platform (Google Classroom, Canvas, Class Dojo), thereby pushing out assignments (mathematics word problems, research projects, science experiment designs, and so on) with the question sets as scaffolds with the click of a button.

Further, with these tech tools, students can write down their thinking step by step, and teachers can easily monitor and assess student responses, progress, and completion while providing the practice opportunities students need. Parents find the technology tools particularly useful when responding to their own children's academic, social, and emotional problem solving as the question sets empower them to be more like a third-party, objective guide on the side.

Finally, the technology tools also allow users to customize our default SELf-question sets by providing the capacity for all users (teachers, students, and parents) to design their own step names and SELf-questions, which also accelerates the process of gradual release and autonomy.

Plan and Act

This step asks the questions: *What do I do first, second, and so on? Does this work? Is this working?*

Because we were literally building the foundations for what would become our SELf-questioning strategy as we went, our plan-and-act process wasn't exactly conventional and occurred simultaneously with our gathering of information, brainstorming, and evaluation. In 2012, the Metuchen School District in New Jersey (a suburban district of 2,300 students) hired Rick as its director of curriculum and principal of Mildred B. Moss Elementary (the Moss School). Determining a means to provide half-day kindergarten teachers time for SEL instruction was one of his first big priorities.

His half-day kindergarten teachers at Moss School told Rick that they wanted professional development on teaching social skills but said they feared that the rigorous academic demands of the recently adopted Common Core State Standards (CCSS) would eliminate the already limited instructional time they had to teach social skills. To save instructional time and ease his teachers' concerns, Rick proposed linking the most common cognitive verbs from the CCSS with the matching thinking skills within responsible decision making. (See Link Thinking Skills, page 9, and the "Linking Cognitive Verbs in CCSS and SELf-Questions" reproducible on page 222.)

This was the beginning, and as you are about to read, Moss School's teacher implementation of the first version of the academic and social SELf-questions would go on to experience great success.

Reflect

This step asks the questions: *Did it work? How do we know? Do we need to go back and try again?*

Reflection is, in part, about assessing the journey. Our experiences and successes with structured SELf-questioning can be observed by listening to students' independent application of linked thinking and utilizing one structure for solving all kinds of problems in the video Moss School Problem Solvers (visit https://youtu.be/rk8vMjP9QS8.). However, flash forward from the start of our work in 2012 to 2018, numerous iterations on SELf-questioning later, and the Moss School received both National and State Character Awards from Charter.org and the Moss School Problem-Solving Curriculum was awarded a National Promising Practice Award (also from Character.org).

During this time, Metuchen's Campbell Elementary School for grades 1–4 also adopted structured SELf-questioning with encouraging results. Based on these initial successes in elementary classrooms, the Metuchen School District district superintendent and the board of education set goals to adopt the strategy districtwide.

These, however, are just our headline success with structured SELf-questioning. The day-to-day successes we experienced stretch across the realms of the social and emotional, academic, and instructional.

Social and Emotional Successes

We think the best way to sum up the social and emotional experience that comes from successful SELf-questioning is best understood through the real example of a young student who internalized the SELf-questioning strategy she first learned via mathematics instruction and transferred toward an emotional problem without any prompting from an adult. Throughout this book, you will read about numerous examples like this one that derive from real-world scenarios. Many of these are based on our first-hand experiences, but for anonymity and to keep the focus on the classroom process, we refer to teachers involved by their initial.

In December 2018, a second grader who had been struggling throughout her schooling with anxiety and school phobia found herself in the counselor's office (and not for the first time). The counselor, Mrs. H., began trying to talk to her and ask her questions. The student waved her hands wildly in front of her face and shut her eyes tight. She told Mrs. H.

she needed some time and space and that she was too upset to talk. Mrs. H. went to her computer at her desk to give the student the time and space she needed.

In a few minutes, Mrs. H. saw that the eight-year-old had grabbed a blank piece of paper and pencil and had written in the upper left-hand corner, "What is the problem?" Though she was technically using a mathematics question set, she wrote about the problem she was dealing with emotionally. She then went on to write the next question of the second-grade questioning set that her mathematics teacher had been teaching her on a daily basis to support her ability to solve complex word problems: "What do I know?" She then wrote down some information that she knew about the problem and continued to the next SELf-question, "What are some possible solutions?" She proceeded to write down three possible solutions to the problem she was currently facing, just as she had learned to do in mathematics.

When she was done writing, she called over Mrs. H., who asked her which solution she was going to try. The student circled the one possible solution of the three that was seemingly the least effective, or least likely to succeed, perhaps intentionally. The student pointed down and looked up at Mrs. H. for a reaction. Mrs. H. simply encouraged her to make the best choice and try the solution that she picked on her own. Mrs. H. ended the session by telling the student to try it out, see what happens, come back to her afterward to let her know how it went.

In 2020, that same student is doing much better with anxiety and school phobia, and her mother breaks into joyful tears when talking about her daughter's growth. Due to this students' efficacy in transferring the one strategy and SELf-question set from academic content to social and emotional contexts, she was asked to serve as a Campbell School Peace Squad peer mediator, which utilizes the academic and social SELf-question set taught in class to help students resolve social conflicts on the playground during recess. In doing so, she served as a model for her peers and younger students.

Academic Successes

We believe teaching linked thinking skills via one set of common problem-solving steps has shown numerous benefits for students in the Metuchen district schools. For example, after deploying this strategy in ELA K–12, the district saw dramatic increases in academic achievement on the New Jersey Student Learning Assessments (NJSLA). In 2017, with support and training from one of the coauthors, Deanne, all sixth-grade ELA teachers piloted the use of structured SELf-questioning, resulting in a dramatic 19 percent increase in proficiency in ELA scores in one year (Cohen, Peragallo, McPeek, Porowski, Evans, & Khoudja, 2019). On the 2019 NJSLA ELA tests, Metuchen High School ninth and tenth grades increased the percent of students scoring as *proficient* by 29 percent when compared to proficiency percentages from 2015. The data in table I.1 show dramatic increases in student performance on state tests from 2015 to 2019 across all of grades 4–10.

Table I.1: Metuchen School District ELA Achievement Data, 2015–2019

ELA Grade Level	Percent Proficient in 2015	Percent Proficient in 2016	Percent Proficient in 2017	Percent Proficient in 2018	Percent Proficient in 2019
Grade 4	68%	72%	78%	69%	77%
Grade 5	65%	76%	80%	85%	83%
Grade 6	67%	68%	87%	81%	88%
Grade 7	77%	77%	77%	84%	84%
Grade 8	70%	80%	80%	77%	87%
Grade 9	56%	73%	89%	72%	85%
Grade 10	44%	65%	64%	70%	73%

Source: Cohen et al., 2019.

Metuchen's state test data also show that dramatic increases in student-growth scores were first observed in grades 4–6 on ELA state tests taken at the end of the 2016–2017 school year, with gains of ten or more percentile points at each of those three grade levels (Cohen, 2019). Table I.2 lists the average mSGP scores (the percentile growth in performance from one year to the next, as opposed to percent proficiency at the end of one scholastic year) students achieved.

Table I.2: Metuchen School District ELA Median Student Growth Data, 2015–2019

ELA Grade Levels	Median Student Growth Score 2015	Median Student Growth Score 2016	Median Student Growth Score 2017	Median Student Growth Score 2018	Median Student Growth Score 2019
Grade 4	56	56	66	60	80
Grade 5	52	56	70	71	81
Grade 6	67	68	81	69	70
Grade 7	54	56	54	42	53
Grade 8	55	55	55	49	60
Average mSGP score	57	58	65	58	69

Source: Cohen, 2019.

To explore these data further, consider that the average of the median student growth percentiles (mSGPs) of all tested Metuchen students grades 4–8 in 2019 was 11 percentile points higher than the average mSGP in 2016 (the year prior to our first pilot of SELf-questioning). These data support Durlak and colleagues (2011) research that shows when SEL interventions are embedded into core content curriculum and taught over multiple years, student academic achievement increases by 11 percentile points.

Although we cannot directly connect the dramatic increase in student proficiency and growth on state tests in Metuchen to classroom use of structured SELf-questioning, evidence statements that report more detailed results show that the district saw the greatest gains from 2015–2019 in the standards of writing expressions (a 15 percent increase in proficiency) and reading informational text (a 13 percent increase in proficiency; Cohen, 2019). These were targeted areas for linked thinking and structured SELf-questioning in Metuchen.

The district also experienced successes in mathematics in the areas of mathematical thinking, reasoning, self-monitoring, and mathematics problem-solving skills. Figure I.1 charts the grades 3–5 Metuchen School District achievement in mathematics over a five-year period across four different subscore areas: (1) major content, (2) additional and supporting content, (3) modeling and application, and (4) expressing mathematical reasoning. This data set dates back to the 2014–2015 school year. For the 2018–2019 school year, teachers implemented the structured SELf-question sets across grades K–5 as a department goal. After just one year of implementation, increases in student achievement were the most dramatic in the subscore of expressing mathematical reasoning, which structured SELf-question sets target for development.

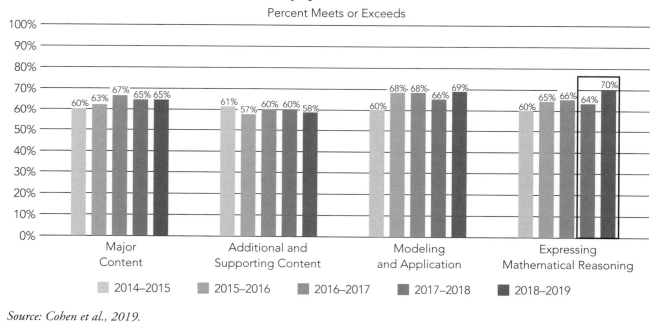

Proficiency by Subscore Grades 3–5
Percent Meets or Exceeds

Source: Cohen et al., 2019.

Figure I.1: Metuchen mathematics achievement results, 2015–2019 for grades 3–5.

Instructional Successes

While test scores are encouraging, even more encouraging is what the K–5 teachers said about the approach of teaching structured SELf-questioning. At the May 24, 2019 Metuchen in-service day, we put the following question to a group of grades 1–4 teachers: *Reflect— What about using the problem-solving process and SELf-question sets worked this year?* Here is a summary of some of the responses teachers offered.

- Helps students with a structure to organize their thoughts

- Allows students to see and experiment with different ways to solve the problem

- Allows students to think-pair-share, and explain how they got to the answer

- Empowers students to rely on *their* strengths

- Allows students to brainstorm a lot of different ways to solve one problem and try them

- Good for small groups with struggling students

- Helps students who struggle with decision making

- Great for sharing ideas and comparing

- Motivates students to really stop and think before just acting on impulse

- Allows for self-reflection

- Assesses (formative and summative) mathematics problem solving and thinking

One reason we believe so many teachers report such success implementing the academic and social as well as the emotional SELf-question sets is because the questions are so easily transferable to different kinds of subjects, problems, age ranges, classroom management styles, and teacher preferences. The universality of the structure, steps, and questions, along with the limited number or quantity of questions, make interdisciplinary lessons and differentiation easier for teachers and independent practice and transfer much smoother for students.

And there is one more teacher benefit for teachers implementing structured SELf-questioning: reduced teacher stress. When teachers have processes to reduce both student stress and their own stress, everyone benefits, as does the cause of learning (Greenberg, Brown, & Abenavoli, 2016).

About This Book

This book shows how it is possible to teach all students the mental framework we just explained for successs in the classroom, at school, and in life. You will see and hear from numerous teachers in every core academic content area and across all grades about how the far-reaching and seemingly impractical ideals dreamed of in this book's introduction are realized every day. *The Metacognitive Student: How to Teach Academic, Social, and Emotional Intelligence in Every Content Area* will show you why so many teachers are now saying they are doing the best teaching of their lives.

Here, you will find everything you need to successfully use structured SELf-questioning to embed and teach SEL and metacognition within your existing curriculum, without the need for additional instructional time in the classroom. As you read, you'll learn about the SELf-questioning framework and our two core SELf-question sets: (1) academic and social and (2) emotional. Research-based and anecdotal evidence support this content, along with practical guidance for how to teach it and depictions of scenarios derived from actual classroom usage. These scenarios illustrate teaching SELf-questioning in a variety of environments across all grade bands and core content areas. The scenarios also demonstrate how easy it is to implement engaging real-world project-based learning (PBL) and inquiry-based learning (IBL) activities through structured SELf-questioning. All of these resources and examples have already led to the successful implementation of this simple strategy in K–12 classrooms, schools, and many individual students' lives. The chapters break down as follows.

Chapter 1 further explains structured SELf-questioning as an innovative metacognitive strategy and why it works. The chapters that follow explain how to embed this strategy into each core academic content area across K–12. This topic progression may seem counterintuitive at first, and you may certainly adapt it differently for your students, but this progression reflects a natural learning curve in using structured SELf-questioning in different contexts.

Chapter 2 starts out by detailing the use of our academic and social SELf-question set with a mathematics curriculum. The focus on problem solving in mathematics makes it an ideal place to set a foundation for using structured SELf-questioning. To introduce you to the social component of the academic and social SELf-question set, chapter 3 focuses on using this strategy in social contexts. We chose to start first with the mathematics chapter as a clear concrete example of how academic and social SELf-questioning naturally works in academics, followed immediately by the social problem-solving chapter to show how easily this one set of academic and social SELf-questions transfers across academic to social contexts.

With a solid foundation for academic and social SELf-questioning established, we turn our attention to ELA, which provides numerous opportunities to expand students' use of the strategy. Because of this, we divide our exploration of this content area into multiple chapters: chapter 4 focuses on embedding SELF-questioning within instruction for reading comprehension, chapter 5 highlights its use with reading decoding, and chapter 6 centers on writing.

As your understanding of using SELf-questioning grows, we shift from the academic and social SELf-question set to our emotional SELf-question set. Chapter 7 begins by showing the utility of this set for helping students with emotional regulation. Chapter 8 expands on that work to showcase its use for emotional problem solving. In this way, teachers and students gradually and consistently build their comfort and skill with using all facets of SELf-questioning.

As teacher and student experiences grow, their ability to apply their use of SELf-questioning to new contexts grows right along with it. That's why we dedicate chapter 9 to refining teachers' and students' ability to naturally transfer use of both the academic and social SELf-question set and the emotional SELf-question set to new contexts inside and outside the classroom. Of particular relevance for this transfer are the subject areas of social studies (chapter 10) and science (chapter 11). Both of these subjects represent a crossroads of academic, social, and emotional learning that not only tap into avenues of historical and scientific thinking but also existing knowledge and experience with literacy, mathematics, and human behavior. This makes them ideal subjects to explore after teachers and students have built experience with SELf-questioning and can comfortably transfer that knowledge across disciplines.

Ultimately, the structured SELf-question sets we provide and model in this book are not scripts. The goal is for students to find the questions so useful that they internalize them to the point they can unconsciously shuffle through the questions like a deck of cards to come up with an answer to a problem. To that end, teachers and students can make their own problem-solving step names, create new SELf-questions, and develop new visuals. Chapter 12 explains how teachers and students can design and autonomously apply SELf-questioning to fit their own style and any situation they face.

Beginning in chapter 2, each chapter also provides a series of scenarios focused on a real-world application of the SELf-questioning strategy for each grade band, K–2, 3–5, 6–8, and 9–12. (Chapter 12 changes this up a bit, for reasons we explain there.) Following the scenarios in each chapter, you'll find a Character Corner section that further connects SELf-questioning to aspects of the CASEL (n.d.) core competencies. This section reflects on how teaching SELf-questioning helps students internalize the attitudes, skills, and behaviors characteristic of a particular value or character trait, such as self-control, self-regulation, responsibility, perseverance, self-empathy, and peace.

Lastly, although there are benefits to understanding the application of SELf-questioning in all of the topic areas we explore in this book, you don't even need to read this book cover to cover to understand how to implement the strategy effectively in your classroom. Instead, target the chapter topics most essential to your work and the unique challenges of your classroom.

Teaching For Intelligence and Character

More than ever, students need to be able to take a step back (metaphorically speaking) and have a think about their thinking and feelings, a phrase you will see throughout this book as the essence of metacognition. They also need the confidence to more independently face the day-to-day stressors and low-level anxieties of school and life. With the knowledge and tested strategy of structured SELf-questioning we provide in this book, you can develop your students into academically strong, socially and emotionally healthy, confident, flexible, adaptive, persistent and responsible critical thinkers, problem solvers, and decision makers. Through structured SELf-questioning, all teachers can empower all students to face life head on and prepare them for greater success by developing their students' academic, social, and emotional intelligence as well as their character. The benefits will not only serve students, but they will also reduce stress and anxiety for teachers as classroom disruptions reduce and learning thrives.

We close this introduction with the poignant words of Martin Luther King Jr. (1947) when he wrote on the purpose of education, "Intelligence plus character—that is the true goal of education" (p. 124). Until now, the dream of teaching students intelligence plus character has seemed only aspirational because teachers across the nation have found it almost impossible to add anything else to their already overloaded curriculum and job demands. This book shows how it is possible to help move education from intelligence *plus* character to intelligence *and* character.

Metacognition and SELf-Questioning: The Underpinnings of the Strategy

"So few people are really aware of their thoughts. Their minds run all over the place without their permission, and they go along for the ride unknowingly and without making a choice."

—Thomas M. Sterner

The human brain is wonderfully designed to step back and have a think about its thinking. As we established in this book's introduction, this ability is called *metacognition*. The prefix *meta-* means about the thing itself. *Cognition* is "the mental action or process of acquiring knowledge and understanding through thought, experience, and the senses" (Lexico n.d.c). Although most educators are familiar with the concept of thinking about one's own thinking, we like the following definition of metacognition: "Awareness and management of one's own thought" (Kuhn & Dean, 2004, p. 270). After all, of the five social-emotional core competencies, the first four relate directly the concepts of awareness and management: (1) self-awareness, (2) social awareness, (3) self-management, (4) responsible decision making, and (5) relationship skills (CASEL, n.d.).

Therefore, metacognition means thinking about and managing your thoughts, experiences, and what your senses are telling you; it is also something that teachers might easily skip over in the classroom. As we've said, time is always a factor, but in a fast-paced world of precooked bacon and 280-character tweets, educators *especially* need to teach students to stop and think about their thinking. Because we designed our SELf-questioning strategy to facilitate teaching metacognitive processes in a way that it is easy to internalize and transfer from one situation to another, using and internalizing our strategy ultimately saves time rather than wastes it.

We begin this chapter by establishing *why* teaching metacognition is important, especially in a 21st century classroom where learning critical-thinking and decision-making skills plays a vital role. We follow this examination with a look at how you can begin teaching metacognition in the classroom.

Why Teaching Metacognition Is Important

For the purposes of this book, metacognition includes the following characteristics (Stevens, 2012).

- Knowing when you know
- Knowing when you don't know

- Knowing what you need to know

- Knowing how to solve problems

- Knowing how to think about your own thinking to improve learning and life decisions

Advances in neuroscience show that people can actually change how their brains function by directing their thinking (Leaf, 2013) and that metacognition "actually changes the structure of the brain, making it more flexible and open to even greater learning" (Price-Mitchell, 2015). In other words, with directed or guided thinking, people can strengthen some neural pathways, form new connections, and effectively erase others. Scientists refer to this as *neuroplasticity*. This is critical, because if students don't believe that they can change as learners, why should they invest in metacognitive thinking or put a lot of work into learning something new? What would be the point?

Knowing that the brain is highly plastic makes it worth the effort to learn about oneself and how to manage one's thinking and learning to grow academically, socially, and emotionally. Carol Dweck (2016) coined a term for this: *growth mindset*. Combining the metacognitive skills of our directed thinking process in SELf-questioning with the metacognitive skill of having a growth mindset helps students hit home runs with their thinking!

Consider the following.

- Authors and educators Douglas Fisher, Nancy Frey, and John Hattie (2016) rank metacognition fourteenth among 150 educational influences.

- Students as young as age three can learn to use metacognition (Wilson & Conyers, 2016; Shure, 2001).

- Some students require explicit training and coaching to learn such skills as metacognition, whereas others seem to absorb metacognitive skills alongside other training (Coutinho, 2008).

- Teaching metacognitive skills is one of the cheapest learning interventions that schools can make, with learners averaging seven months of additional progress in learning per school year (InnerDrive, n.d.).

- Metacognitive approaches to instruction increase student transfer to new situations, such as when students transfer their learning of how to determine the volume of a cube to learning how to determine the volume of a pyramid without the need for explicit prompting (Wiggins, 2012a).

- "Metacognition about mindsets offers teachers an opportunity to give students the gifts of a lifetime—the belief that they can overcome any learning obstacles if they just persevere, that their intelligence is not fixed but actually malleable, and that learning is sometimes hard but not impossible" (Peak, 2015).

These are just some of the many reasons we believe it's imperative that teachers across all grade levels and content areas make metacognition a priority. We could fill pages more with additional examples and resources, but these encapsulate the essential evidence as to the importance of teaching metacognitive skills to students. Now that you understand the *Why?*, let's take a look at the *How?*

How to Teach Metacognition in the Classroom

When it comes to teaching and applying metacognition, we find that using structured SELf-questioning shows the best results. You want to teach students how to think about their thinking in a logical, directed manner that works well for most, if not all, situations. As such, your first goal is to teach students to question themselves through a logical, process-oriented, and structured sequence. Figure 1.1 shows two structured SELf-question sets: one question set for academic and social problem solving and one for emotional problem solving.

Step	SELf-questions for Academic and Social Problem Solving	Step	SELf-questions for Emotional Problem Solving
1. Select a Focus	What is the problem? What is the question? What is the task?	1. Self-Empathy	What am I feeling? How do I feel?
2. Gather Information	What do I know? What do I need to know? What is similar, and what is different?	2. Gather Information	What is causing this feeling?
3. Brainstorm	How can I solve this problem? What are possible solutions? What can I do?	3. Brainstorm	What strategies can I use to make myself feel better?
4. Evaluate	What is the best way to solve this problem? Does this make sense?	4. Evaluate	Has this strategy helped me in the past? How did it help? How did I feel after?
5. Plan and Act	What do I do first, second, and so on? Does this work? Is this working?	5. Plan and Act	What do I do first, second, and so on? Does this work? Is this working?
6. Reflect	Did it work? How do I know? Do I need to go back and try again?	6. Reflect	Did it work? How do I know? Do I need to go back and try again?

Figure 1.1: The two structured SELf-question sets.

Visit go.SolutionTree.com/instruction for a free reproducible version of this figure.

With teacher support (as needed), students review and answer each question one at a time to solve a problem or understand a challenge they're facing. You'll notice that the two sets of questions are identical except for the starting action, which differentiates between selecting a focus and establishing self-empathy. From this point, the structured progression is the same in both SELf-question sets; only the questions associated with each prompt change. It's worth noting that we've chosen the term *self-empathy* (Niezink & Train, 2020) because we believe empathy toward one's self connotes compassion more than terms like *awareness* or *recognition*, and it's our hope that students will build compassion for themselves as they learn to recognize their feelings.

We created and tested these structured SELf-question sets to apply across grade levels while ensuring they are general enough to apply across many disciplines. As you can see, each step of the process has a name (an action to complete) and a visual cue (the icons). This is purposeful, because labeling a skill increases the learning of that skill. As Butler and colleagues (2011) state, "a visual prompt for the actual problem-solving steps . . . when paired with adult-facilitated cueing, leads to increased skill internalization and generalization" (p. 13). The combination of visual prompts, simple steps, and SELf-questions should help students internalize the steps quickly.

There are two approaches we believe are essential to helping students learn to use these two SELf-question sets: (1) modeling and (2) using gradual release of responsibility. We explore each of these in the following sections.

Modeling

If metacognition is the underpinning of quality learning, teachers must ask themselves if they are purposefully and explicitly teaching metacognition. This requires understanding that the most effective way to teach metacognition is through modeling. When you model metacognition, you let students take a peek inside your brain as you think out loud. In "Character and Academics—How to Integrate," education consultant Rebecca Sipos (2016) shows what modeling self-questioning in any subject area or context looks like:

Displaying thinking postures and inspiring emotions. Rubbing the chin, looking contemplative, and showing delight, excitement, and curiosity make it clear that what the teacher is pondering requires deep thought and is naturally fascinating.

Framing problem-solving steps as questions that can be asked and answered (thinking out loud). For example: Let's see, what is the problem? What are some solutions? What might happen if . . . ?

Making comments about their own thinking. For example: Maybe I shouldn't take this idea as a given. I'm not at all sure about it. I think there may be other ways of looking at it. Let's think of some alternatives.

Identifying times when they are using a disposition. For example: Let's think about how we're going to tackle this problem (strategic).

Here's an example of modeling from a high school ELA class in which Sue taught students T. H. White's (1958/2016) novel *The Once and Future King*.

Sue read aloud the following passage:

> Boar-hunting was fun. It was nothing like badger-digging or covert-shooting or fox-hunting today. Perhaps the nearest thing to it would be ferreting for rabbits—except that you used dogs instead of ferrets, had a boar that easily might kill you, instead of a rabbit, and carried a boar-spear upon which your life depended instead of a gun. (White, 2016, p. 143)

After reading the paragraph, she modeled structured SELf-questioning by stating the questions and her thoughts that came from answering them.

What do I know? What do I need to know?

I think boar-hunting sounds really dangerous, and I'm wondering if I need to know what covert-shooting is. I don't think so, because it just seems to be another type of hunting.

How can I solve this problem?

I have to read the rest of the paragraph slowly.

Did it work?

OK, I get it! The author is comparing various types of hunting to boar-hunting. In this kind of hunting, you use dogs and a spear, and the boar might kill you!

Sipos (2016) also suggests that teachers display thinking dispositions visually. To accomplish this, we recommend making both SELf-question sets simple and clear for students by presenting the steps through any standard visual, such as an anchor chart, poster, bookmark, and so on. There are several examples of anchor charts, posters, and visual representations throughout the book and and in the appendix (page 215).

We encourage you to identify how you, as a teacher, envision problem solving as a metacognitive process for your curriculum. Some teachers are linear and sequential, so they display the structure from top to bottom, some use a six-square graphic organizer, and some teachers put the structure into a loop or circle. How you choose to visually represent the structure and steps of SELf-questioning is up to you. What is imperative is that the question sequence remains consistent so that the structure of students' thinking is consistent, which helps internalization. Once students internalize the common structure and steps, teachers or students can autonomously adapt or modify the SELf-question sets. (See chapter 12, page 195.)

Modeling is vital, and teachers should never skip it, but beware of modeling long passages. Students' eyes often glaze over when a teacher goes on for too long using a single passage. However, every single time Sue skipped modeling SELf-questioning with students, and thus skipped showing her students what metacognitive thinking looks like, she regretted it. Every single lesson flop she ever had, Sue can trace back to a lack of modeling.

Gradual Release of Responsibility

In addition to modeling, we recommend teachers apply Pearson & Gallagher's (1983) gradual release of responsibility when teaching SELf-questioning. Through gradual release of responsibility, you can introduce students to structured SELf-question sets one by one, beginning where you see the greatest need in your particular classroom or in the area you feel the most comfortable modeling your thinking. Figure 1.2 (page XX) illustrates this model, which offers a steady, four-step transition from modeling (shown here as *I do, you watch*) to including students in the modeling (*I do, you help*) to students taking action with teacher guidance (*You do, I help*) to the students taking full ownership of the task with teacher oversight (*You do, I watch*).

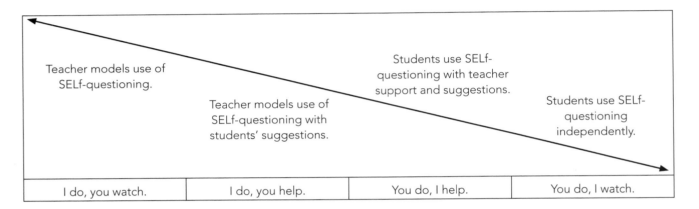

Teacher models use of SELf-questioning.

Teacher models use of SELf-questioning with students' suggestions.

Students use SELf-questioning with teacher support and suggestions.

Students use SELf-questioning independently.

| I do, you watch. | I do, you help. | You do, I help. | You do, I watch. |

Source: Adapted from Pearson & Gallagher, 1983.

Figure 1.2: Gradual release of responsibility applied to SELf-question sets.

The first phase (I do, you watch) is the stage where the teacher models the SELf-questioning steps for students. During this and the following phases, the teacher is not only modeling questions and answers but also his or her metacognitive thinking during the process. During the second phase (I do, you help), the teacher might lead the student through SELf-questioning by asking students for their input as well as giving prompts to help the student. In the third stage (you do, I help), students lead the way through SELf-questioning with only an occasional prompt from the teacher. And, in the final stage (you do, I watch), the student operates with autonomy, and the teacher is an appreciative audience.

There are times when the stages become a little muddy. Here's an example from Sue's experience that falls in the grey area between the second phase (*I do, you help*) of gradual release and the third phase (*You do, I help*). One day, Sue accompanied seventeen-year-old Kaye's father to pick Kaye up from a three-month stay in a mental healthcare facility. Kaye, whom Sue loves very much, immediately became furious because her father would not take her an hour out of the way (they were three and a half hours from home already) to pick up her phone. When the three stopped for lunch, she and Sue chatted about how malleable brains are and the work Sue was doing with structured SELf-questioning. Then, Sue pulled up our SELf-Q app on her own phone, chose the emotional SELf-question set, and they named the set *Phone*. Here is what happened as they worked through the set.

- **Self-empathy: What am I feeling?**

  Kaye answers, "Annoyed." This was interesting, because she was acting *much* more than annoyed.

- **Gather information: What is causing this feeling?**

  Kaye answers, "Just the fact that *he* (disdainfully indicating her father) can find the time for anything for himself, but can't go twenty minutes out of the way for me." You see that her reality was skewed because getting the phone would have added an hour to their journey, but Sue didn't challenge her on this point and dispassionately filled in the app.

- **Brainstorm: What strategies can I use to help myself feel better?**

  Kaye shouts, "I DON'T KNOW!" Sue asked if she could throw a few ideas out since Kaye couldn't come up with any, and Kaye agreed. Sue suggested that Kaye could use her old phone, which was already at her house or that the people who had the newer phone could overnight express mail it to her. (These are options that her dad had already mentioned in the car. It seems that dealing with the situation through an app was easier for her than through conversation—at least with her dad.)

- **Evaluate: Has this helped me in the past?**

  Kaye answers, "How did it help? How did I feel after? This is a new situation which has never happened before." Sue decided to wait for another time to address how Kaye reacts when she doesn't get exactly what she wants.

- **Plan and act: What do I do first, second, and so on?**

  Kaye answers, "Reset the old phone for now, and get my newer phone sent to me." Kaye came up with this herself, and as soon as she did, the tension and anger melted away.

- **Reflect: Did it work? How do I know?**

  They decided to approach reflection on another day. When Sue saw Kaye a few days later, she asked if Kaye had been able to reset the phone. Kaye told Sue she had and that it had been really easy. Her aunt had also mailed the newer phone to her, so the intervention was a success.

This was the first time Kaye had attempted to use the SELf-question set to solve a problem, but under the high-tension circumstances, Sue chose to skip the first stage in gradual release of responsibility (I do, you watch) and instead chose to jump directly to a messy mix of stage two (I do, you help) and three (you do, I help). Although Sue was already a believer in the SELf-questioning strategy, this interaction with a severely troubled teenager was remarkable in action for both Kaye's father and Sue. This metacognitive strategy does not promise magic, but we can promise that this is an effective tool for your students—and perhaps even you—to use.

Next Steps

Ultimately, we believe the explicit teaching of metacognitive skills benefits all students, but it is something we find lacking in many classrooms. Students at every grade level can learn to apply metacognition through structured SELf-questioning, but for them to truly learn these skills, we believe teachers must use modeling and gradual release of responsibility to support that learning. As you engage with the following chapters, you will learn much more about teaching discipline-and context-specific applications of SELf-questioning in the classroom.

As you approach this teaching, it is also important to remember that metacognition is developmental. Brain researcher and author David Perkins (1992) proposes four levels of metacognitive learning: (1) tacit, (2) aware, (3) strategic, and (4) reflective. In their study of metacognition, education experts and authors Arthur L. Costa and Robert Garmston (2016) explain Perkins's metacognitive levels as follows:

> Tacit learners are unaware of their metacognitive knowledge.
>
> Aware learners know about some of the kinds of thinking they do—generating ideas, finding evidence—but are not strategic in their thinking.
>
> Strategic learners organize their thinking by using problem solving, decision making, evidence seeking, and other types of strategies.
>
> Reflective learners not only are strategic about their thinking, but also reflect on their thinking in progress, ponder their strategies, and revise them. (p. 144)

As teachers, our job is to move students along this continuum of metacognitive levels as they are ready. The ensuing chapters demonstrate how the metacognitive strategy of structured SELf-questioning helps every teacher move every student along this continuum while developing all students as strategic and reflective learners and thinkers in academic, social, and emotional contexts without the need for additional instructional time.

Structured SELf-Questioning for Academic Problem Solving in Mathematics

2

> *Many teachers, faced with long lists of content to cover to satisfy state and federal requirements, worry that students do not have enough time to explore math topics in depth. Others simply teach as they were taught. And few have the opportunity to stay current with what research shows about how kids learn math best: as an open, conceptual, inquiry-based subject.*
>
> —Jo Boaler and Pablo Zoido

Both critical thinking and problem-solving skills are inherent in SEL skills and mathematics. You'll also find certain critical-thinking or problem-solving skills employed throughout almost every content area in every K–12 unit. This continues when school ends. The World Economic Forum ranks complex problem solving as the single most valued skill of employers, with the second most valued skill being critical thinking (Gray, 2016). Students also need to apply both with a degree of cognitive flexibility to be independent mathematical thinkers and successful mathematics problem solvers. We cannot stress enough the importance of effectively teaching students critical thinking and problem solving, combined with flexibility and persistence, particularly in mathematics.

Unfortunately, the bad news is that U.S. students' performance of critical thinking and problem solving in mathematics isn't where most would like it to be. The United States is slightly under the Organisation for Economic Co-operation and Development (OECD) average on the Programme for International Student Assessment (PISA) test (PISA, 2018).

This chapter explains how structured SELf-questioning provides a practical approach to teaching students critical-thinking and problem-solving skills for a mathematics unit or class. It also demonstrates how to teach students structured SELf-questioning with an eye toward responsible decision making, a core SEL competency that enhances mathematic performance (CASEL, n.d.). As part of this demonstration, we provide a series of grade-band scenarios showing the use of this chapter's SELf-question set in action. We conclude with a Character Corner section on the value of perseverance that use of this SELf-question set instills.

The Importance of Teaching a Metacognitive Strategy for Mathematics

The NGA and CCSSO (2010b) developed the CCSS to set standards that were focused on critical-thinking and problem-solving skills. For example, the word *solve* appears over one hundred times in the CCSS. The NGA and CCSSO also developed and included in the CCSS eight Standards for Mathematical Practice. Of these eight practices, the first on the list is, "Make sense of problems and persevere in solving them" (MP1; NGA & CCSSO, 2010b). Presumably, this was an attempt to promote the development of character traits such as persistence in problem solving that would enhance students' ability to work through complex, multistep mathematics problems.

Despite years of widespread adoption of standards focused on critical thinking, problem solving, and perseverance, U.S. students still struggle to compete with their international peers. Let's think about the results from the PISA, which is a test of fifteen-year-olds designed to evaluate education systems of seventy different industrialized countries around the globe. According to the 2015 PISA test results, U.S. students' performance of critical-thinking and problem-solving skills in mathematics are below average when compared to their international peers (Richmond, 2016). In mathematics, the United States ranked thirty-ninth out of the seventy industrialized countries PISA surveyed (The Hechinger Report, 2017). After analyzing the 2015 PISA results, the OECD director of education and skills, Andreas Schleicher, stated that "as soon as [U.S.] students have to go deeper and answer the more complex part of a problem, they have difficulties" (as cited in Richmond, 2016). Three years later, results from the 2018 PISA tests show no improvement (Schleicher, 2019). With regard to the 2018 results, *New York Times* correspondent Dana Goldstein (2019) quotes Schleicher: "If you look to mathematics, there is a little fluctuation but nothing significant." So, eight years after forty-five states adopted the CCSS and the Standards for Mathematical Practice, no shift or improvements have occurred in students' performance of critical thinking, problem solving, or perseverance in mathematics.

Some potential reasons for the lack of progression in students' performance in the area of mathematical thinking and problem solving on PISA in mathematics could be because of an inability of students to demonstrate transfer and flexibility among a wide range and quantity of mathematical thinking, reasoning, and problem-solving skills; because teachers feel unsure of how to effectively teach critical-thinking and problem-solving skills or develop character traits such as perseverance; or because teachers struggle to tap into best practices when it comes to teaching mathematical problem solving. This chapter focuses on the last item and the possibilities for improving these practices through the use of the metacognitive strategy of structured SELf-questioning.

How to Teach a Metacognitive Strategy for Mathematics

As we wrote in chapter 1 (page 21), human brains are wonderfully designed to step back and have a think about their thinking. But not every brain finds it easy to step back and focus on the issue at hand, think sequentially with ease, check for understanding each step of the way, and persist all the way toward a final resolution. Often, when students see a mathematics word problem, the text overwhelms them, and they shut down. Other times, students read the word problem but are not sure of what the problem is asking them to solve. Then there are the students who persevere through the text of the word problem but struggle to understand exactly what operation or procedure to apply or what to do first, second, and so on.

Clearly, there is a need for a metacognitive strategy to help students structure their critical-thinking and problem-solving skills and to use that structure to make sense of and persevere through complex mathematics problems. In "*How Did You Solve It? Metacognition in Mathematics*," Sam Rhodes (2019) writes:

> Metacognition undergirds nearly every aspect of problem-solving. When students are presented with opportunities to monitor and regulate their thinking during problem-solving, they are not only refining their metacognitive skills, but may also even be more successful in solving the problem. . . . After all, it's the question—How did you solve it?—and not the answer that is at the heart of mathematics learning.

In "Why Math Education in the U.S. Doesn't Add Up," widely recognized mathematics expert Jo Boaler and economics analyst Pablo Zoido (2016) write how learning to problem solve is much more important than simply learning steps and following them:

> In every country, the memorizers turned out to be the lowest achievers, and countries with high numbers of them—the U.S. was in the top third—also had the highest proportion of teens doing poorly on the PISA math assessment. . . . The U.S. actually had more memorizers than South Korea, long thought to be the paradigm of rote learning. Why? Because American schools routinely present mathematics procedurally, as sets of steps to memorize and apply. . . . Further analysis showed that memorizers were approximately half a year behind students who used relational and self-monitoring strategies.

Self-monitoring strategies? In mathematics? We find that self-monitoring in mathematics is a skill set that involves self-awareness (of procedural knowledge and one's mathematical thinking) as well as self-management (of one's procedural application and mathematical thinking). What Boaler and Zoido (2016) are really saying is that students need to be more aware of their mathematical knowledge and better managers of their mathematical thinking throughout the multiple steps of problem solving.

This is where structured SELf-questioning comes in. Academic SELf-questioning helps students' brains take a step back, stay focused, be aware of the need for and management of multiple cognitive processes, self-monitor understanding, think flexibly, and persevere through challenging problems. The following lists our academic SELf-questioning set from figure 1.1 (page 23), which easily embeds into state standards–aligned curriculum for grades K–12 mathematics instruction.

Select a focus: What is the problem? What is the question? What is the task?

 Gather information: What do I know? What do I need to know? What is similar, and what is different?

 Brainstorm: How can I solve this problem? What are possible solutions? What can I do?

 Evaluate: What is the best way to solve this problem? Does this make sense?

 Plan and act: What do I do first, second, and so on? Does this work? Is this working?

 Reflect: Did it work? How do I know? Do I need to go back and try again?

This academic SELf-question set is not a script. There is one structure for all examples in this book, but there is boundless freedom for teachers' and students' thinking and creativity within that one, evidence-based structure. In the four grade-band scenarios of academic SELf-questioning in mathematics we present after this section, you will notice that we or the teacher involved modified some of the names of the steps and wording of the questions to fit the grade level, content, and context. For example, in one of the scenarios, the teacher adapts the brainstorming SELf-questions to better meet her style and students by asking, "What are ways I can solve this?" instead of asking, "How can I solve this problem? What are possible solutions? What can I do?" We encourage you to use these types of adaptations, so the steps and SELf-questions feel right for you and your students.

This example highlights one reason why we believe so many teachers report such success implementing the academic SELf-question set in mathematics: the questions are easily transferrable and adaptable to different kinds of mathematics problems and grade levels. Even better, the SELf-question set is just as transferable across other academic content areas (such as reading and science) and contexts (such as social and emotional). The universality of the structure, steps, and questions, along with the limited number or quantity of questions, make differentiation easier for teachers. Thus, the academic SELf-question set serves as an excellent intervention strategy for students struggling with mathematical reasoning and expression and accelerates internalization, independent practice, and transfer.

When teaching this set for mathematics, look for opportunities to use it simultaneously with applicable social situations. Its applicability for both is why we refer to it as the academic *and* social SELf-question set. Here is one small example of how teachers and students in mathematics use this SELf-question set to solve both academic and social problems at the same time.

To begin her morning meeting with her first-grade students, Mrs. E. poses a hypothetical mathematics problem in which she has three cookies and wants to share them with five of her friends. Notice how the second piece of this problem invokes a social component. Through a think-aloud, she asks herself the SELf-questions and answers herself out loud question by question to demonstrate for students how structured SELf-questioning helps her take a step back and have a good think about this mathematics and social problem. She does the following.

1. Mrs. E. asks herself, "What is the problem?" and answers, "I need to find a way to share three cookies with five of my friends in a way that is fair."

2. She asks herself out loud, "What do I know?" and answers, "Well, I know if I don't give all my friends an equal, fair amount, some of my friends will be sad and maybe mad at me. I don't want that, so I have to brainstorm."

3. Mrs. E. continues, "What are ways I can solve this?" She answers, "I can draw a picture, use a number line, or I can use manipulatives."

4. She then asks herself, "What is the best way to solve this problem?" and answers, "I think manipulatives will be the best." She provides her students with the manipulatives, a collection of cubes that connect to each other and can be separated. For this activity, Mrs. E. gives student groups three strips of ten connected cubes and asks them to try to share the three cookies with six people (themselves and their five friends) in a way that is fair.

5. Mrs. E. asks herself, "Does this make sense?" In response to this question, she can demonstrate how students can use manipulatives to learn fractions (which is rigorous for first grade), while at the same time teach her students how to use the academic SELf-questioning set for mathematics to solve a social problem that involves sharing equally.

6. Mrs. E. asks herself, "Did this work?" as she looks around the classroom. "Yes," she says, "It did work because everybody got the same amount of cookies."

With structured SELf-questioning, what begins feeling like a complex problem is made much simpler through structured thinking, especially for students who typically struggle with complex, multistep problem solving.

Now, let's take a look at how different teachers have used the structure, steps, and questions of the academic SELf-question set in mathematics classrooms across all the grade bands to help students become better problem solvers of mathematics problems.

Scenario: Grades K–2

Class or subject: Second-grade classroom (Ms. A; teacher)

Objective:

- Analyze word problems to identify whether to add or subtract.

Standard:

- Fluently add and subtract within 100 using strategies based on place value, properties of operations, and/or the relationship between addition and subtraction. (2.NBT.B.5; NGA & CCSSO, 2010b)

On her smartboard, Ms. M. posts an anchor chart of steps and questions built on the academic SELf-question set. To begin her whole-group instruction, she also posts the following word problem of the day:

> *Elana put thirty-two marbles on the table and then went to get a bowl to put them in. When Elana came back to the table, there were only eight marbles left on the table. How many marbles fell on the floor?*

Ms. M. asks her students to write answers to each SELf-question in their mathematics journals. As they do, she walks around, peering over her students' shoulders, or kneeling down next to them when they get stuck. Here is the process she followed.

SELECT A FOCUS

Question: What is the question?

Ms. M. observes that many students have written in their journals, *How many marbles are on the floor?* Some students struggled to identify what the problem was (addition or subtraction) because some students were accustomed to seeing the question "How many more?" or "How many less?" Ms. M. models for these students at their side what using the first SELf-question looks and sounds like and how it helps them with mathematics word problems by saying out loud, "Let's ask ourselves, What is the question?" She then says her thinking out loud, "I know one way to find the question. I will look for the question mark." Ms. M. asks these students to go back and reread the sentence with the question mark. If they are still not sure, she directs them to go to the next step to gather more information.

GATHER INFORMATION

Question: What do I know?

This box of their journals says, "What do I know?" Most students successfully write in their journal some variation of, *There were thirty-two marbles on the table and then only eight marbles left on the table.* Students who struggle to answer the first question receive support from Ms. M. or turn to their partners for help. Often, mathematics teachers will go over the initial SELf-question steps with the whole class and have students turn and talk each step of the way through the strategy. This gives students practice asking and answering the SELf-questions and practice expressing their mathematics thinking in words.

BRAINSTORM

Questions: How can I solve this problem? What can I do?

In reviewing students' answers, Ms. M. observes two or three approaches most students thought of, such as *count on*, *number line*, and *make a drawing*.

EVALUATE

Question: What is the best way to solve this problem?

Students who were able to brainstorm multiple ways to solve the problem decide which of the options they come up with they want to use and circle it in preparation for the next step. It is OK for students to only brainstorm one possible solution or strategy. When possible, however, it's good for teachers to support students in trying to brainstorm three possible solutions. (See the example in the Brainstorming section of this book's introduction, page 8.) In this case, when students only have one solution, Ms. M. tells them to try and solve it with their solution but to be sure to reflect and go back and check that the one solution worked.

PLAN AND ACT

Questions: What do I do first, second, and so on? Does this work? Is this working?

Students use their selected approach to work out a solution to the problem. Their work includes number lines and drawings with thirty-two tiny circles in rows of ten inside a square. After drawing the circles, these students crossed out either eight or twenty-four circles. On the bottom of this work, many students also wrote out an equation, *32 - 8 = 24*. Some wrote *32 - 24 = 8*.

REFLECT

Questions: Did it work? How do I know? Do I need to go back and try again?

Ms. M. instructs students to exchange their journals with a partner to check each other's work. This is a common approach teachers can use to help promote the practice of precision. In this example, you can see how structure helps students be sequential, ensuring students know what the mathematics problem or question is or what to do next if they're unsure. The SELf-questions prompt and cue students' cognitive flexibility by asking them to find out what else they might know when they don't see key words, like *more* and *less*, that help them identify the mathematical procedure. By utilizing the academic SELf-question set in daily mathematics, students have a scaffold they can internalize to help them develop as flexible thinkers and persistent problem solvers at even the youngest ages.

Scenario: Grades 3–5

Class or subject: Fifth-grade classroom (Ms. D.; teacher)

Objectives:

- Use inequality symbols to compare decimals to the thousandths place.

- Use place-value relationships to round decimals to the nearest hundredth, tenth, and whole number.

Standards:

- Compare two decimals to thousandths based on meanings of the digits in each place, using >, =, and < symbols to record the results of comparisons. (5.NBT.A.3.B; NGA & CCSSO, 2010b)

- Use place value understanding to round decimals to any place. (5.NBT.A.4; NGA & CCSSO, 2010b)

In Ms. D.'s fifth-grade mathematics class there is an anchor chart both hanging on the wall and posted on the smartboard that is built on the academic SELf-question set for mathematics. Based on a quick reread of state standards (listed at the start of this section) she plans to teach, she sees that the cognitive thinking skill the first standard focuses on is for students to *compare*. The second standard also asks students to *use understanding*. Asking students to use their prior knowledge (in this case, prior knowledge of place value) and apply that understanding to accomplish a new task (round to decimals in any place value) is a metacognitive task because students must demonstrate self-awareness of their prior knowledge and self-management to apply that prior knowledge with accuracy and precision in a new situation. The strategy of structured SELf-questioning makes such a complex, multistep, multicognitive process possible for teachers to teach and students to learn and apply independently over time and with practice. Then, when teachers ask students to apply (transfer) this same strategy to other mathematics learning or other content areas, they naturally think strategically about their own thinking and strategies, which is a metacognitive task.

In this lesson, Ms. D. models how to use the structured SELf-question set as a strategy to guide students in self-talk through the following mathematics problem.

> *Billy walks 3 and 275/1000s or 3.275 kilometers to school. Sarah walks 3 and 240/1000 or 3.240 kilometers to school. Who walks farther?*

Ms. D. asks her students to write answers to each SELf-question in their mathematics journals.

SELECT A FOCUS

Questions: What is the problem? What is the question?

Ms. D. says, "When solving the problem, the first thing I want you to do is just read the problem." She hands out the problem and asks, "You read all the juicy info, but what does the problem actually say? The first thing you are trying to do is think, 'What is the problem trying to find out?'"

One student answers, "Who walks farther?"

Ms. D. confirms, "Yes, the question is who walks farther to school."

GATHER INFORMATION

Questions: What do I know? What do I need to know? What is similar, and what is different? What information is important?

Ms. D. asks the following questions: "What is the same? What is the same about the numerator of the fraction and the digits to the right of the decimal point?" She tells students, "Explain how you can use what you know about comparing 240 and 275 to help you compare 3.240 with 3.275. What is the difference between whole numbers and decimals? What place value is this referring to?" When teachers regularly ask questions like "What is similar?" and "What is different?" the questions help students develop more cognitive flexibility.

BRAINSTORM

Questions: How can I solve this problem? What can I do?

Ms. D. encourages her students to look at the brainstorm step and question on the anchor chart, which she has posted on the smartboard. She encourages students to use the SELf-questions for this action step (*How can I solve the problem?*) to help them independently think of ways to solve the problem. Here is where we recommend modeling the use of thinking dispositions like those referred to in the Modeling section (page 24) of chapter 1. Modeling helps students understand that sometimes the best way to solve a problem does not just jump off the page. Mathematics teachers can help students immensely by demonstrating how they think about their knowledge, strategies, and by how they sometimes make up their own ways to solve a mathematics problem.

EVALUATE

Questions: What is the best way to solve this problem? Does this make sense?

As students work on ways to solve the problem, Ms. D. sees some students needing additional support and asks them questions that she adapted from the academic SELf-question set. She asks specific students variations of, "Why would you do that?" "Do you have to look at the whole numbers?" "Can you cross off the whole numbers and just compare the decimals?" "Does this make sense?" By asking additional open-ended questions, Ms. D. models for the students the value of extending one's thinking and persisting through SELf-questioning. For this mathematics problem, which was more difficult and contained content new to the students, Ms. D. determined more scaffolding would benefit student thinking. So, she made the open-ended questions more specific and targeted to more directly prompt student thinking in the right direction.

PLAN AND ACT

Questions: What do I do first, second, and so on? Does this work?

Students work on solving the problem. To reinforce self-monitoring, Ms. D. asks what she calls a *pulse check* question: "Which place values do we look at first when we are comparing numbers? Why? Does this work?" Some students do struggle to identify which place value to look at first. Ms. D. uses those observations to build small groups for reinforcement of place values when conducting free learning, choice centers, and teacher conferences later in the week.

REFLECT

Questions: Did it work? How do I know? Do I need to go back and try again?

At the end of this lesson, and after students have shared ways they solved the problem to the whole class, Ms. D. asks a slightly adapted version of the reflect SELf-question to the class: "Did you do it a different way?" A few students raise their hand, and she invites them to the front of the room to show the class the different ways they solved the problem. This practice is great for showing students how their peers model cognitive flexibility. It reinforces and demonstrates that there are often multiple possible solutions and how great mathematical thinkers often think of more than one possible solution, evaluating which is the best.

Scenario: Grades 6–8

Class or subject: Sixth-grade algebra (Mrs. T.; homeschool teacher)

Objectives:

- Use algebraic reasoning to show growth in a pattern.
- Use modeling to solve a problem.
- Look for and make use of structure.

Standards:

- Algebra 6–8 Expectations: Represent, analyze, and generalize a variety of patterns with tables, graphs, words, and, when possible, symbolic rules. (National Council of Teachers of Mathematics [NCTM], n.d.)
- Model with mathematics. (MP4; NGA & CCSSO, 2010b)
- Look for and make use of structure. (MP7; NGA & CCSSO, 2010b)

Reygan is a sixth-grade, homeschooled student who is a bubbling brook of joy. Her teacher presents her with a task from youcubed (www.youcubed.org), which is depicted in figure 2.1. This site is connected to the Stanford University Graduate School of Education, for which Jo Boaler—mathematics guru supreme—is the faculty advisor. It contains many high-interest and low-entry problems for all grade levels.

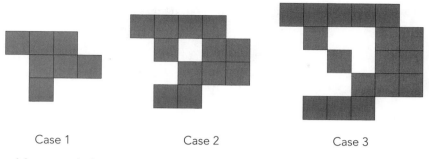

Case 1   Case 2   Case 3

Source: Adapted from youcubed, 2018.

Figure 2.1 Middle school problem.

This task, as presented in youcubed (2020) is more complex, but because Mrs. T. knows that Reygan isn't used to this kind of mathematical thinking, she has Reygan just draw the fourth case. During the week following, they'll draw other cases and write this algebraically. The following sections describe how Reygan uses SELf-questioning to solve the problem. Mrs. T. intentionally does not model this process for Reygan as she wants to get a baseline for her thinking.

SELECT A FOCUS

Question: What is the problem?

Reygan states, "The number of squares that are in the fourth case."

GATHER INFORMATION

Question: What do I know? What do I need to know?

Reygan states, "I know you need to show a pattern. I need to use the first three cases to know how many squares would be in the fourth case."

BRAINSTORM

Question: How can I solve this problem?

Reygan states, "The only thing I can think of is to estimate or to count." Mrs. T. wants to ask here, "Estimate what?" but she stops herself. Mrs. T. wants to understand exactly where Reygan's mathematical thinking and communication skills are at, so Reygan can also mentally visualize cubes of other sizes. Mrs. T. can then identify any of Reygan's misconceptions and address them via modeling in their next lesson.

EVALUATE

Question: What is the best way to solve this problem? What can I do?

Reygan states, "The best way to solve is to estimate, not counting because if you sit there and count the squares, that will take a long time."

PLAN AND ACT

Question: What do I do first, second, and so on?

Reygan works for a few minutes on the fourth case, producing the result in figure 2.2.

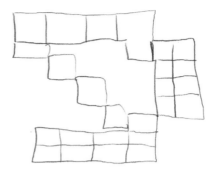

Figure 2.2 Reygan's attempt to solve a mathematics problem.

REFLECT

Question: Did it work? How do I know? Do I need to go back and try again?

Reygan explains, "See, case 1 has no diagonals, case 2 has two, and case 3 has three. So, I knew that case 4 would have four." Mrs. T. comments, "I like your thinking! Reygan, did you notice that you actually used counting and not estimating to determine how many squares should be in the diagonal?"

Mrs. T. also mentions that she might want to look at other progressions, and Reygan realizes that she has made a mistake on the top row. Reygan states, "If I had counted the top row, I would have seen that it increased by one in each case and that case 4 should have six squares across the top."

Teachers need to know the baseline of their students' thinking in the process of using the SELf-questions and explaining their responses. It is most helpful to wait as students work through a problem at the beginning of using SELf-questioning so they determine when students have a mathematical misconception or simply difficulty communicating their mathematical thinking. In a class setting, teachers can do this with handouts for the students to fill out that list each step.

Scenario: Grades 9–12

Class or subject: Ninth-grade algebra (Mrs. S.; tutor)

Objectives:

- Construct a viable argument about the process for solving this problem.

- Draw reasonable conclusions about a situation being modeled.

Standards:

- Grades 9–12 Expectations: Draw reasonable conclusions about a situation being modeled. (NCTM, n.d.)

- Construct viable arguments and critique the reasoning of others. (MP3; NGA & CCSSO, 2010b)

Most education books contain highly successful student examples, and Mrs. S. often wonders what would happen if things don't go so well during real-world application, particularly with her own students. Because of this, she chose Kayden, an introverted and not very self-aware ninth grader with whom to use SELf-questioning during a tutoring session.

Kayden, a freshman in honors mathematics, hates CCSS mathematics because she equates it with having to explain her answers, which was the purpose of providing her with tutoring. (NCTM standards also call for explaining one's reasoning.) Figure 2.3 presents another task derived from youcubed. Mrs. S. presents the question: "Imagine that we paint a 4 x 4 x 4 cube gray on every side. How many of the small cubes have three gray faces? How many have two gray faces? How many have one gray face? How many have not been painted at all? How many faces would be painted in a cube of any size? Think visually!"

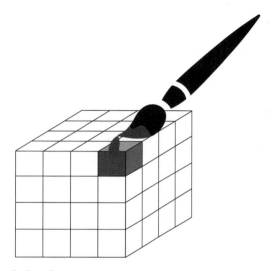

Source: Adapted from youcubed, n.d.

Figure 2.3: Problem illustration.

She adds to Kayden, "Before we start, let's think about why it is important to explain how you got your answer. I know you dislike doing it, but there are valid reasons for explaining our thinking. For one thing, it helps us to think mathematically. Two, it also helps develop critical-thinking skills. In a way, it is like teaching, and we remember a huge amount of what we teach. There are more reasons than this, but let's start with these."

SELECT A FOCUS

Question: What is the question?

Mrs. S. says, "Before we start on your problem, let me model a simple problem for you: A school bus can hold twenty-four students. There are 132 ninth graders going on a field trip. How many buses will they need?" Mrs. S. pauses and then continues, "OK, I need to know how many buses the students will need. I know it seems pretty basic, but when we work on more difficult problems, finding what the problem is asking can be more difficult. How would we apply this thinking to your problem?"

Kayden says, "I need to know many sides of each mini-cube are covered in paint." Mrs. S. observes that she answered with a shrug and a that's-pretty-obvious attitude.

GATHER INFORMATION

Question: What do I know? What do I need to know?

Mrs. S. says, "Back to my problem. What do I know and what do I need to know? I know how many students there are, and I know how many students the buses can hold. I'm going to have to divide the number of students by the number of students a bus can hold. Then I'll have to figure out what to do with the remainder if there is one. What about your problem?"

Kayden is quiet, so Mrs. S. has to prompt her: "For example, You know the whole outside of the cube is covered with paint." Kayden then adds, "So, I want to know how many cubes are covered on three sides with paint, how many with two sides, how many with one side, and how many have zero sides covered with paint."

BRAINSTORM

Question: How can I solve this problem? What can I do?

Mrs. S. says," There are many ways to divide. I could do long division, short division, make equal groups, or skip count. How could you solve your problem?"

Kayden answers, "The best way is to look at it, and count the squares." When Mrs. S. asks her how else she could solve the problem, Kayden replies, "There aren't any other ways." Mrs. S. says, "I could also write this as an algebra problem, couldn't I?" Kayden answers, "Maybe, but I don't know how."

Since she is just at the beginning of trying to overcome Kayden's resistance, Mrs. S. decides to let that lie for now.

EVALUATE

Question: What is the best way to solve this problem?

Mrs. S. says, "I would choose to do long division for my problem, because it would be efficient. What about you?"

Kayden replies, "The best way would be to visualize and count."

PLAN AND ACT

Question: What do I do first, second, and so on?

Mrs. S. says, "I would divide the number of students (132) by the number of students a bus can hold (twenty-four), which would give me five buses with twelve students left over. Since those twelve students need to go too, I would need a total of six buses. How about you?"

Kayden looks at the problem for about three seconds and then correctly announces the answer. She quickly identifies the pattern and shows she can also mentally visualize cubes of other sizes (such as 5 x 5 x 5) and give the correct answer. Mrs. S. asks her to explain exactly what she counted, and Kayden answers, "Well, you would first count the corners, and that would give you the number of cubes with paint on three sides. Then you would count the cubes on the edges that aren't on the corners, and that would give you the number of cubes with paint on two sides. Finally, you would count the number of cubes on the faces that aren't on the edge, and that would give you the number of cubes with paint on one side. The cubes on the inside of the big cube would have no paint on them."

REFLECT

Question: Did it work? How do I know? Do I need to go back and try again?

Kayden says, "I know it worked because of common sense." When Mrs. S. pushes her to reflect on her thinking, Kayden states, "I don't think when I do math. I just know the answer."

In this instance, she isn't being difficult; she just doesn't know how to identify and voice her thinking process. For students lacking the skill of explaining their thinking, we have found that it is best to continue to model the SELf-questions in mathematics several times using problems that increase in difficulty. At the same time, have them use SELf-questioning to explain their process. Over time, students begin to reflect more deeply on the process and see its usefulness.

Mrs. S. says, " We said at the beginning that it is important to understand the process by which we solve a problem. I know my problem worked because I checked my answer by multiplying six times twenty-four and then adding twelve. That equals 132 students. Do you think that other students would understand how to do this problem if they listened to your explanation? " She answers, "No…I don't think so."

Teachers have often told Kayden to explain her thinking, but she has never heard *why* she should do it. After all, she thinks, *I got the right answers, so what difference does it make?* Students like Kayden need to be explicitly taught the value of this process.

Character Corner: Perseverance

Developing students' character traits, such as perseverance, are foundational (Elias, Ferrito, & Moceri, 2016). To that end, this and the remaining chapters include a Character Corner like this one to show how embedding the metacognitive strategy of structured SELf-questioning and the use of SELf-question sets intertwines best practices in character development.

In writing this chapter, we inferred that the intent of the CCSS developers in adding the Standards of Mathematical Practice was to guide mathematics teachers to develop their students' ability to persevere through problem solving. We have seen first-hand how structured SELf-questioning and supporting students' internalization of the academic and social SELf-question set not only improves their performance in mathematics but can also lead to improved perseverance in problem solving. Moss teachers often reported students trying five or six different strategies to figure out an unknown word before giving up and moving on to the next word.

In the book introduction (Social and Emotional Successes, page 13), we told a true story of a second grader who had learned to use the academic and social SELf-question set to solve both mathematics problems in class and a personal problem in the guidance counselor's office. Not only did the student in that story demonstrate independent transfer of the strategy from academic to social and emotional problem solving, but she continues to show perseverance with mathematics problems just as she successfully perseveres in managing her anxiety and school phobia with increasing independence.

Structured SELf-Questioning for Social Problem Solving

"For apart from inquiry, apart from the praxis, individuals cannot be truly human. Knowledge emerges only through invention and re-invention, through the restless, impatient, continuing, hopeful inquiry human beings pursue in the world, with the world, and with each other."

—Paulo Freire

In chapter 2, we demonstrated how the metacognitive strategy of structured self-questioning helps students guide their self-talk through complex *academic* problem solving. In this chapter, we demonstrate how the use of that same metacognitive strategy, supported by the same SELf-question set, helps students guide their self-talk through complex *social* problem solving. Once students internalize the academic SELf-question set in their classrooms, they are simultaneously empowered to guide their own self-talk through challenging social problems and pressures outside the classroom.

In this chapter, we show how you can accomplish two goals.

1. How to take the research of Elias and his colleagues (Butler et al., 2011, Elias & Arnold, 2006; Elias et al., 2016) and easily infuse best practices from the field of social psychology into your classroom through structured SELf-questioning. In particular, note that Butler and colleagues (2011) specifically teach that decision making and problem solving are the exact same process. If you teach academic problem solving, you have also taught the social decision-making process at the same time.

2. How to easily and productively provide authentic opportunities for students to transfer and apply the academic SELf-question set to real-world social problem solving and responsible decision making in your classroom.

In the following sections, we more fully examine the importance of teaching a metacognitive strategy for social problem solving, how to teach that strategy using academic and social SELf-questioning, and how this learning develops the character trait of responsibility. The models in this chapter demonstrate how to develop students' ability to cope with and solve social pressures, conflicts, and problems in class, school, and life.

The Importance of a Metacognitive Strategy for Social Problem Solving

Life in and out of school has always posed social pressures, challenges, conflicts, and problems for students of all ages. However, it seems like the number of these factors students have to deal with are increasingly widespread, and this was before a global pandemic shook the world we knew.

A consistent trend line from the 20th century into the 21st century reveals an increasing socioeconomic status (SES) achievement gap, with students living in poverty-stricken communities often labeled *at-risk* (Chmielewski, 2019). The social problems students from poverty experience in school, at home, and throughout their communities are not new, and numerous resources document them (Brendtro, Brokenleg, & VanBockern, 2019; Colburn & Beggs, 2021; Jensen, 2019). However, in the 21st century, the student groups educators widely consider at-risk have increased and widened in scope to include students from even affluent communities. According to *Washington Post* reporter Jennifer B. Wallace (2019):

> Emerging research is finding that students in "high-achieving schools" . . . are experiencing higher rates of behavioral and mental health problems compared with national norms. . . . While the stressors are markedly different, researchers are finding that both [low SES and affluent students groups] are "at risk" for elevated levels of chronic stress that can affect health and well-being.

One factor in these findings is the volume of teens who own smartphones. According to a recent Pew Center poll, "Smartphone ownership has become a nearly ubiquitous element of teen life: 95% of teens now report they have a smartphone or access to one . . . 45% of teens now say they are online on a near-constant basis" (Anderson & Jiang, 2018). According to psychologist Jean M. Twenge (2017), cell phones and social media pose additional social pressures and problems for almost every student:

> Rates of teen depression and suicide have skyrocketed since 2011. It's not an exaggeration to describe iGen as being on the brink of the worst mental-health crisis in decades. Much of this deterioration can be traced to their phones.

Given the degree to which this preponderance of factors contributing to students' social stress and anxiety can negatively impact learning and lead to more behavior issues in the classroom, teaching students how to cope with and deal with these challenges is essential for student learning and success in the classroom. The silver lining in all this is that these real-world social pressures, conflicts, and larger societal problems can be some of students' strongest learning opportunities and teachers' greatest teaching tools. Also fortunate, we know from psychologists like Elias and Shure how to turn social pressures and social problems into great learning experiences in any classroom that aligns academic instruction with developing students' social problem-solving and decision-making skills.

Butler and colleagues (2011) suggest the following for productively and efficiently turning real-world social pressures and problems into highly valuable teaching and learning experiences in the classroom.

1. **Introduce a general strategy for guided self-talk:** You have likely guessed the first component, teaching a general strategy, aligns perfectly with using structured SELf-questioning to serve as a vehicle for guided self-talk through social problem solving and social decision making.

2. **Explore each element of the strategy as a separate skill:** Teach each of the six steps in the academic and social SELf-questioning set separately, one at a time.

3. **Practice each skill in varied contexts, such as engaging in hypotheticals, providing age-appropriate scenarios, and engaging in open-ended choice and conflict situations:** This component of teaching social problem-solving skills gives students opportunities to practice the strategy of structured SELf-questioning. In particular, we focus this chapter on the use of open-ended choice and conflict situations in the classroom. In doing so, we explore how teachers can use numerous models of common, real-life conflict situations as opportunities for students to practice the overall strategy for guided self-talk inside and outside the classroom.

Does the prospect of helping students confront complex social problems in your classroom sound a little frightening? Scary? Chaotic? Without providing students an overarching strategy, along with the right amount of structure and support, it can be just these things—a lesson we have learned the hard way. For instance, when Rick was a first-year teacher in Phoenix, Arizona, in 1996, he didn't understand the importance of providing both structure and a strategy for his students. All he knew was, the first two days of his teaching career went great. So, he made the social decision to let his students have a little fun on the third day of school, at the end of the day, on Friday.

He thought it would be a fun reward, a good idea even, to teach his seventh-grade students the scientific method, scientific data collection, and measurement by directing students to make various designs of paper airplanes, fly them around the room and hallway, and collect data on flight distances of their different designs. In the name of open-ended choice, those were the directions he gave students. What ensued were numerous conflict situations that did not help achieve the lesson's designed objective. Students intercepted other students' planes in midflight or launched themselves off chairs to better smash planes that had landed. There was no structure, no strategy, and no parameters, so students made them up. Rick did not end up smiling again until after the holiday break.

So yes, posing and confronting social problems with students can be very chaotic, even scary, but it need not be so if teachers provide a strategy, structure, and supports for students when posing open-ended choice and conflict situations in the classroom. With just the Goldilocks amount of structure and support—not too much, not too little—students can rise to the occasion and practice their higher-order critical-thinking skills and problem-solving strategies in ways you may never have thought possible. To that end, the advantages of the SELf-questioning metacognitive strategy are twofold.

1. The versatility of the academic SELf-question set provides one structure for students' critical-thinking and problem-solving skills applicable to both academic and social problems in the classroom.

2. The academic SELf-questions provide one set of prompts for the exact type of critical thinking skills students need each step of the way for scaffolding both academic and social cognitive processing.

Teachers we've worked with have found that the strategy of structured SELf-questioning provides each individual student the necessary amount of structure and support without over-scaffolding since the questions are open-ended. By providing one set of SELf-questions for both academic and social problems, the sheer quantity of questions students need to internalize is very limited, making internalization more efficient and accessible as students confront both academic and social challenges inside and outside the classroom.

Through multiple practice opportunities, applications, iterations, and reflections, students become more fluent with the strategy and question set, thereby developing through time and practice the ability to respond (response-ability) more independently to all kinds of problems. With practice, structured SELf-questioning becomes a habit of mind, and responsible decision making becomes more the norm in the classroom when problems or conflicts arise. Because students have a particular strategy at the forefront of their minds and are more familiar with what to do when problems occur, students have greater success when attempting social conflict resolution and responsible decision making at school. With practice using the steps and SELf-question set to better resolve social conflicts, students gain more confidence. As a result, stress and anxiety decrease without the need for additional instruction or time.

How to Teach a Metacognitive Strategy for Social Problem Solving

You may be wondering how it looks in the classroom to teach the same SELf-question set for both academic and social challenges. How can students productively guide their own self-talk through complex, multistep social problem solving without chaos and without the need for more instructional time?

To help you incorporate the teaching of social problem solving into your existing curriculum with structure and a strategy, we ensured the same steps we offered in chapter 2 (page 29) for academic SELf-questioning apply equally well to social situations. Any teacher can use these same steps and questions to formulate the open-ended, initial questions that will structure and support students' self-talk through either academic or social problem solving. This simplifies transfer of the strategy across academic and social contexts for both students and teachers. Let's briefly review the steps and questions.

 Select a focus: What is the problem? What is the question? What is the task?

 Gather information: What do I know? What do I need to know? What is similar, and what is different?

 Brainstorm: How can I solve this problem? What are possible solutions? What can I do?

Evaluate: What is the best way to solve this problem? Does this make sense?

 Plan and act: What do I do first, second, and so on? Does this work? Is this working?

 Reflect: Did it work? How do I know? Do I need to go back and try again?

With the structure and support this SELf-question set provides, teachers are empowered to gradually release responsibility for social problem solving in the classroom to their students. When teachers pair gradual release of responsibility with initial think-alouds as part of their academic instruction (see the example we provided in chapter 2, page 29), students receive just the right amount of scaffolding they need to internalize, transfer, and apply independently that same strategy and self-questioning set to social problem solving. By then giving students opportunities to transfer and practice their academic problem-solving skills on social situations, teachers can serve as coaches on the side, which is imperative if students are to use the strategy when the teacher is not there, like at recess, at lunch, at home, or in the community. Consider the following sequence of events.

In the spring of 1997, Rick's seventh-grade students (the same ones who flew the airplanes around the room) told him they wanted to do something about the social problems they faced at school. He asked, "What are the problems at school?" They said drugs, gangs, and violence. Next, he asked them, "What do you know about drugs, gangs, and violence?" They told him more than he wanted to know. Then, he asked them, "What are possible solutions to address drugs or gangs or violence at school?" They had a bunch of good ideas.

One of those ideas involved the students volunteering to teach younger students after school about the social problems they may soon face and what they would need to know about them. As part of a trip to visit incoming students, and while playing chess, face painting, or giving them break-dancing lessons, Rick's students asked the younger students, "What do you know about drugs? Do you know what they do to your body and brain? What do you know about gangs? What do you think you could do if a gang member asks you to join their gang?"

Another idea focused on reducing fighting at school, so student volunteers also trained as peer mediators and volunteered during lunch to help their peers resolve social conflicts at recess peacefully. To serve as peer mediators of social conflicts at school, his students asked their peers a series of structured open-ended questions, such as, "What are possible solutions?" and, "What is the best way to solve this problem?"

After three years of providing these activities at Loma Linda Elementary School (a K–8 public school in Phoenix, Arizona's Creighton School District), between 1997 and 2000, the school's discipline office reported a 60 percent reduction in suspension for drug, gang-related, and fighting violations. In 1999, Rick's program was awarded the Creighton School District's Exemplary Program Award. It wasn't until 2010 that Rick became familiar with the work of Elias and realized that the tactics he had implemented out of pure desperation in Phoenix were actually evidence based (Butler et al., 2011; Elias & Arnold, 2006; Elias et al., 2016).

Let's take a look at the different ways teachers can utilize the academic and social SELf-question set so all students can not only guide their self-talk through social conflicts and problems inside the classroom but also support themselves through state standards-aligned curriculum, PBL, IBL, research, and service-learning projects.

Scenario: Grades K–2

Class or subject: Kindergarten classroom (Mrs. A.; teacher)

Objective:

- Solve a social conflict without support using a previously modeled conflict-resolution strategy.

Standards:

- With prompting and support, ask and answer questions about key details in a text. (RI.K.1; NGA & CCSSO, 2010a)

- Responsible decision making: The abilities to make caring and constructive choices about personal behavior and social interactions across diverse situations. (CASEL, n.d.).

In a balanced literacy classroom, two six-year-old students go to the library center (while their teacher works with a small group of students in guided reading). They encounter a simple yet real-world social problem: they both want to sit in the same chair. The students both try going through their learned academic critical-thinking and problem-solving skills to attempt to solve this social conflict. In this iteration of the SELf-questioning actions, notice how the students grouped specific actions together.

SELECT A FOCUS AND GATHER INFORMATION

Questions: What is the problem? What do I know?

At the library center, there is only one remaining red chair, and both students want to sit on it (the focus of the social problem). They also both know that the other student wants to sit on it. Neither is sure who was first. Even as they determine their focus (the chair), they simultaneously gather information about it. In this case, they observe the chair is square on all sides and has a flat solid surface on three sides.

BRAINSTORM, EVALUATE, AND PLAN AND ACT

Questions: How can I solve the problem? What is the best way to solve this problem? What can I do? What do I do first, second, and so on?

On their own, the students come up with an idea. They realize that if they turn the chair over onto one of the three flat surfaces (the top), there will be a flat surface big enough for the two of them to sit on. They engage in a four-step process to solve the problem.

1. The two students flip the chair over.

2. They try sitting on the one flat surface sticking up in the air.

3. They turn and face opposite directions and sit back to back.

4. They begin reading their books.

Here, we see that sometimes students do not always need to go through every step or every question in the SELf-questioning set. Here, the students combined the *focus* and *gather information* steps and then grouped the *brainstorm*, *evaluate*, and *plan and act* steps. This is implicitly possible because, even at a young age, students can perform multiple thinking skills and steps fluidly. In this case, they came up with the idea, loved the idea immediately, and enacted the idea.

REFLECT

Question: Did it work? How do I know? Do I need to go back and try again?

When the time for the center rotation ends, Mrs. A. notices her two students sitting back to back reading at the library center. Curious, she asks the students why they are sitting that way. They respond by telling her how they solved the problem each step of the way.

While all of this complex real-world, social problem solving was occurring amongst two six-year-olds at a reading center, Mrs. A. never stopped her teaching. No one disrupted small-group instruction, and the students had a meaningful, relevant, authentic opportunity to practice and transfer the problem-solving strategy they had already learned during academic instruction to a real-world social problem in the classroom. Once students demonstrate memory of the steps independently, if they tell the teacher about a social conflict, then the teacher can always ask students if they have tried to use their problem-solving strategy to encourage them to try transfer on their own first. If students can't transfer on their own, the teacher can pose the SELf-questions to students (changing *I* to *you*)

If a teacher were to observe that the students did attempt using their problem-solving steps and questions to resolve a social conflict without adult support and were not successful, it's time for the teacher to engage. Butler and colleagues (2011) recommend that teachers "first try to *ask* open-ended questions, then *suggest* options from which students can choose, and then *tell* students [how to resolve the conflict], if necessary" (pg. 17).

Scenario: Grades 3–5

Class or subject: Third-grade classroom (Ms. H.; teacher)

Objective:

- Use a written T-chart to reflect and improve on a behavioral issue.

Standard:

- Make sense of problems and persevere in solving them. (MP1; NGA & CCSSO, 2010b)

- Look for and express regularity in repeated reasoning. (MP8; NGA & CCSSO, 2010b)

- Responsible decision making: The abilities to make caring and constructive choices about personal behavior and social interactions across diverse situations. (CASEL, n.d.)

Students sometimes do not make the best choices at school. This is not news to any teacher. Those bad choices, however, can be the best learning experiences. To maximize the learning opportunities that each bad choice presents, without requiring the teacher to stop teaching and intervene, Ms. H. utilizes the social SELf-questioning set as a *think sheet*. This is a T-chart with the steps and questions on the left side and blank boxes on the right side of each for student-written responses. (See "Academic and Social Problem-Solving Think Sheet: Design 1" in the appendix, page 218, for an example.)

In this scenario, an otherwise adorable third grader in Ms. H.'s class isn't making such adorable choices. As a result, he receives a think sheet from Ms. H. that requires him to think through the first three SELf-questioning steps. The following sections detail how the student addressed each SELf-question on the think sheet.

SELECT A FOCUS

Question: What is the problem?

The student writes, *I was talking. Also, I was arguing with other students. I made faces at other people.*

GATHER INFORMATION

Question: What do I know?

The student writes, *I was interrupting other people.*

BRAINSTORM

Question: How can I solve the problem?

The student writes, *To not talk when other people are talking. To come up with suggestions when I am arguing with other people.*

By adapting the academic and social SELf-question set into a think sheet for students to fill out, Ms. H. challenges her students to think about their own behavior, take responsibility for their mistakes, and brainstorm better ways to handle the problem next time. For these goals, Ms. H. only uses three of the steps and SELf-questions because she intends to play a more active role in the other steps in the future.

Once a student has filled out the form, Ms. H reviews it briefly and decides whether the form is ready to go home for parent review and signature. By having students take their sheets home, students present a classroom rule violation to their parents in a solution-oriented fashion. In doing so, parents receive information about what happened while also seeing how they might reinforce the use of structured SELf-questioning at home. Note that this process is made even more effective when teachers present it along with a sample think sheet to parents at the start of the school year (either printed or digitally).

Through the process depicted in this scenario, Ms. H. accomplishes many objectives for social problem solving with little to no additional instructional time and little to no additional professional time (such as making phone calls to parents, spending time in the hallway discussing with students, and so on). In addition to utilizing the academic and social SELf-question set for social-conflict resolution and reinforcement of classroom routines, Ms. H.'s school also utilizes the SELf-questioning set for its peer-mediation program and for restorative justice practices. You can read more about this in chapter 7 (page 113), which is about using the emotional SELf-question set for emotional recognition.

Scenario: Grades 6–8

Class or subject: Title I BrainSTREAM (science, technology, reading, engineering, art, mindfulness) classroom (Mr. C. and Ms. L.; director and teacher)

Objective:

- Apply the social SELf-questioning set to solve a real-world social problem at school.

Standards:

- Write narratives to develop real or imagined experiences or events using effective technique, well-chosen details and well-structured event sequences. (CCRA.W.3; NGA & CCSSO, 2010a)

- Develop and strengthen writing as needed by planning, revising, editing, rewriting, or trying a new approach. (CCRA.W.5; NGA & CCSSO, 2010a)

- Conduct short as well as more sustained research projects based on focused questions, demonstrating understanding of the subject under investigation. (CCRA.W.7; NGA & CCSSO, 2010a)

- Responsible decision making: The abilities to make caring and constructive choices about personal behavior and social interactions across diverse situations. (CASEL, n.d.)

A middle school principal feels her school's students are acting too much as bystanders instead of upstanders when bullying incidences occur. Mr. C., a program director in the district, and Ms. L., a classroom teacher, take up this call with their students by having them seek an answer to the question, How can we serve as upstanders against bullying and teach our peers what to do if they see a peer being bullied?

SELECT A FOCUS:

Questions: What is the problem? What is the question? What is the task?

Mr. C. says to a student group, "The task we have is to turn our school's students into upstanders instead of bystanders when bullying occurs in school."

GATHER INFORMATION

Questions: What do I know? What do I need to know? What is similar, and what is different?

Mr. C. continues, "Think for a minute and write down what you know about bullying." Students begin writing in their journals what they know about bullying. With prompting from Mr. C. and Ms. L., some students share their experiences with the whole class. Mr. C. then asks, "What do you need to know?" Students say they need to know "more ways to be an upstander." They say they will gather information by researching on the internet, interviewing the vice principal, and asking their peers.

BRAINSTORM

Questions: How can I solve this problem? What are possible solutions? What can I do?

Students get to work gathering information from the resources they chose. They write down ideas in their journals, share them with a partner, and then, as a whole group, discuss different ways to be an upstander. Collectively, they brainstorm four solutions derived from the information they gathered: (1) help after the incident, (2) tell a trusted adult, (3) pull the victim away, and (4) block someone cyberbullying you and others.

EVALUATE

Questions: What is the best way to solve this problem? Does this make sense?

The students decide to make videos to teach their peers how to apply the four best solutions in different bullying situations. They feel this solution is best because they can distribute the videos to all students at school efficiently, and they think that a quick video will be more interesting to their peers than classroom presentations.

PLAN AND ACT

Question: What do I do first, second, and so on? Does this work? Is this working?

First, students get into groups and pick one of the four ways to be an upstander. Second, students write narratives in their journals and then do some shared writing to develop a skit or scenario. Third, they write scripts with a clearly identifiable bullying situation along with a clearly identifiable solution representing a way for any middle school student to act as an upstander. Fourth, students use their tablet computers to make their videos (there are four videos in all). Fifth, after some peer review and teacher feedback of student video productions, students make final revisions and combine all four clips into one video. They post the video set to the district website, and the principal agrees to show the video to all students. (Visit https://youtu.be/8b7slHb5Gow to see the actual video that students created for Edgar Middle School, in Metuchen, New Jersey, using the SELf-questioning process for exactly this purpose.)

REFLECT

Questions: Did it work? How do I know? Do I need to go back and try again?

Mr. C. and Ms. L. ask students to write in their journals what they did and what they learned, focusing on the problem-solving process they learned as much as content, and how they personally would handle a bullying situation in the future.

Not long after this exercise, a mother of one of the students came up to Mr. C. and said her son had helped her to see a mistake she had made with one of her daughters. She explained that one night, while eating dinner as a family at home, one of her daughters was describing a bullying situation that had occurred that day at the middle school cafeteria. She explained that she had directed her daughter to stay out of it. Immediately, her son said, "Mom, you are teaching her the wrong thing. You are teaching her to be a bystander. You have to teach her to be an upstander and tell her to inform a trusted adult at school." The parent welled up with tears as she told the story and expressed that she felt the lessons her child learned from the program were invaluable.

Scenario: Grades 9–12

Class: Twelfth-grade health (Ms. B. and Mr. U.; teachers)

Objective:

- Use collaborative decision-making skills to identify and research a topic; teach the topic to younger students to demonstrate healthy decision making and behaviors..

Standards:

- Students will demonstrate the ability to use decision-making skills to enhance health. (Standard 5; Centers for Disease Control and Prevention [CDC], 2019)

- Determine the value of applying a thoughtful decision-making process in health-related situations. (Standard 5.12.2; CDC, 2019)

In a health class, students utilize structured SELf-questioning to guide a student-directed, inquiry-based research-and-service project by conducting their own research into vaping. Their goal is to create their own lesson to teach younger students in middle school and elementary school about the dangers and consequences of vaping. Ms. B. and Mr. U. instruct students to use the academic and social SELf-questioning set as their guide for their collaborative inquiry-based research process and lesson. During the classroom implementation of this project, for which they set aside a week to accomplish, Ms. B. and Mr. U. don't teach ELA, health content, or research skills. Instead, they encourage students to use their knowledge from prior instruction and research, and they scaffold students' self-talk by providing them with the structured SELf-question set.

This scenario presents how the teachers wrote the curriculum to align with the use of the SELf-questioning framework. The following scenario steps include excerpts from the curriculum itself to show how the academic and social SELf-question set aligns with the necessary parameters for the project and to scaffold students' SELf-questioning.

SELECT A FOCUS

Questions: What is the problem? What is the question? What is the task?

For this project, teachers, administrators, and school board members collectively chose vaping as the topic for students to focus on because vaping had become a major problem in the high school and community.

GATHER INFORMATION

Questions: What do I know? What do I need to know? What is similar, and what is different?

With support from the academic and social SELf-question set, Ms. B. and Mr. U. expect twelfth graders to know how to independently perform the necessary critical-thinking skills and information-gathering process. They do not provide direct instruction on how to research; they only support students through the process as needed. However, they do explain to students they have high expectations for the complexity, quality, and reliability of the work students need to do. The teachers include the following specific criteria, which appear in both teacher and student assessment rubrics.

- Determine the truthfulness and efficacy of the information you find.

- Develop critical-thinking questions about the information you discover.

- Organize the information logically using graphic organizers and outlines.

BRAINSTORM

Questions: How can I solve this problem? What are possible solutions? What can I do?

The curriculum sets the expectation for this step, and teachers present the expectation to students via a project rubric with the following statement: *Collaborate with others to develop evidence of your findings and to propose solutions to these global concerns.*

EVALUATE

Questions: What is the best way to solve this problem? Does this make sense?

Once again, the curriculum already determines the expectation for this step, and teachers present the following expectation to students accordingly: *Present your findings in the form of an oral presentation to the class.*

PLAN AND ACT

Questions: What do I do first, second, and so on? Does this work?

Again, the curriculum sets an expectation, which teachers present as the following statement: *Collaborate with others to present their findings to other middle school and elementary school classes.*

REFLECT

Questions: Did it work? How do I know? Do I need to go back and try again?

The curriculum further enables reflections by assigning students the following tasks.

- *Engage in peer and metacognitive self-assessments to reflect upon your research methods, problem-based learning skills, and presentation.*

- *Engage in ongoing revision throughout the duration of the inquiry process.*

For this grades 9–12 scenario, and others like it in any content area, it is intended that twelfth-grade students transfer the structured SELf-questioning strategy they learned as an academic problem-solving and inquiry-based research process into a strategy students can apply to guide their healthy decision making when they encounter real-world social pressures and problems like vaping and substance abuse. By having the students independently apply the strategy in a health class using a real-world social problem, students practice transfer and application of the strategy toward real-life social issues and situations in a controlled environment. However, they still have a teacher by their side to guide them where necessary. Further, by engaging students in teaching the strategy to younger students, the high school students maximize their own retention and become even less dependent on having a teacher's support, all while promoting transfer to younger students. This mastery of the metacognitive process of structured SELf-questioning is the curriculum's expectation and is a deliberate component in the health curriculum.

Character Corner: Responsibility

The more practice students get applying the academic and social SELf-questioning set at school, the more responsibility they develop. CASEL (n.d.) defines the capacity for students to make responsible decisions as being able to adhere to three criteria when making choices related to personal behavior and social interactions: (1) employ ethical standards, (2) consider safety, and (3) adhere to social norms. CASEL (n.d.) includes the following actions in this process.

- *Identify* solutions.

- *Analyze* information, data, and facts.

- *Anticipate* and *evaluate* consequences.

- *Recognize* opportunities for critical thinking in and out of school.

- *Reflect on* one's role in decisions and consequences.

- *Evaluate* impacts of decisions personally, for the community, and for institutions.

If you reflect on this list, you may note that the cognitive (italicized) verbs listed here are the exact same cognitive verbs involved in both academic and social problem solving. (See also the "Linking Cognitive Verbs in CCSS and SELf-Questions" reproducible on page 222.) Our SELf-questions explicitly correlate to and target the execution of these thinking skills. By teaching students one strategy for guiding self-talk through this one set of core critical-thinking skills for academic and social problem solving, teachers can simultaneously develop students' ability to employ all three criteria for responsible decision making. Hence, it is possible for any teacher of any grade level and any content area to simultaneously teach state or provincial standards, provide authentic opportunities for students to transfer their academic critical-thinking and problem-solving skills to social situations, manage their classroom behavior, and develop their students' responsible decision-making abilities.

Structured SELf-Questioning in Reading Comprehension

4

Proficient readers, sometimes automatically, sometimes purposefully, must first be metacognitive: they must be aware of their own comprehension.

—Elin Keene and Susan Zimmermann

In the same way that we walked through using SELf-questions with mathematics (chapter 2) and social skills (chapter 3), we now enter the wonderfully complex world of reading. Taking a metacognitive step back is an asset for students engaged in decoding and comprehending text. *Decoding* has to do with understanding the individual words on the page and includes phonics, sight words, and sounding out words. *Comprehending* moves beyond decoding to include the understanding and interpretation of the text. In other words, comprehending involves what the individual words mean when readers put them together into sentences, paragraphs, and chapters. According to Reading Rockets (n.d.), an initiative dedicated to supporting child literacy:

> To be able to accurately understand written material, children need to be able to (1) decode what they read; (2) make connections between what they read and what they already know; and (3) think deeply about what they have read.

The academic and social SELf-question set we established in chapters 2 and 3 helps in all three of these areas. Therefore, in this chapter, we stress the importance of modeling thinking about reading comprehension. We provide you with how-to information about teaching this form of thinking and walk you through the question set with examples across the grade levels. We conclude this chapter with a character corner about self-efficacy.

The Importance of Teaching a Metacognitive Strategy for Reading Comprehension

Metacognition is what readers use to monitor their understanding and make adjustments as they read. It comes into play in additional components of reading, such as making connections, questioning, visualizing, inferring, synthesizing information, and evaluating. Metacognitive thinking also helps readers choose when to apply a certain strategy. As Annemarie Sullivan Palincsar and Ann L. Brown of the Center for the Study of Reading at the University of Illinois find, "Metacognitively skilled readers seek to establish 'meaningfulness' in their reading and value careful selection of appropriate strategies and careful monitoring of their comprehension" (as cited in Kolencik & Hillwig, 2011, p. 88).

When reading, metacognition is what takes readers beyond mere identification of words into a sphere where they truly understand what the author has written, discuss (internally or out loud) the author's ideas or message as they read, determine the author's purpose, or evaluate what they are reading for quality thinking and writing. Our SELf-questions don't just help students solve problems in various areas of life; they also help students move beyond merely understanding a text to become thinking, metacognitive readers.

Consider this: the OECD (2019) reports that across the education system, students perform better academically if they have a growth mindset. More specifically, the OECD (2019) states:

> This is especially true for 15-year-old students in the United States. Students who disagreed or strongly disagreed with the statement "Your intelligence is something about you that you can't change very much" scored 58 points higher in reading than students who agreed or strongly agreed with the statement, after accounting for students' and schools' socio-economic profile" (p. 2).

For students, having a metacognitive strategy at the ready when they read a text helps them develop the necessary mindset for academic growth.

How to Teach a Metacognitive Strategy for Reading Comprehension

Before teachers can use the academic and social question set in reading comprehension, they need to have a clear idea of what each step entails. In *select a focus*, students need to explicitly learn what it means to understand and not to understand. As a first grader, Sue's great-nephew, Gunner, had advanced-level decoding skills for his age. He's also the son of a former Marine reconnaissance soldier. Sue asked Gunner to bring her a book that would be a *little* difficult for him to read, and he brought her his copy of *Jane's Aircraft Recognition Guide* (Endres & Gething, 2007)—a book for adults. Gunner could flawlessly read the following passage:

> Short-fuselage version of A320, officially launched in June 1993 and first flown at Hamburg on August 29, 1995. Entered service with Swissair on April 30, 1996. First ACJ (Airbus Corporate Jetliner) variant was announced at 1997 Paris Air Show and made its maiden flight on November 12, 1998. First delivery to customer November 8, 1999. A319LR delivered to PrivatAir May 2004. Total delivered: 930 (ordered 1497). (Endres & Gething, 2007)

The fact that a first-grade student could read this without error and with expression is amazing, but when she asked him if he could tell her about what he had read, he couldn't say, "This was about the development of an airplane." He could give a lot of details about the aircraft that he had memorized from reading the specifications on the facing page, but those specifications had no real-world meaning to him. Gunner is an expert decoder but did not comprehend what he read. The question is, Does *he know* that he doesn't understand?

Although understanding seems obvious to us, it is not always obvious to students, who can struggle with the concept of making sense—a problem that Ellin Oliver Keene (2008) grappled with in *To Understand* after a second-grade student, Jamika, challenged her during a reading conference. When Keene asked Jamika if the book she was reading makes sense, she answered, "None a y'all ever say what make sense mean [sic]" (Keene, 2008, p. 2).

The whole idea of modeling is key to the first step of our question set: *select a focus*. People have a human need to pose questions and seek answers, and readers can apply that need to help them decide if they understand what they read. Modeling with examples and non-examples via think-alouds is foundational to teaching.

In the case of modeling understanding, the teacher first models the type of thinking he or she does when he or she *does* understand a text. For example, when teaching this concept in grades 3–5, Sue might grab a copy of Marguerite Henry's (1948) classic, *King of the Wind*. In the following scenario, she reads a passage out loud to students and stops at regular intervals to reflect out loud about what she read, giving students a window into her brain.

> **Passage:** *"The morning fog had lifted, giving way to a clear day. Nearly all the people of Windsor, Ontario, and thousands of visitors were surging into Kenilworth Park, filling the stands and overflowing to the infield." (Henry, 1948, p. 1)*
>
> **Teacher think-aloud:** *I wonder why so many people were going to the park. It must be a special event.*
>
> **Passage:** *"It was the greatest crowd ever to attend a race in Canada." (Henry, 1948, p. 1)*
>
> **Teacher think-aloud:** *What kind of race?*
>
> **Passage:** *"For this was the day of the match race between Man o' War, the great American horse, and Sir Barton, the pride of Canada." (Henry, 1948, p. 1)*
>
> **Teacher think-aloud:** *Oooh, it's about a horse race! So far I understand what's happening.*

Next, she models something that she *doesn't* understand so that students can see the difference in her thinking when comprehension breaks down. For this example, she selects the science textbook *Chemistry* (Flowers, Theopold, Langley, & Robinson, 2019).

> **Passage:** *"The basic principles of physics are essential for understanding many aspects of chemistry." (Flowers et al., 2019)*
>
> **Teacher think-aloud:** *Hmm, I think physics is about how things move and chemistry is about mixing chemicals together. How do these two fit together?*
>
> **Passage:** *"there is extensive overlap between many subdisciplines within the two fields, such as chemical physics and nuclear chemistry." (Flowers et al., 2019)*
>
> **Teacher think-aloud:** *I know a subdiscipline would mean various types of chemistry, but how does this fit in?*

Passage: *"Mathematics, computer science, and information theory provide important tools that help us calculate, interpret, describe, and generally make sense of the chemical world." (Flowers et al., 2019)*

Teacher think-aloud: *I really don't understand what I'm reading! I know the words, but I still don't understand the text. Let me see if I can understand this if I use SELf-questioning.*

Notice how, in the first example, Sue models understanding of a text and that she can continue reading. In the second example, she not only models a lack of understanding but also the *realization* that she needs to work through the SELf-question framework.

In the *gather information* step, teachers need to model for students how to determine what they know and what they need to know. Sue remembers conversing with a student's father once about whether his son needed to understand each and every word on a page. Her stance was that the student can determine if a word was necessary to know. He believed, rather staunchly, that you should look up each and every word that you do not precisely know. She explained that when she read mysteries in Spanish, she only looked up words that she didn't know if they seemed to be part of a clue or if they were repeated several times. She explained that she could follow the gist of the story, and looking up every single word would ruin the joy and the flow of reading. It got a little heated, and they finally agreed to disagree.

Looking back, she thinks they were both right. There are circumstances in reading where each word and phrase is of the utmost importance—for example, legal documents, the U.S. Constitution, religious texts, and much poetry. In these instances, readers must comprehend each word to understand the meaning of the full text. This is usually not the case in a novel or children's book, in which readers can derive the meaning and author's purpose without necessarily stopping to ensure they understand every word.

Returning to the example of the chemistry text Sue did not understand, she might model her thinking this way:

> *What do I understand? Hmm, I understand all the words.*
>
> *What do I need to understand? I do not understand how the concepts fit together. For example, how are chemical physics and nuclear chemistry related to one another?*

For the *brainstorm* step, students need to determine an approach, a strategy, to their reading. This means they need at least a few strategies in their toolboxes (such as building background knowledge or rereading complex text) before they start using SELf-questioning. As students learn such strategies, we suggest teachers post them in the brainstorming section of an anchor chart for students to choose from. If any students still have no idea what to do for this step, start the ball rolling with an idea or two of your own. Some of the comprehension strategies we suggest include the following.

- **Change reading pace:** Understanding can sometimes be clarified by speeding up (when reading is syllable by syllable) or by slowing down (to carefully look at words and punctuation). Say, "Try reading slower or faster, and see if it helps your comprehension."

- **Use background knowledge:** Background knowledge (schema) is everything you bring to a book, your life experiences, relationships, and everything you believe. Ask, "What do I *already* know about this that will help me understand?"

- **Visualize:** When students read, they create mental images based on the text, and they continue to do so after reading. Say, "Try making a movie in your mind of what you're reading to help your understanding."

- **Infer:** Students infer at the word level using context clues and word substitution to determine what the author has implied. Say, "Maybe you need to make an inference to understand." Then, ask, "Why did the character do or say that?" or "Why do you think the author wrote this?"

- **Predict:** Predicting is technically part of inferring, and learning to make reasonable predictions is a key to reading engagement. Say, "Can you make a reasonable prediction about what will happen next?"

- **Question:** Proficient readers ask questions to clarify meaning, show skepticism, and consider text-inspired rhetorical questions. Say, "Constantly self-question when you are reading, and look for answers to those questions."

- **Determine importance:** A critical aspect of nonfiction reading is understanding the difference between important information and what is merely interesting to read (Mackenzie, n.d.). For fiction reading, readers must understand the significance of the setting, main characters and their relationships, the problems or conflicts in the story, and so on. In either case, say, "What is important?"

- **Summarize:** Summarizing is relating the most important part of a text in your own words. Say, "Can you summarize what you have read so far?"

- **Synthesize:** Synthesizing is how readers combine background knowledge and their evolving understanding of one or more texts to reach complete understanding of what they've read. Even students as young as age 3 can learn to use metacognition (Miller, 2002). Ask, "Can you synthesize what you've read along with your feelings about what you've read?" or "Can you synthesize what you've read in these texts?"

- **Evaluate:** This reading strategy includes forming opinions and developing ideas from what you are reading. Ask, "Why does this matter?"

- **Keep reading:** Sometimes authors leave you with questions on purpose that are answered later in the text. Say, "Why don't you keep reading and see if your confusion clears up?"

- **Reread:** Rereading is the most commonly used reading strategy and one of the most effective. Say, "Go back to where your understanding broke down and reread."

With several reading strategies to choose from, students can select a few of them and *evaluate* which of the strategies is likely to be the most helpful. Returning to the previous example, in which Sue did not understand the text, she might model her thinking for students this way.

> *What is the best way to solve this problem? I think I am missing some fundamental background information about the relationship between physics and chemistry. Why don't I search online to find out about the relationship between physics and chemistry to see if that will help?*

In the *plan and act* step, students find out what works. Here is how Sue might model her thinking, continuing from the previous example.

> *What should I try first? When I first searched for "What is the relationship between chemistry and physics?" I could only find either a Wikipedia article or extremely deep scientific articles that were even more confusing than my text.*

> *Second, to improve my results, I instead searched for "Relationship between chemistry and physics for kids" and found a video on the differences and similarities that helped me understand that there is a lot of overlap between physics and chemistry. They both study the structure and properties of matter. Physics uses more mathematics and looks at how things hold together, and chemistry looks more at reactions.*

> *Third, if I did not have access to the internet, I would try to find a book, textbook, or knowledgeable person who could give me the information I need.*

The *reflect* step is where students again step back and think about their achieved outcome to see if their actions brought them to a place of understanding or even just greater understanding than before. Returning to the example of the text Sue did not understand, she might model her thinking this way.

> *Did it work? How do I know? The quick online search I did gave me an understanding that physics and chemistry are much more closely related than I originally thought. Although everything is not crystal clear, I think it is clear enough to continue.*

At this point, teachers should gauge students' grasp of the process to see if they need more modeling to understand the basics or if they're ready for increased release of responsibility to read their texts.

For reading comprehension using the academic and social SELf-question set (see figure 1.1, page 23), and as alluded to earlier in this section, we find it helpful to make an anchor chart of the questions and refer to it often in whole-class and small-group discussions, as well as in individual reading conferences. Accomplished readers may utilize some or all of the steps by SELf-questioning with a degree of automaticity. Because of this, passionate readers may not see the necessity for explicit teaching of the steps; however, teachers must consider the less-passionate readers in the classroom and ensure they receive explicit teaching (modeling and gradual release of responsibility) for using SELf-questioning to enhance reading comprehension.

Now that we've looked at an example of how to model SELf-questioning, let's start with an example based on teaching grades K–2 learners and expand on it for subsequent grade bands.

Scenario: Grades K–2

Class: Second-grade international school classroom in Ecuador (Mrs. T.; teacher)

Objective:

- Determine characters' motives and points of view.

Standard:

- Acknowledge differences in the points of view of characters, including by speaking in a different voice for each character when reading dialogue aloud. (RL.2.6; NGA & CCSSO, 2010a)

In this scenario, an Ecuadorian school is populated by well-off, suburban children from many countries with many levels of English-language competency. You will see dual problem solving as Mrs. T. uses the question set for herself to determine her teaching strategy in the moment, as well as to question students.

To begin, Mrs. T. reads the following text to her second-grade class using E. B. White's (2014) *Charlotte's Web*:

> "Where's Papa going with that ax?" said Fern to her mother as they were setting the table for breakfast.
>
> "Out to the hog house," replied Mrs. Arable. "Some pigs were born last night."
>
> "I still don't see why he needs an ax," continued Fern, who was only eight.
>
> "Well," said her mother, "one of the pigs is a runt. It's very small and weak, and it will never amount to anything. So your father has decided to do away with it." (p. 1)

As Mrs. T. reads the passage, a student raises her hand and asks, "What does 'do away with it' mean?" Mrs. T. answers, "It means 'kill.'" Several students immediately shout, "That's mean! Why would he kill a pig? I don't understand!" At this point, Mrs. T. decides this is a good time to use SELf-questioning with the class to help the students understand. Here is the SELf-questioning process she followed.

SELECT A FOCUS

Questions: What is the problem? Does this make sense?

Mrs. T. says, "It seems we have a problem understanding the motives of Papa. "Is he being mean or is he doing the right thing?" The students affirm their feeling that he's being mean.

GATHER INFORMATION

Questions: What do I know? What do I need to know?

Mrs. T. understands that, in the primary years, a lack of comprehension most often signifies a decoding issue, a lack of vocabulary, or lack of background knowledge, as in this case. Given these considerations, and rather than engage students directly, Mrs. T.

posits a SELf-question to herself: *What do I know?* She knows that students understand that the pig is going to be killed. She asks herself the next question: *What do my students need to know?* She knows most of her students, being from suburban families, have no idea *why* a farm animal might need to be killed, so they are likely misunderstanding the father character. Turning to the students, she says, "Let's see, we know the pig is going to be killed. We need to know why he is going to be killed. Does that make sense?" The students nod, and she moves on to the next step.

 ### BRAINSTORM

Questions: How can I solve this problem? What are possible solutions? What can I do?

To help students understand, she says, "Let's try and figure out why the father would kill the pig. We need to brainstorm a few different possibilities. One thing that might help us is if we had some background knowledge about how farms work to answer that question. But also, sometimes authors leave us with questions so that we keep reading. When that happens, we can find an answer if we just keep reading."

 ### EVALUATE

Questions: What is the best way to solve this problem?

Mrs. T. says, "Which strategy should we try first?" The students vote to keep reading. Mrs. T. continues, "If keeping reading doesn't help, we can always go back and look up some information about farms. OK?"

 ### PLAN AND ACT

Questions: What do I do first, second, and so on? Does this work? Is this working?

Mrs. T. continues to read from the book, which includes the following passage:

> "Do away with it?" shrieked Fern. "You mean kill it? Just because it's smaller than the others?"
>
> Mrs. Arable put a pitcher of cream on the table. "Don't yell, Fern!" she said. "Your father is right. The pig would probably die anyway." (White, 2014, p. 1)

After reading this passage, Mrs. T. pauses for a moment and says, "I think continuing to read worked out for us. This passage shows us that Fern's dad is not just being mean or killing the pig because he wants to but because the pig would die anyway. He realizes the pig is too small and weak to survive." She continues, "I think this tells us that farmers have to think of their animals differently than the way we think about our pets. What do you think?" The students again erupt with dismay, but she suggests they move to the next page and reads a small selection out loud in which Fern is arguing with her father:

> "Fern," said Mr. Arable, "I know more about raising a litter of pigs than you do. A weakling makes trouble. Now run along!" (White, 2014, p. 3).

Mrs. T. says, "I don't think the farmer wanted to kill the pig, but in his experience, a weak pig causes trouble. More important, we learned how an author might present us with a problem or challenge that we don't understand. However, if we're patient, he or she might soon give us the information we need."

REFLECT

Questions: Did it work? How do I know? Do I need to go back and try again?

The class agreed that even though they didn't like the idea of the pig being killed, they understood that the farmer wasn't doing it to be mean but to avoid trouble on the farm. Mrs. T. concludes the lesson by saying, "So, readers, do you think you can remember to do this the next time you read about a character you think is being mean? Or rude? Can you remember to use the SELf-question set to help you learn more about the character?"

Scenario: Grades 3–5

Class: Fifth-grade international school classroom in Costa Rica (Mrs. B.; teacher)

Objective:

- Make sense of an unfamiliar book setting.

Standard:

- By the end of the year, read and comprehend literature, including stories, dramas, and poetry, at the high end of the grades 4–5 text complexity band independently and proficiently. (RL.5.10; NGA & CCSSO, 2010a)

In this scenario, Mrs. B. sits down with Juan, a fifth-grade student, for a reading conference about *The Thief Lord* by Cornelia Funke (2000). Juan is a grade-level reader in a class full of above-grade-level and highly motivated readers. He is reading this particular book because he wants to be part of his group of friends who have all read and enjoyed it.

SELECT A FOCUS

Questions: What is the problem? Does this make sense?

Mrs. B. asks Juan to talk to her about *The Thief Lord* (Funke, 2000). He says he's really bothered by it, so Mrs. B. engages him in SELf-questioning about his disconnect. Juan says he feels quite disgusted with himself because the book confused him, even though many of his friends read and loved it. This establishes the focus for their discussion.

GATHER INFORMATION

Questions: What do I know? What do I need to know?

To gather information, Mrs. B. questions Juan about what he understands and what he doesn't understand. He understands the characters, and he understands the words. He says, "But I don't get what's going on. One moment they're on a street, and the next moment they're in a boat."

BRAINSTORM

Questions: How can I solve this problem? What are possible solutions? What can I do?

The next step is to brainstorm what solutions or strategies might address this problem. Juan could not come up with any strategies that would help him, but Mrs. B. notices that the book takes place in Venice. She asks him what he knows about Venice. He replies curtly, "Nothing!" She says, "Then we need to build some background knowledge!"

EVALUATE

Questions: What is the best way to solve this problem?

As the lack of background knowledge about Venice seems to be Juan's primary disconnect, Mrs. B. decides not to brainstorm further options. Instead, she evaluates options for building that background knowledge. She suggests they try together to learn a little more about Venice so that Juan can better understand the setting's geography using either a phone to look up information or visit the library for a travel book about Venice. As the more expedient option, they choose the former.

PLAN AND ACT

Questions: What do I do first, second, and so on? Is this working?

Together, Mrs. B. and Juan search for pictures of Venice on Mrs. B.'s phone, and soon he understands he was missing the needed context of Venice's canals and streets to better understand the text.

REFLECT

Questions: Did it work? How do I know? Do I need to go back and try again?

With this bit of background, Juan contentedly returns to his silent reading, problem solved. His whole comprehension problem was one of geography. Once he has the teacher's support in using SELf-questioning to solve his issue, he speeds through the rest of the book. With just this small intervention and through conversation with his friends, Juan successfully makes it through the book, which was actually above his reading level. He also begins to see the importance of the SELf-question set as a practical aid to reading comprehension.

Scenario: Grades 6–8

Class: Seventh-grade ELA (Mr. O.; tutor)

Objective:

- Make sense of epigraphs and their relationship to a chapter.

Standard:

- By the end of the year, read and comprehend literature, including stories, dramas, and poems, in the grades 6–8 text complexity band proficiently, with scaffolding as needed at the high end of the range. (RL.7.10; NGA & CCSSO, 2010a)

In this scenario, Mr. O. sits down with Hannah, a seventh-grade student, to have a reading conference about *Chains* by Laurie H. Anderson (2008). He asks Hannah to read the epigraph at the beginning of the chapter:

> Youth is the seedtime of good habits,
>
> as well in nations as in individuals . . .
>
> —Thomas Paine, *Common Sense* (as cited in Anderson, 2008, p. 3)

Hannah does not understand the meaning or purpose of the epigraph. Together, she and Mr. O. engage in SELf-questioning to address this gap in reading comprehension.

SELECT A FOCUS

Questions: What is the problem?

After reading the epigraph, Hannah makes a face, showing she's clearly confused. Mr. O. asks, "What is the problem? Do you understand this passage?"

Hannah answers, "No. I don't get it!"

Note that there is nothing wrong with scaffolding your students' thinking as you are teaching them to use the SELf-question sets. That is why Mr. O. stops her and asks her if she understands. Since the epigraphs at the beginning of each chapter fit with the content of each chapter, Mr. O. encourages Hannah to do a little extra work to understand this particular epigraph.

GATHER INFORMATION

Questions: What do I know? What do I need to know?

Hannah thinks about what she knows and says, "I understand the first line. It means that you learn, or plant, good habits when you're young." She then thinks about what she needs to know, saying, "I don't understand the second line."

BRAINSTORM

Questions: How can I solve this problem? What are possible solutions? What can I do?

Hannah pauses as she brainstorms possible solutions to this problem. She says, somewhat shakily, "I could make an inference?" It's clear she needs a moment to think of a strategy. She then continues, "I could look online for an easier version of the quote. Or, I could ignore it." Mr. O. sees that Hannah is struggling with coming up with other options, so he suggests that perhaps Hannah could simplify the statement herself. Hannah answers, "Maybe I could instead break it apart and try to put it in my own words? I could also read it over and over."

EVALUATE

Questions: What is the best way to solve this problem?

After mulling over (evaluating) her options, Hannah says, "I think I will try reading it over and over." When Mr. O. asks why, she answers a little impatiently, "Cause that's what I'm doing, and it's working." Mr. O. realizes that Hannah is responding a bit testily because she is new to having her thinking pushed like this. He smiles and says, "I sometimes get cranky when people push my thinking too. But let's keep on pushing. It's good for your brain."

PLAN AND ACT

Questions: What do I do first, second, and so on? Is this working?

Hannah reads the passage a couple more times and says, "I think I'm starting to get it. It's talking about how good habits are planted for groups of people and for individuals when they're young." "You've got it!" Mr. O. says. He then further encourages Hannah, adding that it is a difficult passage to understand because, when this was written, the United States itself was quite young, and the writing style was different.

REFLECT

Questions: Did it work? How do I know? Do I need to go back and try again?

With total comprehension blooming on Hannah's face, she exclaims, "I get it now!" Remember, as students move into more challenging reading, teachers may have to scaffold the question set similarly to how Mr. O. did in the plan and act step. This scaffolding supports students as they face new challenges that require (to them) new solutions.

Scenario: Grades 9–12

Class: Eleventh-grade ELA (Ms. A.; teacher)

Objective:

- Use SELf-questioning to decipher challenging text from William Shakespeare.

Standard:

- Cite strong and thorough textual evidence to support analysis of what the text says explicitly as well as inferences drawn from the text, including determining where the text leaves matters uncertain. (RL.11-12.1; NGA & CCSSO, 2010a)

Regina and Bayley are assigned the following passage to decipher from *King Lear* (Shakespeare, 1608/1994) in their small group discussion in an eleventh-grade ELA class. They are struggling to understand Goneril's speech about her father, King Lear:

> The best and soundest of his time hath been but rash. Then
> must we look from his age to receive not alone the
> imperfections of long-engrafted condition, but therewithal
> the unruly waywardness that infirm and choleric years
> bring with them (Shakespeare, 1994, p. 11).

Since the girls worked together to resolve their difficulties with this text, without a teacher's intervention or guidance, the following account paraphrases and describes their discussion. The class had previous experience using the SELf-questioning set, and in this scenario, Ms. A. is floating from group to group to listen in on students' problem-solving efforts.

SELECT A FOCUS

Questions: What is the problem?

To establish a focus on the problem, Regina states, "Well, we know all of those words, but we do not understand the passage. Therefore, we need to engage in quite a bit of metacognitive wrestling." Note that the class had just discussed metacognition and using the academic and social SELf-question set to clarify understanding. Bayley answers, "Which leads us to the next question."

GATHER INFORMATION

Questions: What do I know? What do I need to know?

Bayley continues, "We understand that the first part says, at his best, my father has been rash and unthinking. And we understand that the last part means that, as people age and become infirm, their character traits tend to become exaggerated. Lear is more angry, or choleric, than ever." Regina says, "Yes. I think what we don't understand is the middle part. That might be important. Let's think of ways to solve this problem."

BRAINSTORM

Questions: How can I solve this problem? What strategies could help me understand? What can I do?

Regina thinks for a moment and says, "Perhaps rereading slowly will help. Using our background knowledge about old people and angry people, like how I tell stories about my grandpa, might also help. We might also think about determining importance and if we need to understand."

EVALUATE

Questions: What is the best way to solve this problem?

Bayley thinks about the options Regina suggests and concludes, "To solve this problem, we need to determine the meaning of Goneril's short speech. I think the best choice is to reread slowly while applying our background knowledge about old and crabby people."

PLAN AND ACT

Questions: What do I do first, second, and so on? Is this working?

Regina reflects and says, "First, we'll try reading the portion that we don't understand slowly while applying background knowledge. Second, if that doesn't work, we'll determine the importance of the part that we do not understand. We think the 'long-engrafted condition' refers to Lear's habits, so we must be looking at his habit of rashness. He makes terrible decisions without much information."

Bayley chimes in, "Yes, I also think that, as we look at King Lear's age, we must realize that he is probably not going to recognize his habit of anger and rash acts, just like your grandpa when he can't see how crabby he's getting."

REFLECT

Questions: Did it work? How do I know? Do I need to go back and try again?

After thinking through these ideas, the two turn to their teacher. Bayley says, "We think we finally understand Goneril's speech, and combining our background knowledge of Regina's grumpy grandpa with a slow and careful reading helped us understand. It took four or five slow, careful readings to understand it—and that's when we already knew the vocabulary!"

Notice the grit they showed when working through this passage and the rush they felt when they nailed it. These are the kinds of benefits a strong SELf-questioning strategy can provide.

Character Corner: Self-Efficacy

Although students received teacher guidance in many of this chapter's scenarios when working through the academic and social SELf-question set to improve reading comprehension, the overarching educational goal is twofold: (1) for students to learn to use the question set independently while working through a reading comprehension problem, and (2) for students to internalize the questions and transfer them to other academic, social, and emotional areas. This is exemplified by an increasing sense of *self-efficacy*, which is an individual's belief in their capacity to have self-control over their motivation, behavior, and social environment (Carey & Forsyth, 2009).

Consider the examples from this chapter's scenarios: Juan realized that his understanding could increase if he just knew a bit more about the geography of Venice, Hannah worked out the meaning of an epitaph, and Regina and Bayley correctly interpreted a portion of a play by Shakespeare. In doing these things, they all added to their storehouses of self-efficacy. They knew they could use SELf-questioning to solve reading comprehension problems.

SELf-questioning and its inherent self-talk leads to self-efficacy, as exemplified in the following email from the parent of a student at Moss Elementary School. His five-year-old son Cassidy, whose mom had worked with him for years with using SELf-questioning for a variety of purposes, had learned to apply it for himself.

> *Rick,*
>
> *Good morning, sir! I wanted to pass this along as it made my morning. This evening Cassidy is going to go to the science fair at my wife's school. To say he is excited would be a huge understatement.*
>
> *This morning, he said to me, "Dad, if mom's students are having a hard time with their projects, I will show them how to do self-talk." He then proceeded to put his hand on his head and say, "I am smart. I can do it."*
>
> *He has done this many times on his own around the house, but this was the first time he applied it to possibly helping others.*
>
> *Have a great day!*
>
> *William Veit (personal communication, 2/27/2020)*

Cassidy obviously had developed self-efficacy through the self-talk and wanted to pass on to his mother's students the value of telling yourself, "You are smart, and you can do it too!" It's a remarkable demonstration of self-efficacy and a growth mindset from such a young mind.

In the following chapter about reading decoding, you'll see how the academic and social SELf-question set also works to help students with reading decoding challenges.

Structured SELf-Questioning in Reading Decoding

Fluent, accurate decoding is a hallmark of skilled reading. . . . Automatic word recognition, which is dependent on phonic knowledge, allows the reader to attend to meaning.

—Louisa C. Moats

In chapter 4, we looked at how the metacognitive strategy of structured SELf-questioning helped students with reading comprehension. This chapter shows how that same strategy and question set can also help students in reading decoding. Note that we put the decoding chapter after the comprehension chapter because reading comprehension precedes word identification. Think of how very young children process a picture book while sitting on a parent's lap. Like comprehension, decoding is a life-long skill that increases in complexity as students read increasingly complex texts.

A National Reading Panel (2000) report posits the following big-picture interactive and essential elements of reading instruction that remain relevant.

- **Phonemic awareness:** Recognizing and manipulating the sounds of spoken words

- **Phonics:** Understanding the connections between the sounds of spoken language and the letters of written language

- **Fluency:** Reading text quickly and accurately, with expression

- **Vocabulary:** Understanding the words that you are hearing and speaking

- **Comprehension:** Creating meaning from text

These elements weave together like fine tartan fabric to make students into readers. *Decoding* has to do with making words out of the letters written on a page and includes phonics and fluency, as well as chunking and sight words in reading practice. All of these are firmly rooted in students' *phonemic awareness*—their ability to hear sounds in the spoken word. From *cat* to *antidisestablishmentarianism*, decoding is a lifelong skill. Figure 5.1 (page 76) illustrates the interaction between the essential elements to decode a simple word. Note how the elements are not always sequential and might even require the reader to revisit an element.

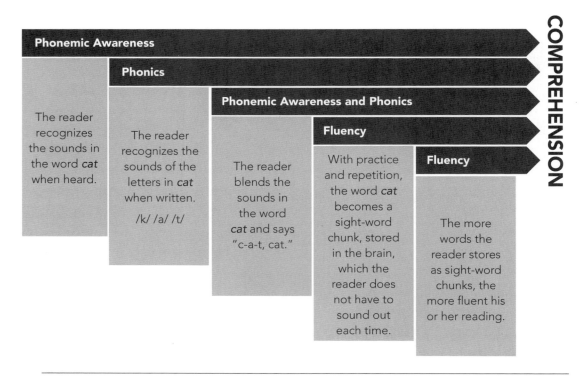

Figure 5.1: The decoding process.

It is important to note that while decoding is necessary to understand a text, it is not a prerequisite. This may sound contradictory, but we'll explain. Many decoding skills develop concurrently and are interdependent with one another, meaning readers need to learn how to use multiple decoding strategies simultaneously to identify an unknown word. For example, readers often need to use their comprehension of phonics to decode. When a second grader reads the sentence, *The scary dog showed his sharp teeth*, he or she might pause before reading the word, *scary*, because he or she has not yet learned the *r*-controlled phonics skill for /ar/. However, the reader can use the beginning blend /sc/ with comprehension of the first part of the sentence, *The sc____ dog showed his . . .* to think about what the dog might show that begins with the /sc/ blend. Further, the reader could also use picture clues that show an aggressive-looking dog with sharp teeth to help him or her determine the word is *scary* without sounding or stretching each part of the word. Thus, this second-grade reader actually utilizes three skills simultaneously to decode the word: (1) phonics by knowing the initial blend /sc/, (2) picture clues, and (3) comprehension.

As in chapter 4 (page 59), this chapter stresses the importance of modeling the metacognitive strategy of structured SELf-questioning to help students be aware of and manage multiple reading and decoding skills simultaneously. We also walk you through how to teach using the academic and social SELf-question set to support students' metacognitive functioning in decoding with scenarios across the K–12 grade bands. Finally, we connect the character trait of grit to the process of using structured SELf-questioning for reading decoding.

The Importance of Teaching a Metacognitive Strategy for Decoding

Although much of decoding is more cognitive than metacognitive, metacognition enters the picture when students determine if a word makes sense or sounds right in a given context. Although parents often encourage their children to sound or stretch words out to decode, teachers need to empower readers with a broader repertoire of decoding strategies to identify unknown words in a text. Because parents seldom prompt their children to use any other strategies besides producing the sounds for each individual letter in a word, it is essential that educators teach students other strategies, model those strategies, and query students as to which strategy is best when they are stuck on a word. Teachers should also guide students to think about how the strategies interact with each other and reflect on why a particular strategy was or was not successful in identifying an unknown word. In the next section, we list several of these strategies and explain how students can use the academic and social SELf-question set to select one.

Whether students are just learning to read or just learning to read a language new to them, they should have more experiences learning to decode during *authentic reading*—students engaging with text that is relevant, meaningful, and useful—than they do learning phonics in isolation (Allington, 2012; Bridges, 2018). There is a widespread misconception that decoding is phonics instruction and only relates to letter-sound relationships. While phonics instruction is a strong component of all primary reading instruction, it is only one component to build strong word-attack skills. Reading specialists agree that students across grades benefit from instruction that is a planned sequence taught in a systematic approach (Morrow & Gambrell, 2019). Cognitive scientists Anne Castles, Kate Rastle, and Kathleen Nation (2018) further write, "There is strong scientific consensus on the effectiveness of systematic phonics instruction during the initial periods of reading instruction."

School districts often consider purchasing a commercial phonics program to support and increase their students' decoding skills in a systematic way. While consistent phonics instruction does support students' word-attack skills, we contend it is far more vital to ensure teachers have a consistent approach to teach decoding strategies, where sound-letter relationships (phonics) are just one of the pieces of information readers can use to identify an unknown word.

How to Teach a Metacognitive Strategy for Reading Decoding

Before teachers can use the academic and social SELf-question set for reading decoding, they need to have a clear idea of what each step entails. Remember, even if your more proficient readers approach the SELf-question steps with a degree of automaticity, teacher modeling and use of gradual release of responsibility will benefit students who feel challenged practicing decoding while using SELf-questions. Let's carefully walk through the question set and see how teachers can put it to use when teaching reading decoding. (See figure 1.1, page 23, to revisit the full academic and social SELf-question set.)

To *select a focus* for the purpose of decoding, the student simply needs to identify the word that he or she does not understand. This is pretty simple and self-evident.

During the *gather information* step, the student primarily determines if he or she needs to know the word for the text for it to make sense. In books for emergent and early readers, including students learning English, students need to understand most if not all words for comprehension to take place. Education scholars Irene C. Fountas and Gay Su Pinnell (2001) assert it is necessary for students to decode with 90 to 94 percent accuracy to determine their instructional reading level, often referred to as a *just-right text*. Students at this level can still comprehend and make meaning of a text without the ability to automatically and accurately identify 6 to 10 percent of the words a text presents to them. As emergent readers reach approximately a third-grade reading level, they become *transitional readers* (students moving from learning to read words to reading to learn) and can learn to determine which words are important enough to be worth the effort to stop and look up and which are not. For example, in the sentence, *The dulcimer, banjo, and the fiddle are popular instruments in the Appalachian Mountains*, it is not necessary to take the time to decode and look up the word *dulcimer*. The context tells the proficient reader that it is probably a musical instrument of some kind.

To *brainstorm*, students need strategies in their toolboxes to choose from. Some decoding strategies for emergent readers we recommend include the following.

- Study the picture, if the book has images, for clues.
- Match letters to a sound, such as *m* = /*m*/, *o* = /*o*/, or *p* = /*p*/.
- Slide through the word, such as *s-t-o-p*.
- Flip the vowel (short to long or vice versa), such as /*bak*/ or *bake*.
- Chunk the word into parts (syllabification), such as *stand—ing*.
- Get your mouth ready to make the first sound (poppers).
- Reread the word.
- Skip the word.

Similarly, teachers can use many of the aforementioned strategies for transitional readers, especially chunking a word into syllables. This is known as *syllabification*, such as /syl-lab-i-fi-ca-tion/. As students learn these strategies, teachers can create an ongoing anchor chart of strategies as a brainstorming resource.

It is quite common for different school districts to utilize different names for the decoding strategies that readers need to apply automatically. For example, when attempting to decode an unfamiliar word, some teachers identify the exact same strategy as "get your mouth ready," "use the popper," or "look at the beginning sound." This is fine. However, it is helpful for students, as they move from grade to grade or school to school, for districts to maintain internal consistency in naming these strategies.

In the same vein, education scholar Lucy Calkins (2015) and her colleagues at the Reading and Writing Project (https://readingandwritingproject.org) suggest labeling decoding strategies as *superpowers*, such as *we have pointer power* and *we have partner power*. Some districts and schools create their own strategy sets. Although consistent naming is helpful, readers ultimately need to be autonomous in selecting and utilizing decoding strategies, whatever they're called. Once students internalize the decoding strategies, those strategies become the toolkit that readers utilize to brainstorm and evaluate which works best when using the academic SELf-questioning set.

During the *evaluate* step, students simply choose which strategy will work best and follow that selection with *plan and act* by giving it a go. They choose what they will try first, second, and so on, and see how it works.

Finally, in the *reflect* step, students check to see if what they've done helps make sense of what they are reading or if they need to try something else.

Let's take a look at how teachers can use this SELf-questioning set to help guide students' self-talk through reading decoding problems.

Scenario: Grades K–2

Class: Kindergarten classroom (Mrs. D.; teacher)

Objective:

- Utilize multiple cueing systems, including combining picture clues and initial sounds to decode unfamiliar words to build fluency.

Standard:

- Know and apply grade-level phonics and word analysis skills in decoding words. (RF.K.3; NGA & CCSSO, 2010a)

Ryan, an early emergent reader, is struggling during guided reading to decode the word *hop* in the level A text, *I Can, We Can* by Don L. Curry (2002). His nonverbal cues clearly demonstrate that he has difficulty using the picture clues to decode the word *hop* in the sentence *I can hop*. He blankly stares at the page with the picture of a girl jumping rope. Mrs. D., a literacy coach, gently prompts him to employ the SELf-questioning set by exaggerating her words as she points to the wall where a poster of specific problem-solving steps is displayed for students to use as a reference. (See the "Academic and Social Problem-Solving Poster" reproducible in the appendix, page 216, for an example of this poster.)

The complexity of decoding for a kindergarten student at the emergent level is quite different than the decoding skills of a second-grade transitional reader. Emergent readers rely heavily on utilizing the combination of picture clues and initial sounds, referred to as *poppers*. In an emergent text, students can often identify words by analyzing the picture and getting their mouth ready for the first sound. Often, the word pops right out without sounding or stretching each sound, thus the name *popper*.

SELECT A FOCUS

Questions: What is the problem? Does this make sense?

Mrs. D. says, "Ryan, it seems like you stopped reading, which means you must be thinking. What is the problem? Please share your thinking with me."

Ryan responds, "Oh yeah. When I stop, I need to use my problem-solving steps to help me *stop and think*." He giggles to himself as he says this and uses hand signals to abruptly make a stopping motion with his arms as a crossing guard would do. This kinesthetic motion prompts students to automatically initiate the structured SELf-questioning they need to support their problem solving in all contexts, including decoding. Ryan continues, "So, what's my problem?" Ryan seems to shout as he throws his right hand up in the air and points to the word, *hop*, with his left hand. "Well, I am stuck on this word!"

Mrs. D. celebrates that Ryan, a struggling reader, used the stop sign from the displayed poster to ask himself the first SELf-question. She waits patiently for him to move to the next step.

GATHER INFORMATION

Questions: What do I know? What do I need to know? What is similar, and what is different?

After several seconds, which feel like minutes, Ryan looks at the same poster on the wall, and he points to the *gather information* step, which is an illustration of a man collecting sticks. Mrs. D. asks Ryan, "How can you gather information?" as she purposefully glances over at the decoding strategy cards displayed in the center of her table. Previously, she had created a strategy card with a visual for each decoding skill and placed them at this table. She used this as a prompt for readers to gather information in order to decode an unfamiliar word, such as looking at picture clues and the beginning sound (popper) of a word, as shown in figure 5.2. Although the goal is for Ryan to automatically ask himself, "How can I gather information?" Mrs. D. notes the extended wait time and chooses to ask him the question to continue the process without frustration. This is common early in kindergarten, as students need significant modeling and prompting before internalizing a process. Mrs. D. barely has the word *gather* out of her mouth before Ryan exclaims, "Oh yeah. Gather information from the picture *and* the popper!"

Look at pictures for clues

plus

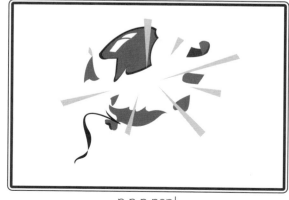

p-p-p-pop!

Figure 5.2 Strategy cards for poppers.

BRAINSTORM

Questions: How can I solve this problem? What are possible solutions? What can I do?

With the information he needs to proceed, Ryan instinctively looks at the poster on the wall again and whispers, "I know the next thing is to say, How can I solve this problem?" He immediately looks perplexed as he scrunches his face and shares, "But I think it should be the word *jump* because she's jumping rope, and my sister does that!" He can only think of one solution, so he proceeds to evaluate whether it might be correct.

EVALUATE

Questions: What is the best way to solve this problem? Does this make sense?

Ryan continues without further prompting from Mrs. D., "I thought the word *jump* was my favorite and the best choice, but when I asked myself if it makes sense, I know it just *can't be jump!*" When Mrs. D. asks why, he points to the letter *h* in the word hop and responds, "The popper says /h/ and *jump* does not start with /h/."

Mrs. D. immediately documents this observation in her anecdotal notes as it's strong evidence that Ryan is using the decoding strategies she's taught. Ryan is automatically using the question set to improve his decoding skills. Essentially, he is combining the decoding strategies of using picture clues and poppers to monitor his reading. Yet, he hasn't arrived at an answer that works, and he knows it.

PLAN AND ACT

Questions: What do I do first, second, and so on? Does this work? Is this working?

Mrs. D. asks Ryan what he should do next. He again looks at the chart and SELf-questions, "Well, what do I do next? I really didn't pick my favorite because I only brainstormed the word *jump*. I know it's a picture of a jump rope because my sister has one." Figure 5.3 shows the picture sequence Ryan is referring to as well as his thinking sequence as he resolves the word.

Figure 5.3: Pictures to help students isolate word sounds.

Mrs. D. shows Ryan the picture in isolation (the left-most image), and he begins to brainstorm other words, such as *skip*, *hop*, and *jump*. He is still convinced it should say jump and does not give up on the word.

Next, Ryan looks at only the initial letter *h* on the second card and makes the sound /h/ with wide eyes.

Ryan literally jumps out of his seat as he shouts the word *hop*. He yells, "It's hop! It's hop! And it popped right out! Hop and pop even rhyme!"

Mrs. D. confirms his use of the multiple decoding strategies by complimenting Ryan for using the picture and popper to read the word rather than use the sound for each individual letter. This was extremely important for Ryan, who has yet to learn vowel sounds. Therefore, sounding and stretching the consonant-vowel-consonant word would not have been productive. Mrs. D. makes sure she emphasizes his use of SELf-questioning by stating, "Ryan, you need to kiss your brain for working so hard and not giving up. When you asked yourself all those questions for problem solving, you realized that you needed to brainstorm more words using the picture and popper. Good for you!"

REFLECT

Questions: Did it work? How do I know? Do I need to go back and try again?

Ryan returns to the page in the book and fluently rereads the sentence, *I can hop*. He beams brightly, providing evidence that he feels empowered and successful with his accomplishment.

As this scenario demonstrates, even early-emergent kindergarten readers can build their metacognitive skills using SELf-questioning. By using the poster of the problem-solving steps on the wall and asking himself the questions for each step, Ryan is able to monitor his own reading, employ multiple decoding strategies, and experience success. Most importantly, SELf-questioning becomes a tool to build grit and perseverance. It empowers Ryan with the necessary tools and thinking processes to problem solve by asking him the questions to attack an unknown word in context.

Scenario: Grades 3–5

Class: Third-grade pull-out reading instruction (Mr. L.; reading tutor)

Objective:

- Apply word-attack skills that have been a part of ongoing learning.

Standard:

- Know and apply grade-level phonics and word analysis skills in decoding words. (RF.3.3; NGA & CCSSO, 2010a)

The classroom teacher has given Leia and Mr. L. a reading tutor, a reading test to work on in the hallway. Leia consistently struggles with multisyllabic words and was recently diagnosed with a word-tracking problem, and so breaking words into syllables when decoding can be challenging to her. Mr. L. is allowed to cue her but not reveal any words as they work on the test.

Leia tries to read the sentence, *Suddenly, the boy stood up.*

SELECT A FOCUS

Questions: What is the problem?

Looking at the sentence, the word *suddenly* brings Leia to a screeching halt, as do most words longer than two syllables. She asks herself, "What would make sense?" Leia's recognition that context affects meaning shows that she is monitoring her reading. This self-monitoring also prompts her to recognize that she doesn't know the word suddenly. In the past, Leia would have probably kept on reading without decoding the word. Mr. L. is seeing growth here.

GATHER INFORMATION

Questions: What do I know? What do I need to know?

"So you don't know this word," Mr. L. says while pointing at the word *suddenly*. "Do you think you need to know this word for this text to make sense?" In this case, sometimes asking students a follow-up question can help them clarify their thinking. Leia answers, "Since it's a test, I think I need to know all the words." Although Mr. L. doesn't think Leia necessarily needs to know the word in the context of the article, he notes that Leia shows good reasoning about the importance of the test, so he moves Leia forward to the brainstorming stage.

BRAINSTORM

Questions: How can I solve this problem? What are possible solutions? What can I do?

After Mr. L. asks, "How can you solve this problem?" Leia experiences difficulties brainstorming and generating a strategy. Therefore, Mr. L. prompts her with a follow-up question: "What strategies helped you decode long words in the past?" Leia responds, "I could break it apart or sound it out." From our experience, many students experience difficulties with brainstorming at first but become much better with consistent modeling and practice.

EVALUATE

Questions: What is the best way to solve this problem? Does this make sense?

Mr. L. nods at the options and asks Leia what she thinks is the best way is to solve this problem. Leia answers, "Break it apart. That helped me before."

PLAN AND ACT

Questions: What do I do first, second, and so on? Does this work? Is this working?

Leia breaks the word apart like this: *sudd/en/ly*. In doing so, she naturally moves into her sounding-out skills to figure out the individual syllables. She then slides through the syllables to come up with the word *suddenly*. Mr. L. knows the word is not divided into syllables correctly, but since the division would not affect Leia's process, he doesn't say anything. Instead, he jots down a note for them to work on syllabification in a few weeks.

REFLECT

Questions: Did it work? How do I know? Do I need to go back and try again?

Leia is delighted with her work and quickly realizes that the word now makes sense in her sentence. Although she and Mr. L. have been working with breaking words into parts for the previous few weeks, combining that with the SELf-question set equips her with the tools to use with any number of strategies in the future.

Scenario: Grades 6–8

Class: Seventh-grade ELA (Mrs. F.; tutor)

Objective:

- Correctly utilize various decoding strategies.

Standard:

- By the end of the year, read and comprehend literature, including stories, dramas, and poems, in the grades 6–8 text complexity band proficiently, with scaffolding as needed at the high end of the range. (RL.7.10; NGA & CCSSO, 2010a)

While working with Mrs. F. on his reading, Joel, a seventh-grade English language learner, reads out loud the first page of *Chains* by Laurie H. Anderson (2008) and stumbles on the word *peculiar* from the following passage: "My sister, Ruth, sat next to the coffin. Ruth was too big to carry, plus the pastor knew about her peculiar way of being, so it was the wagon for her and the road for me" (p. 3).

SELECT A FOCUS

Questions: What is the problem?

Joel reads the word *peculiar* as *plain*, and he knows that doesn't make sense.

GATHER INFORMATION

Questions: What do I know? What do I need to know? What is similar, and what is different?

Joel says, "I'm figuring out that this is in olden days because a wagon is pulled by mules, that someone has died, and that someone's sister is riding in the wagon. I don't understand this word." He points to *peculiar* and tries to pronounce it again.

BRAINSTORM

Questions: How can I solve this problem? What are possible solutions? What can I do?

Joel decides to write down a list of options, and the list amuses Mrs. F. because it's so very middle school.

I could Google it.

I could use my best pronunciation and say it in my phone and see what pronunciation my phone says.

I could ask my mom.

I could break it into syllables. (Mrs. F.'s suggestion)

I could ignore it.

After Mrs. F. adds that it is really important to understand the first chapter of a book because it sets the stage for the rest of the book, Joel says, "When it seems like it's pretty important, I might really look at it, but I would usually ignore it."

EVALUATE

Questions: Which is the best choice? Why?

Joel says, "I think I'll *really* look at it."

PLAN AND ACT

Questions: What do I do first, second, and so on? Does this work? Is this working?

He takes a closer look at the word and tries various ways to divide it into syllables, verbally, until he hears a word he knows. "Oh, it's *peculiar*!" he says with joy.

REFLECT

Questions: Did it work? How do I know? Do I need to go back and try again?

Joel rereads the sentence and is pleased to find that it now makes sense. Students are often taught skills in isolation, and it is difficult for them to choose which strategy to use. The SELf-question sets provide students with a framework with which to choose a strategy that will most likely work and provides them with some steps—plan and act and reflect—where they can circle back if the first strategy they choose doesn't help.

Scenario: Grades 9–12

Class: Tenth-grade ELA (Mr. W.; homeschool teacher)

Objective:

- Use prior knowledge about Greek and Latin roots to decipher challenging words.

Standard:

- Cite strong and thorough textual evidence to support analysis of what the text says explicitly as well as inferences drawn from the text. (RL.9-10.1; NGA & CCSSO, 2010a)

Sam and Kimmy are tenth-grade homeschool students who receive their homeschool ELA instruction from a certified teacher. Neither of them self-identify as readers and seem to look at reading as something to trudge through. Thus, Mr. W. is seeking extremely engaging books and lessons for them. This day, they are doing an exercise for class that comes straight from Kelly Gallagher's (2003) wonderful book, *Reading Reasons*. In this exercise, they needed to decode and construct a definition for the word *pneumonoultramicroscopicsilicovolcanoconiosis*.

SELECT A FOCUS

Questions: What is the problem?

Almost in harmony, Sam and Kimmy exclaim, "We don't know this word!"

GATHER INFORMATION

Questions: What do I know? What do I need to know? What is similar, and what is different?

They continue, "What do we understand? Nothing. What do we need to understand? Everything."

BRAINSTORM

Questions: How can I solve this problem? What are possible solutions? What can I do?

Sam says, "We'll need to divide this into word parts and then use our knowledge of Greek and Latin roots to help us. We could also look at words that are similar to the word parts and see if that can help us."

EVALUATE

Questions: What is the best way to solve this problem? Does this make sense?

Kimmy states, "Yeah, we should use both of those strategies together." Note that sometimes the *brainstorm* and *evaluate* steps flow together.

PLAN AND ACT

Questions: What do I do first, second, and so on? Does this work? Is this working?

The girls worked through the problem using the following procedure, with each of them contributing different pieces:

> *First, we'll divide it into word parts. Pneumo has something to do with breathing or the lungs. Think of pneumonia. Volcano is obvious, and niosis after words sounds like some kind of disease. We see the word microscopic, which means really small. Oh! I just noticed ultra between pneumo and microscopic. Since ultra comes before microscopic, it probably means really tiny. Second, if we put that all together, I think we get the breathing of really small parts of a volcano, which makes you sick.*

REFLECT

Questions: Did it work? How do I know? Do I need to go back and try again?

The girls were absolutely amazed at what they could accomplish with their background knowledge of Greek and Latin roots to figure out such a long, unknown word. Mr. W. points out that without the structure of the SELf-question set, they might have struggled more with this task. The more students perceive the benefits of SELf-questioning, the more determined they are to internalize the steps and the more apt they are to pull it out of their personal toolboxes when they have a problem to solve.

Character Corner: Grit

As you have seen in this chapter, you can use this question set as a problem-solving metacognitive structure for students and teachers alike to solve decoding problems. Where perseverance (see chapter 2's Character Corner, page 43) is often characterized as the determination to master skills necessary to complete a task, *grit* is the amount of effort, interest, and stamina to achieve a long-term goal (Building Learning Power, n.d.). Students develop grit as they independently use the academic and social SELf-question set to attack unknown words in a text. Kindergarten teachers we've worked with have reported students using five and even six different decoding strategies until they are able to figure out the unknown word.

One way to define grit is for a person to have resolve (Duckworth, 2016; Jensen, 2019). To that end, SELf-questioning helps students and teachers access strategies and tools that develop and support that resolve. When teachers train students to apply SELf-questioning to decode unknown words, students can successfully take a step back, have a think about their thinking, and go back and re-solve the problem of the unknown word. This prepares students to transfer the strategy to any academic or social problem.

Through the practice of grit, students also learn to be self-reliant in decoding unknown words. They reduce their dependence on the teacher to help them slide or stretch a word out, find a chunk or part they know, divide into syllables, use affixes, find a little word within a big word, use Greek and Latin roots, and so on. We have also found that this question set is a great resource for parents who want to assist their child in problem solving but not give away the answers or over-rely on phonics as the only decoding strategy. Over time, and with practice utilizing SELf-questioning, students develop grit and resolve naturally as a habit of mind.

Structured SELf-Questioning for Inquiry-Based Research Writing

> *If you think about it, almost everything we write throughout our lives is expository—writing to inform, explain, describe, propose, amuse, remind, direct, teach, persuade. Students need to master this genre for academic success and, subsequently job success.*
>
> —Marcia S. Freeman

In chapters 4 and 5, we focused on utilizing the academic and social SELf-question set to support readers in both comprehension and decoding. In this chapter, we demonstrate how the use of that same metacognitive strategy and same SELf-question set helps guide students while writing, with a specific focus on the complex task of inquiry-based research writing. As Fountas and Pinnell (2001) confirm in *Guiding Readers and Writers, Grades 3–6*, "It is important for students who need more support to engage in investigations. As they conduct their own research, they can follow their interests and develop their knowledge of informational texts" (p. 509).

Regardless of grade level, both traditional research and inquiry research require students to locate, evaluate, analyze, and document information about a topic. However, inquiry-based research writing increases student engagement, motivation, and ownership by additionally challenging students to self-generate driving questions, identify complex problems to explore and evaluate, seek relevant information from multiple sources to further their investigation, and communicate their findings for a relative audience (Daniels, 2017).

To better prepare students for college and career, the entire education system has shifted to emphasize informational reading and writing skills, a shift that is inherent in CCSS standards (NGA & CCSSO, 2010a). Fortunately, the academic and social SELf-question set is something teachers and students can utilize when providing instruction in every genre of writing.

In this chapter, we highlight the importance of teaching metacognitive strategies for research writing, how to teach these strategies for use with research writing, some ways to apply our strategy to writing assignments across academic disciplines, and how writing skills supported with a strong metacognitive strategy further students' self-confidence.

The Importance of Teaching a Metacognitive Strategy for Research Writing

Most formally educated individuals can recall their experiences in utilizing the following stages of the writing process.

- **Prewriting:** Brainstorming topics and ideas, researching information, organizing information

- **Drafting:** Documenting the ideas or information from prewriting, which some refer to as *sloppy copy*, *first draft*, or *flash draft*

- **Revising:** Adding, deleting, moving, or substituting information and ideas to improve the quantity, quality, clarity, and organization of writing for the reader

- **Editing:** Correcting the mechanics of writing to reflect formal language rules, such as fixing spelling, capitalization, punctuation, grammar, and so on

- **Publishing:** Sharing the work with an audience in various formats either in physical or digital text

In *A Guide to the Common Core Writing Workshop: Primary Grades*, Lucy Calkins (2013) asserts that "the writing process is fundamental to all writing; therefore, it is important that children of every age receive frequent opportunities to rehearse, draft, revise, and edit their writing" (p. 34). She equates students' ability to identify, understand, and utilize the steps in the writing process with their understanding of the steps in the scientific method (question, research, hypothesize, experiment, observe, conclude, and communicate). We agree. However, we question why every content area and discipline needs all these different processes.

Consider this: scientists and science teachers maintain that students need the scientific method, mathematicians and mathematics teachers maintain their process for solving complex word problems, counselors provide a set process for addressing social and emotional issues, and English teachers maintain that productive writing is often a result of engaging in the writing process. It is no wonder that students often experience challenges or "use and confuse" these steps and processes. Often, students just use the steps in these processes because teachers direct them to. Yet, the most valuable knowledge lies in understanding how and why each step is a valuable tool to support their thinking and output. How can educators teach and expect transfer for mastery and long-term understanding when so many similar but different processes exist with different labels? What do they all have in common? The answer is that, although they each make different adjustments and use different labels for each discipline, the *process* between them is no different.

This all points to a need for a singular metacognitive process for students to internalize and ultimately apply with autonomy across all content areas. It is especially important to empower students with a specific metacognitive strategy for research writing, which is one of the most complex and challenging tasks students face throughout their learning. If they have internalized this one process, they can focus their energy and efforts on the subject-area content they are researching rather than struggle with the craft of writing.

Furthermore, utilizing structured SELf-questioning prompts students to increase their reflection about what is working and what is not working for them when conducting research. This heightened awareness of their research-writing strengths and challenges helps students to monitor, self-regulate, and transfer their learning when research writing in multiple disciplines.

Finally, using one singular metacognitive process prompts students to interact and question the information they research, such as asking themselves, "How can I choose the strongest evidence to support my claim?" or "Which sources are the most credible, current, and reliable?" Rather than simply locating and restating information, metacognitive skills are essential for 21st century learners who can easily access information at their fingertips via smartphones, tablets, and so on. The SELf-questions sets encourage students to question, analyze, and evaluate this readily available information rather than simply locate and regurgitate it.

How to Teach a Metacognitive Strategy for Research Writing

When it comes to teaching the universal academic and social structured SELf-question set in inquiry-based research writing, we recommend using two approaches simultaneously. The first approach entails teachers explicitly supporting students in making the connections between the traditional writing process described in the previous section and the universal academic and social structured SELf-question set, which supports metacognition. We might classify this approach as broad-based since it can be used to show students how they might use SELf-questions and self-talk throughout the entire writing process, from prewriting to publishing. For example, students can enact the prewriting stage in the traditional writing process using the first, second, and third steps in the SELf-question set (select a focus, gather information, and brainstorm).

The following examples demonstrate how a student might utilize SELf-questioning and self-talk during prewriting.

- **Receiving an assignment to write a personal narrative:** If I ask myself, "What is my task?" I can use self-talk to answer that it is to write a personal narrative. Next, I ask myself, "What do I know or need to know?" to gather information for a personal narrative. I answer that *I know* that personal narratives are usually about ourselves or historically significant or otherwise memorable people, places, and events in our lives. *I also know* that the teacher modeled different ways to think of ideas, like how to use a heart map to generate a list of people, places, and events that are special when writing a personal narrative.

- **Understanding an assignment or test instructions:** If I ask myself, "What is my task?" when required to complete an assignment or respond to an essay question, such as during a standardized test, I might immediately use self-talk to look closely at the instructions and articulate exactly what I'm being asked to do. The second SELf-question—What do I know?—could prompt me to state some of the details of the assignment, look for information already at my disposal—including key words—or to access my prior knowledge. In the case of a standardized test essay question that asks me to explain and analyze how another author builds an argument, I might say, "I know I need to analyze Paul Bogard's argument about preserving natural darkness. I also know that one of the ways he builds this argument is with a personal story."

- **Generating questions for inquiry-based research:** If I ask myself, "What is my task?" when engaging in inquiry-based research writing, I might begin by generating a list of my own questions related to a topic.

- **Making a writing plan:** If I ask myself, "How will I organize my information?" I can consider strategies that might help me structure my assignment or see clear relationships between my ideas or concepts. For example, I could make an outline, a Venn diagram, a concept map, or so on.

All these examples demonstrate that students can autonomously engage in prewriting if they understand the thinking behind it and the questions they should ask themselves throughout the process. Asking oneself the SELf-question, "What is my task?" is significantly more open-ended than the traditional teacher-directed prewriting activity where the teacher might pose closed questions or prompts such as the following.

- "Name a favorite memory from the summer for your personal narrative."

- "Next, circle the verbs and nouns in the prompt."

- "Now, research this topic _____ and organize your prewriting information into defined categories using the four-square method or an outline."

Instead, connecting the writing process with a structured SELf-question set fosters thinking and independence as compared to teaching students to simply use the steps in the writing process to complete writing tasks. It is imperative that teachers explicitly share with students the connections between the SELf-question set and the stages in the writing process. Figure 6.1 shows one example of this, although the relationship between the writing process and SELf-questions is not always a one-to-one relationship.

By explicitly stating the connections as well as the differences between the familiar writing process steps and SELf-question set as demonstrated in figure 6.1, students understand the benefits of utilizing SELf-questioning to support independent thinking and problem solving. In utilizing the universal structure of the SELf-question sets, students should be more autonomous in moving through the writing process during inquiry-based research and are better equipped to address challenges they will confront along the way.

While this approach emphasizes the broad connections between the SELf-question set and the entire writing process, another approach utilizes all six steps in the SELf-question set to address more narrow writing challenges that students might confront during just one stage of the writing process. Students do not engage in all stages of the writing process in one day. Writing takes time, especially research writing! For example, consider an eighth-grade student tasked with writing an introductory paragraph to an inquiry-based research assignment about how climate change will affect migration in the coming years. She has gathered and read lots of good information, but she isn't sure how to begin. She's stuck. To get unstuck, rather than relying on the teacher to tell her how to begin, she works through

Writing Process Step	SELf-Question Step	Example SELf-Questions for Writing and Research
Prewriting	Select a Focus	What is my task? How do I select a topic or focus? What questions do I have about my topic or focus? What are my best questions?
	Gather Information	How will I gather information on some or all of my questions? What do I know? What do I need to know? How or where can I find information?
Prewriting and drafting	Brainstorm	How can I organize and present my information?
Prewriting, drafting, and revising	Evaluate	What is the best choice? Why? What is the strongest evidence to support my research? Which sources are the most credible, current, and reliable?
Drafting, revising, and editing	Plan and Act	What do I do first, second, and so on? Is this working? What is the strongest word choice? How can I improve sentence fluency to keep my audience engaged?
Revising, editing, and publishing	Reflect	What was surprising about my research? What did I do well, and how can I improve?

Figure 6.1: Writing steps with SELf-question steps and questions.

each step of the academic and social SELf-question set to overcome this single obstacle. In doing so, she does the following.

- Defines her task
- Gathers what she knows and doesn't know about the task and obstacle
- Brainstorms several ways she might begin or how she might decide where to begin
- Evaluates those ideas and chooses a course of action
- Tries to draft her initial paragraph

- Reflects on the result and whether her writing is working as she imagined it might

This example is just one of the many ways students can use the question sets to tackle a single writing challenge. Let's examine some grade-band scenarios that demonstrate other ways in which teachers utilize our SELf-questioning set's structure, steps, and questions to support students when engaging in the complex task of inquiry-based research writing. Notice the adaptations we've made to the steps and language in each scenario to increase opportunities for transfer across disciplines, which we encourage teachers to do as long as they maintain the basic structure. As in the previous chapters, we stress the importance of modeling.

Scenario: Grades K–2

Class: Kindergarten classroom (Mrs. O.; literacy coach)

Objective:

- Conduct research by asking and answering questions to make a booklet with three to five facts about an animal.

Standards:

- Participate in shared research and writing projects. (W.K.7; NGA & CCSSO, 2010a)

- Use observations to describe patterns of what plants and animals need to survive. (K-LS-1-1; Next Generation Science Standards [NGSS] Lead States, 2013).

Kindergarten students are conducting research on an animal as a component of an interdisciplinary unit that connects their learning about informational writing with learning about animals in a science unit. This approach supports Mrs. O. in addressing both state standards for informational writing and NGSS standards. After Mrs. O. explicitly models how to conduct research on polar bears, each student subsequently researches his or her own animal. The students' task is to draw a picture of their self-selected animal and write information in a three to five-page blank booklet to teach readers about their animal. The objective for the writing lesson is for the students to learn how to ask questions to help them add their own factual information and details using the SELf-question set to support them as research writers.

To support the early emergent writers in her class, Mrs. O. significantly scaffolds the process by providing students with a blank booklet. She prompts them to write specific information on each page. To help students gather information, she frames the questions for the first two pages using the following prompts.

- **Page 1:** "To gather information for page one, ask yourself, 'What do I know about the type of animal? Is it a mammal, bird, fish, reptile, or amphibian?'"

After posing these questions, Mrs. O. answers, "A polar bear is a mammal" and documents the sentence on the first page of her booklet.

- **Page 2:** "To gather information for page two, ask yourself, 'What do I know about what my animal looks like?'" She again models an answer by answering her own question: "Polar bears are big and white." She documents the sentence on page two.

As compared to these first two teacher-directed pages, subsequent pages ask students to generate their own inquiries about their animals. This requires a higher level of thinking and independence that students can achieve by employing their SELf-questions for research writing.

Next, Mrs. O. models how she might *gather* and add *information* to her next blank page in her research book by asking herself, "What else do I know about my animal?" and asking herself lots of questions about polar bears.

As she transitions to the next step, *brainstorming*, she thinks aloud, "I should brainstorm if I can answer any of my questions to add information to my research book." She begins to orally name her answers to her own questions and states, "I know that polar bears have webbed feet, polar bears live in cold places, and polar bears have paws." She models how to add one of her ideas and answers to the next blank page in her book. She then turns students loose to work on their own books with their own animals.

As the students attempt to ask and answer their own questions about their animals, many experience difficulties. Mrs. O. encourages them to use their SELf-question set to help them solve their writing problems. One student, Abdul, joins her for a writing conference to talk about his efforts to research bats. His first two pages include accurate (and adorable) pictures with labels as well as the following sentences with adequate spacing and proper letter formation.

- **Page 1:** *A bat is a mamel.*
- **Page 2:** *Bats are broun or blak. Thay have wings and fer.*

Abdul struggles as he attempts to add his own information to the remaining pages by asking his own questions. He shares, "I tried using my SELf-questions for my writing problem, but I am still stuck." To support him, Mrs. O. asks him to think aloud as he uses the SELf-question set.

SELECT A FOCUS

Questions: What is the problem? What is the question? What is the task?

Abdul began, "I asked myself, 'What is the problem?' and I answered it. My problem is I just can't think of what to write about on the next page." He aggressively points to page three in his booklet, which is blank. He continues confidently, "It's not that I don't know enough facts. The problem is that I asked myself soooo many questions about bats and have soooo many facts in my head, and now I am confused about what to write in a sentence on this page."

GATHER INFORMATION

Questions: What do I know? What do I need to know?

Mrs. O. compliments Abul by sharing that his problem is a great problem to have because he has so much information to teach his reader. She points to the SELf-question set displayed on the wall and prompts Abdul to ask himself the next question. Abdul continues, "See, that is really my problem. When I tried to ask myself 'What do I know?' and 'What do I need to know?' I had too much facts to write. I asked myself, 'When do you see bats?' Then I answered, 'Bats come out at night and that means they are nocturnal.'"

Abdul is especially proud of his fancy word (*nocturnal*) as evidenced by his grin as he says it. Notice also how he adapts the information-gathering question to suit his needs. This customization of the question set shows Abdul has internalized the metacognitive process and confirms his ownership of it to help him solve a problem. He continues, "Then, I just kept asking questions and answering them so I can write so much facts in my book, like bats hang upside down, and they see in the dark, and they can fly, and bats live in caves and trees and roosts." Abdul stomps his foot slightly and raises his hands in the air as he exclaims, "See, how do I write everything I know?"

BRAINSTORM

Questions: How can I solve this problem? What are possible solutions?

Again, Mrs. O. compliments Abdul's extensive knowledge about bats and shares that his problem is one that real authors often have. She explains, "Many times authors have too much research and information to share, so they need to organize it by figuring out what is important." She nods toward the SELf-question chart and directs him to ask himself the brainstorm question, How can I solve this problem?

Abul repeats the question aloud and scratches his head, which he often does when Mrs. O. models thinking. He then offers, "Well, I can just pick my favorite three facts, or I can pick the facts that have the fancy words like *nocturnal* or *roost*. Did you know those words?" He pauses to think before continuing, "I can also solve the problem by using the *Are, Can, Live* chart I made during science." Figure 6.2 shows the chart he's referring to.

EVALUATE

Questions: What is the best way to solve this problem? Does this make sense?

Without prompting from Mrs. O., Abdul automatically applies this SELf-question, stating, "I think the best choice is for me to use the Are, Can, Live chart from science. It makes sense because it will help me make sentences about all this information and most of my questions were about those facts anyway."

PLAN AND ACT

Questions: What do I do first, second, and so on? Does this work? Is this working?

At this point, Abdul clearly thinks he is done, but Mrs. O. points at the SELf-question set chart again, adopting an exaggerated expression to indicate there is more to do. Abdul

Figure 6.2: Abdul's Are, Can, Live chart.

concedes and asks himself, "What do I do first?" He takes out the Are, Can, Live chart and answers for himself, "First, I will write *Bats are nocturnal mammals*, because I want to use my fancy words." He writes the sentence on the booklet's third page and draws a picture of a bat flying around in dark woods with a moon out to show it is night. "Second, on page four, I will write, *Bats can fly*." As he writes the sentence on page four, he elaborates his sentence by adding "*and hang upside down*." He then rereads the entire sentence aloud, "Bats can fly and hang upside down." He smiles up at Mrs. O. and continues on to page five, consulting his Are, Can, Live chart and writing without support, *Bats live in caves and roosts*.

REFLECT

Questions: Did it work? How do I know? Do I need to go back and try again?

When the teacher gathers the students back on the rug to conclude the writing period, she points to the SELf-question set displayed on the wall and prompts all the students to reflect. She directs them to think about their problems during writing, the solutions they devised, and then ask themselves, "Did it work? How do I know? Do I need to go back and try again?" She directs them to share their reflections with a partner and listens specifically to what Abdul shares with his partner. He says, "My plan totally worked because I had too many questions and answers to add facts. I knew too much about bats, so I used the Are, Can, Live chart from science to help me get started writing fact sentences on page three. I was totally stuck before because all my ideas were just one big sentence." He proudly shows pages three, four, and five to his partner.

This scenario exemplifies that even very young writers need to experience empowerment through productive struggle. Abdul felt well-earned pride in his ability to problem solve when he encountered the common challenge that many young writers feel when they have so many ideas to say orally but struggle to transfer those words to paper. The process of SELf-questioning supported Abdul in breaking down the steps and thinking about his thinking, thus building metacognitive skills.

Basically, our goal as teachers is to develop independent thinkers and problem solvers. The success was not in the exceptional product that Abdul created in his animal-research book on bats but in his ability to utilize the SELf-question set to help himself solve problems when writing. Abdul generated the solution to use his Are, Can, Live chart, which he completed during science—a significant example of transfer. We ask you to think about which is more meaningful and transferable for lifelong learning: the teacher helping the student fix the piece of writing about bats or teaching Abdul to teach himself how to solve a problem when struggling with writing.

Scenario: Grades 3–5

Class: Third-grade classroom (Mrs. O.; literacy coach)

Objective:

- Research an individual who contributed to society and present the information to an authentic audience.

Standard:

- Conduct short research projects that build knowledge about a topic. (W.3.7; NGA & CCSSO, 2010a)

Mrs. O. is introducing a six-week informational unit of study in writing that would ultimately result in empowering students with the writing strategies and skills necessary to conduct inquiry-based research. During the first two weeks of the unit, she often models and utilizes think-alouds to demonstrate how to use structured SELf-questioning during students' initial informational writing task. She asks students to produce a writing sample from their schema (background knowledge) on a self-selected topic, which she identifies as *expert writing*. This writing on a familiar topic while also deepening that knowledge through research provides scaffolds that ensure that students internalize the structured SELf-question set during the writing process without the additional challenges of simultaneously conducting research on an unfamiliar topic.

After students utilize the structured SELf-questions to help them complete the initial expert writing task, Mrs. O.'s goal is for students to apply and transfer the structured SELf-questions to a new inquiry-based research writing project. This scenario highlights how students autonomously utilize the entire SELf-question set during the second task in an informational unit of study. After Mrs. O. models how to use each step and structured SELf-question, she assesses students' application during the second task, in which they write a narrative biography by asking questions and researching information about an individual of their choice who significantly contributed to society. To provide an authentic purpose and audience for the research writing, she asks students to present the information during a living wax museum in which they will dress up and teach classroom visitors, including parents and students from other classes, about the individual they researched by reciting a speech when people visit their exhibit.

SELECT A FOCUS

Questions: What is the problem? What is the question? What is the task?

Mrs. O. instructs the students to work with a partner to each select their focus—in this case, the individual they will research. One of the student pairs consists or Tanya and Michael. Tanya begins the conversation by exclaiming, "I will write about JoJo Siwa!" Michael immediately replies by shaking his head side to side to communicate his disagreement. He responds, "We can't just pick our person because we like them. We all know you just love her because you always wear those big bows. We need to ask, 'What is the problem?' or 'What is the task?'"

Tanya, looking slightly disappointed, glances at the smartboard showing the assignment details and concedes by asking herself, "What is the task?" She responds to herself using self-talk as Mrs. O. had previously modeled, "Well, we need to teach an audience about an individual who contributed to society." Mrs. O. notes that Tanya struggles to fluently read *contributed* and *society*. Michael supports her by saying, "That means people who helped the world. Maybe we should each make a list of people that we think have helped the world." Michael begins to list several athletes, such as Derek Jeter and LeBron James, as well as a few significant historical figures, such as Martin Luther King Jr., John F. Kennedy, and Neil Armstrong. Tanya, sticking to her passion for music, includes Taylor Swift, Kesha, Alicia Keys, and yes, one JoJo Siwa.

GATHER INFORMATION

Questions: What do I know? What do I need to know? What is similar, and what is different?

Tanya begins by instructing Michael like a teacher would, "Now we need to ask ourselves questions like 'What do I know?' and 'What do I need to know?'" It's clear that Tanya is very motivated as she quickly divulges all of the information that she knows about JoJo Siwa. She can provide more than ten pieces of information across her fingers and proudly holds up all ten fingers to confirm her extensive knowledge. She also experiments with other individuals on her list, but it's clear that she is set on researching JoJo Siwa.

Michael similarly gathers information by asking himself, "What do I know about each person on this list?" He names facts across his fingers for each person and settles on Martin Luther King Jr., who is the topic of *My Brother Martin* (Farris, 2006), which he recently read. Therefore, he is able to share many pieces of information about this prominent figure, who he understands made societal contributions that eclipsed the athletes on his list.

As Tanya is ready to progress to the next step, *brainstorm*, and the next structured SELf-question, Michael stops her and says, "We still need to ask ourselves, 'What do I need to know?' because that is the information that we will need to research." Tanya candidly replies, "Well, how am I supposed to know what I need to know?" Michael simply responds, "Remember, we just ask each other questions." Michael then asks Tanya several questions about JoJo Siwa that Tanya carefully notes in her writer's notebook, as follows. (Note that the difference between the second and third questions isn't especially distinct, but this is typical of such work at this grade level.)

- Why is JoJo Siwa so famous?
- How has JoJo Siwa helped the world?
- How has JoJo Siwa contributed to society?

Tanya is initially aggravated that Michael does not seem to agree that JoJo Siwa is famous and has contributed to society. In response to "How has JoJo Siwa helped the world?" she claims, "JoJo makes all her Siwanatorz [followers] happy with her great songs and famous big fashion bows." When Michael questions Tanya if that is a significant contribution compared to people like Martin Luther King Jr. and Neil Armstrong, Tanya's immediate reaction is to quip, "It is not a contest!" Despite this, she realizes she has a bigger problem on her hands: proving JoJo Siwa is a philanthropist. Motivated by the SELf-questioning process, Tanya immediately begins to conduct research.

BRAINSTORM

Questions: How can I solve this problem? What are possible solutions?

With awareness that she must conduct research, Tanya looks at Michael and asks, "How can I solve this problem?" Without waiting for Michael to respond, she engages in self-talk and exclaims, "Well, I am going to use that Biography.com website on our resource list or use the book JoJo wrote herself, *JoJo's Guide to the Sweet Life* [Siwa, 2017]. Michael nods but is clearly already engaged in his own self-talk as he asks himself the same question and shares that he thinks everyone should use the *Who Was* series of books as a source of information.

EVALUATE

Questions: What is the best way to solve this problem? Does this make sense?

Michael looks over at this step on the anchor chart and asks himself, "What is the best way to solve the problem?" He replies, "I think the best way is to use the text features to help us look for information about how the people helped the world, so we don't have to read the *whole* book. We can just use the table of contents in the books and the headings in the articles or websites." Mrs. O., who is circulating around the room to support all the partnerships, joins Tanya and Michael and compliments them for independently applying the reading strategies during writing instruction, which is evidence of how SELf-questioning promotes transfer.

PLAN AND ACT

Questions: What do I do first, second, and so on? Does this work? Is this working?

Tanya peers over again at the structured SELf-question anchor chart and asks herself, "What do I do first, second, and so on?" She looks at Michael and confidently begins, "First, I will use the Biography.com website, because they are usually only one page long, so it will be quick. Then I will skim and scan my JoJo book to be a fact checker."

Mrs. O. had previously modeled that, as 21st century learners and researchers, students can't always believe the information they find on the internet. Therefore, to check the validity and reliability of a source, she explains that researchers can fact check by making sure the information is present in two sources. Mrs. O. also encourages the students to write down the information they collect while researching their topic in their writing notebooks, under the questions they generate. She instructs them to place a checkmark next to information if they confirm it appears in a second source. This process takes several days as the students document information, search various sources, and fact check.

REFLECT

Questions: Did it work? How do I know? Do I need to go back and try again?

After two full writing periods dedicated to independent research and fact checking, Mrs. O. directs the partners to reunite to reflect on their work thus far. The room bursts into chatter, demonstrating how motivated the students are to share the information they gathered about their subjects.

After sharing some research about Martin Luther King Jr. and JoJo Siwa, Michael turns to the structured SELf-question anchor chart and asks Tanya, "Did it work? How do I know? Do I need to go back and try again?" He slightly grins and celebrates, "I know it totally worked because all three of my facts from the Biography.com page about MLK were almost the same as the facts from *My Brother Martin*. I didn't even have to reread the whole book or the entire article! I just used the one heading, 'Nobel Peace Prize,' in the article to fact check that part in my book."

Tanya high fives him and is bursting at the seams to tell him that her plan worked as well. She starts by shouting, "JoJo Siwa *did* help the world, and I can totally use her as my topic for the living museum. I know it worked because Biography.com had a heading, 'Hold the Drama' that said that her songs give messages to young girls about having the courage to stand up to bullies." Tanya continues, "*And*, I found a book that had so many text features that helped me prove she helped society, like really big quotes in the middle of the text. My fact-checking quote was, 'Siwanatorz protect each other. If they see someone being bullied, they speak up. Maybe not to the bully herself—but to a parent or teacher'" (Siwa, 2017, p. 3)

The story of Michael and Tanya is not the exception but the norm in this class, where the teacher and literacy coach consistently utilize structured SELf-questioning during writing instruction and across all disciplines. When using the more traditional models of research at the third-grade level, a teacher typically provides a topic and a list of questions or specific information that students need to look up, which usually results in students simply googling the required information. Conversely, students utilizing structured SELf-questioning are empowered with the skills necessary to independently conduct research.

The process of SELf-questioning during each step brings awareness to student thinking, thus building metacognition. The degree of automaticity and decrease of dependency on the teacher confirm success since the intended goal is to develop independent thinkers and problem solvers. Students are ultimately more invested in their writing. They have ownership of their work because their questions drive the content of their research as well as the next steps they take in the writing process.

Scenario: Grades 6–8

Class: Sixth-grade ELA (Mr. K.; literacy coach)

Objective:

- Cite and explain evidence to support a claim using inquiry-based research about an ancient civilization.

Standard:

- Conduct short research projects to answer a question, drawing on several sources and refocusing the inquiry when appropriate. (W.6.7; NGA & CCSSO, 2010a)

Students in a sixth-grade ELA class are to conduct research about ancient civilizations they are learning about in social studies. This assignment emerged after the social studies teachers noticed that students were struggling to select, cite, and explain evidence; they noted this to their colleagues teaching ELA. Mr. K.'s focus is to teach students how to cite and explain evidence that supports a claim they make about an ancient civilization based on their inquiries. As the students ask themselves, "What is my question?" they document their individual inquiries on digital sticky notes using Note.ly (https://note.ly/landing) to compile and view a shared document for all students to access. Some of the overarching questions the students generate include the following.

- Which ancient civilization was the greatest?
- Which ancient civilization most resembles our current society?
- How can we identify the most advanced ancient civilization?
- How did the ancient civilizations progress?
- How were the ancient civilizations alike and different?
- How do we see ourselves and our lives in the ancient civilizations?

Students self-select which overarching question they are interested in researching and continue to generate additional and more specific questions for their possible topics. Over the next two days, the students begin to gather information from at least two sources and formulate their individual theses.

This scenario provides some insight into the work of two sixth-grade partners, Melissa and Ted, who work through the SELf-question set together and come to the realization that they both need to be stronger when presenting their evidence to support their claims about ancient Egypt. Although both their thesis statements need some revision, their use of the SELf-question set during their peer conference successfully guides them forward in their research and writing. In this case, they both feel they are struggling with presenting their evidence and research to support their theses.

SELECT A FOCUS

Questions: What is the problem? What is the question? What is the task?

Melissa says, "My problem is that I am finding it hard to include evidence from my research to support my claim that ancient Egypt was one of the greatest early civilizations due to its focus on mathematics and education. I feel like I am just listing my evidence and research in my writing."

Ted follows suit: "What is my problem? Well, my problem is kind of similar. I need to think of different ways to include my research to support my claim that Egyptian temples showed how their spirituality advanced their technology and engineering."

GATHER INFORMATION

Questions: What do I know? What do I need to know?

Melissa says, "When I asked myself, 'What do I know?' I looked at all the evidence I highlighted in my two sources. Then I made a list of the most important ideas that were in both sources that support my claim." She looks over at Ted and suggests, "Why don't you list what you know like I did? Here is my list based on my research on Egyptians using mathematics." Melissa hands him a list with the following statements.

- I know that Egyptians did complicated mathematics that we still do today, like geometry.

- I know that they wrote books about mathematics and have some of the earliest documented uses for measurement because of fear of the Nile river flooding or droughts occurring.

- I know that Egyptians were the first people to calculate fractions.

Ted takes Melissa's advice and looks at his two sources, which are full of text he highlighted. He says, "I know that Egyptians built temples over 3,500 years ago. I know that the temples were usually to honor gods, goddesses, or kings and pharaohs who might be considered gods after death. I know that Egyptians took a long time to build the temples with the tools they had back then. I also researched the different sizes of the temples, and I know they were huge, which shows how advanced their engineering was given they didn't have the mechanical tools we have today."

BRAINSTORM

Questions: How can I solve this problem? What are possible solutions?

Melissa moves forward into the SELf-question set: "How can we solve the problem that we both have? We have all this information from our sources, but we don't just want to list it. Let's brainstorm ways we can write the evidence to support our claims."

Together the students begin to name the strategies for presenting evidence, which are documented in the Resource section of their writing binders. Ted voices some of the strategies: "We can choose strong words and phrases that help us angle and explain our evidence. Remember, *angle* here means to present facts or information in an argument so that it leans toward our claim. We can also use comparisons between our civilization and other ancient civilizations, and we can name the counterclaim and oppose it."

EVALUATE

Questions: What is the best way to solve this problem? Does this make sense?

Melissa, after asking herself and Ted the next SELf-question, says, "What is the best way to solve this problem?" She looks at Ted and continues, "Even though I think we should probably use all of these strategies in our research-based essays, I think the best way to solve our problem is to choose strong words and phrases that help us to explain and angle evidence. It makes sense for me because I really just listed the evidence I researched." Ted agrees.

PLAN AND ACT

Questions: What do I do first, second, and so on? Does this work? Is this working?

Melissa thinks for a moment and says, "What should I do first? Well, first I need to frame my first piece of evidence." She makes air quotes around the word *frame* as Mr. K. had modeled when demonstrating how to contextualize evidence using sentence frames. "Maybe I should revise my work by adding more supporting information after my evidence and direct quote about how Egyptians were great mathematicians and built pyramids by using their understanding of right triangles."

She writes: *The right triangle is the foundation for geometry and architecture. Without it, many people believe the Egyptians wouldn't have the pyramids that still stand today. The pyramids were built on the mathematical concepts of the 3-4-5 right angle, which was later credited to Pythagoras, who is a famous mathematician.*

Ted listens and watches as she writes and responds, "Next, you should end it with a strong statement connecting the evidence to your explanation like, 'This proves the greatness and advanced math of the ancient Egyptians.'" Ted is clearly proud of this feedback and begins to point to his notebook computer as he requests that Melissa support him in explaining and angling his evidence about Egyptian temples.

REFLECT

Questions: Did it work? How do I know? Do I need to go back and try again?

As Mr. K. circulates around the room, he visits student pairs as they advance to the reflection SELf-question, which provides him with the information necessary to provide additional support where it's needed. By listening to the students interact, he can differentiate and lift the level of conversation by questioning and prompting students as needed based on the content of their peer conferences. When he approaches Melissa and Ted, Ted gives a brief summary of their work, and Mr. K. asks, "How will you know if your plan worked?"

Melissa thinks out loud, "How do I know if it worked? Well, I asked my partner which of my statements most convinced him that Egypt's education and mathematics made it one of the greatest civilizations in the world. Ted said my revised statement with the angled explanation of my evidence was the strongest. I think he's right because, before my revision, I was really just listing the evidence from my research and citing the source. I never connected the research to my claim."

Notice how this partnership demonstrates how powerful it can be for students to work collaboratively with the SELf-question set to address similar challenges they are experiencing with inquiry-based research. As Mr. K.'s other students, not just Melissa and Ted, developed complex writing strategies and skills, they were comfortable taking risks in a socially supportive setting. Their consistent use of the SELf-question set established a community of writers where all students constantly worked through their challenges and collaborated to improve their writing. The student authors felt complete ownership of their process and product. No longer were the outcomes of the research papers a reflection of the teacher's effort as he or she spoon feeds the students with a carefully scaffolded or essentially scripted outline. Where such traditional and teacher-directed models of research all focus on the product, the essays these students produced after engaging in inquiry-based research and using SELf-questions to address their challenges reflect their inquiries, interests, grit, and writing abilities. They allowed students to ultimately produce work they are proud of!

Scenario: Grades 9–12

Class: Eleventh- and twelfth-grade ELA (Ms. S.; teacher)

Objective:

- Use feedback from peers and the instructor to make a revision plan. Use the revision plan to write the final draft.

Standard:

- W.11–12.5: Develop and strengthen writing as needed by planning, revising, editing, rewriting, or trying a new approach, focusing on addressing what is most significant for a specific purpose and audience. (W.11-12.5; NGA & CCSSO, 2010a)

In this scenario, Ms. S. asks students to write a four to six–page research essay on a topic of their choice. One of the requirements for the essay is that students discuss both what is known and what is unknown about their topic. Some students may feel drawn to topics in literature, history, or psychology, while others may explore topics in the natural sciences. Although students could use the academic and social SELf-question set at several points throughout this sort of project, we intend for the example in this scenario to illustrate how the SELf-questions might help a student through the revision process.

For this scenario, assume that all students in the class have written a first draft and that they've each received written feedback from both Ms. S. and at least one peer. Now, they are ready to revise and submit a final draft. Also assume students are familiar with the SELf-questioning problem-solving process and can answer its questions independently, in writing. In addition to their paper, Ms. S. expects them to turn in their written responses to the SELf-question set. Instead of examining what students write about the SELf-question set, let's examine this process from the teacher's perspective.

SELECT A FOCUS

Questions: What is the problem? What is the question? What is the task?

Ms. S. wants students to identify that they are tasked with revising their projects based on the feedback from their peers and instructor. This first SELf-question may also be an opportunity for students to begin expressing a problem or challenge they are having with their essay. Although it may seem like the answer to this question is obvious, it is worth asking, as it may help students clearly articulate the task or a challenge within it. Asking the question also may afford Ms. S. the opportunity to clarify the purpose of the task or the purpose of revision in general. For example, she might ask the whole class, "What is the task?"

After the task is clear and the students have written it down, Ms. S. may have students follow up with a class discussion to answer other questions, such as: "Why are you revising?" "What is the purpose of revision?" and, "How do you make decisions about what to revise?" Once she solicits responses to these questions and the students have taken notes, she asks them to answer the remaining SELf-questions on their own.

GATHER INFORMATION

Questions: What do I know? What do I need to know?

In this step, Ms. S. expects students to explicitly acknowledge the challenges they encountered in making their research essays stronger and the feedback they received on their drafts. She encourages students to get specific about what is working in their essays and what is not. She also encourages them to write down the feedback they receive from others and any information they may need to gather so that they can address that feedback. Finally, she emphasizes that students should clarify anything about that feedback that is unclear or confusing by conferring with her or the student who completed their peer review.

For example, let's say that a student, Ellie, is writing an essay about the relationship between social media and depression. Ms. S. has praised Ellie's writing on what is known about that relationship but asks her to focus more on the relationship's unknown aspects. As a response, Ellie might write:

My instructor says I am doing a good job explaining what's known about social media and depression but this is only half the assignment. Some of the research says that people don't know why social media causes depression, so that is unknown, but I don't know how to make half an essay out of that one idea.

BRAINSTORM

Questions: How can I solve this problem? What are possible solutions?

Here, students brainstorm ways to address the feedback they've received. This included looking for more sources, asking the teacher or peers for clarification, rereading the essay, moving sections of the essay around, eliminating sections, clarifying ideas, and so on. It's worth noting that, when it comes to revision, student writers often need to address several aspects of their text, some of which may not seem directly related. For example, a student may need to restructure their introduction while also making sure that all the paragraphs throughout the essay are coherent, especially those in the body. When this is the case, they may make a list of the top tasks they need to complete or the challenges they need to address as they write the next draft.

In this case, Ellie is confused about how to go into detail about what is unknown about the relationship between social media and depression. Therefore, she decides she could ask her peers for some ways they are talking about the unknown in their essays. She also could ask Ms. S. how one might elaborate on unknowns. Finally, she could reexamine her sources, looking only for places in the texts where the authors discuss remaining questions.

EVALUATE

Questions: What is the best way to solve this problem? Does this make sense?

For this step, students evaluate the options they've come up with in the brainstorming step and select the best option. Sometimes, students might encounter more than one promising strategy and, therefore, choose to enact them either sequentially or simultaneously. Ellie decides asking her peers, two of whom are seated right next to her, about the unknowns in their essays is the best choice, particularly because it is convenient. However, when the information she receives from her peers fails to provide a clear path forward, she can choose an additional viable strategy, such as reexamining her sources. Although Ellie may have begun by choosing what she determined was the best option, after trying it out and reflecting, she finds herself returning to this step to evaluate her options again. This circling back illustrates the recursive nature of our question sets and our problem-solving process, which can help students persevere through extended difficulty. After all, complex problems are not often solved on the first try.

PLAN AND ACT

Questions: What do I do first, second, and so on? Does this work? Is this working?

Since revision is a complicated and often nonlinear process, this step acts as an overall revision plan where students articulate how they plan to address the major points of feedback they've received. In this scenario, Ellie writes, "First, I'll ask my peers about the unknowns in their projects. Then, I'll go through all my old articles. If I still need help, I'll ask Ms. S. how I can say more about what's unknown about my topic." After she spends several minutes completing the first two strategies, Ellie decides she feels confident enough to give revision a try.

When students turn in their revision plans with the revision itself, it can help both them and their teachers to see students' intentions and the execution of those intentions. This step acts as a sort of contract for the revision between students and themselves, between teachers and students, and in the case of group projects, between students and their peers. The revision plan can also help students stay focused and on track, especially when the revision is extensive and complex.

REFLECT

Questions: Did it work? How do I know? Do I need to go back and try again?

In some cases, students may feel tempted to try to answer reflection questions before moving to the revision itself. Here, however, Ellie has taken the necessary time to complete her revision first, before reflecting on it. As Ms. S. suggested to the whole class, she takes her revision plan home and spends some time that evening refocusing her essay on the questions researchers still have about the relationship between social media and depression. After that, she completes the final step of her revision plan:

> *I still don't think my essay is perfect, but I can see now that it's better because I'm actually doing what the assignment says. It took me a while to figure out how to talk about what's not known, but I think I made progress. I'm excited to turn in my revision plan and final draft and hear what my teacher thinks of my changes.*

It's important for teachers to remind students that guided SELf-questioning is an authentic process and that, therefore, they cannot complete their plan until they've completed the revision the preceding questions are designed to support. Once students have a completed revision, they can more accurately reflect on its success, as well as the challenges they encountered along the way. They may also choose to discuss what they would do next if they had more time.

Revision is a challenging process for both novice and expert writers. In this scenario, you can see how a research-writing SELf-question set can guide students through this process, helping them to slow down, think metacognitively, and think more deeply to understand each step. Finally, using this SELf-questioning set for inquiry-based research writing can help a teacher easily structure a complex writing process such as revision. This helps teachers more clearly see each student's thinking process.

Application Across Genres

Although the grade-level scenarios in this chapter focus on inquiry-based research writing, this SELf-question set is a powerful tool across all writing applications and genres. Table 6.1 provides an authentic example of a student at each grade-level band utilizing the first three steps of the SELf-question set for typical problems a student might encounter during narrative writing.

Table 6.1: Using SELf-Questions Across Grade-Level Bands for Narrative Writing

Grade Band	Select a Focus (What is the problem?)	Gather Information (What do I know? What do I need to know?)	Brainstorm (How can I solve this problem? What are the possible solutions?)
Grades K–2	My problem is I have a hard time reading my writing.	I know I need to make my writing readable so I can read it and other people can too. I know I wrote about my trip to the park and store this weekend from my picture because there is a slide there, but I don't remember anything else.	I can make spaces between my words. I can label my pictures to help me remember. I can use a yellow highlighter to draw a yellow line to count the words in my sentences before I write them like the teacher.
Grades 3–5	My problem is that my story and dialogue are boring in my realistic fiction writing.	I know that I shouldn't add dialogue everywhere. I only need dialogue where it contributes to the story.	I can add dialogue to show the characters' inside traits. I can use dialogue to show how a character feels about another character. I can remove dialogue that is unnecessary, like when the characters are greeting each other, which takes multiple paragraphs.
Grades 6–8	My problem is that my narrative includes very cliché figurative language and sensory details.	I know that writers include figurative language to engage the reader and they use sensory details to help the reader visualize the story.	I might use the website that the teacher gave us with all the figurative language examples to use as mentor sentences. I can fill in the sensory image chart and think about what I might hear, see, feel, and smell in the moment. I can try to add one metaphor, one simile, and one piece of personification so I don't feel so overwhelmed.
Grades 9–12	My problem is that I dedicate so much time to describing the characters and setting in the exposition, which usually is my best work in my piece. However, I lose interest, time, and energy in developing the middle part of my narrative, so my rising action and climax always fall flat and bring my grade down.	I know that I need to find a way to improve the middle part of my narrative, including how I develop the plot. I know that describing characters and the setting does not constitute a narrative, as it needs a plot that includes a possible problem to interest the reader. I know that writers carefully plan how they develop their story, all leading to the climax.	I can quickly generate a sketch of the characters and setting and then immediately dedicate my initial time and energy to developing the plot. I can use a plot diagram or story mountain to budget for myself a limited amount of time and energy for each part. I can work backward by starting with the middle. I can brainstorm the climax of the story, develop the rising action, and then draft the exposition where the description of the characters and setting will foreshadow the problem.

Character Corner: Self-Confidence

Structured SELf-questioning doesn't just support students working in various applications and genres of writing, such as the narrative-writing examples in table 6.1 (page 109); help them move along the stages in the writing process, such as in figure 6.1 (page 93); or support them while engaging in inquiry-based research writing. Structured SELf-questioning is so much more. It is a powerful tool that is applicable and transferable to both academic and emotional challenges and helps students build self-confidence in their thinking processes, both in academic and personal contexts. Consider the following example, which demonstrates how a second-grade student, Sydney, utilized the SELf-questioning set to address an integrated emotional and writing problem that helped her build up the self-confidence to share a deeply personal experience.

On a Monday, Sydney was teary-eyed while attempting to write in her weekend journal. She raised her hand and shared with her teacher, "I have a problem, but it is not just about journal writing. I am just sad to write about my weekend because my hamster died, and I feel sad." The teacher quickly hugged Sydney and confirmed her feelings by agreeing that it is hard to lose a pet who is a member of the family. She briefly shared an anecdote about losing her dog. Then the teacher shared, "Every person needs to deal with his or her sadness and grief a different way, so maybe you should try to use the SELf-question set to think of ways to help yourself feel better. It is great that you already did step one, because you already know your problem and what is causing your sadness."

Still in tears, Sydney quietly looked at the SELf-questioning chart and asked herself, "What do I know?" She mumbled, "I know that I loved Snowflake. I know that I have had him since I was really little. I know that I feel really depressed and can't write about my weekend right now. What I need to know is will he be OK? Does Snowflake know I will miss him? Will my mom get me a new hamster? I think she hated him because he smelled sometimes, and she hated cleaning his cage."

At this point, her lip started to tremble, but she persisted. Sydney looked at the SELf-questioning anchor chart and asked herself, "Well, how can I solve this problem?" She began to list some possible solutions in her writing journal.

- I can write a letter to ask my mom for a new hamster like when we did our persuasive writing to ask our parents for a holiday gift.
- I can write a poem about Snowflake to tell my feelings.
- I can write Snowflake a letter and read it at his funeral after school.

Sydney then asked herself, "What is the best way to solve this problem?" She looked up with her glassy eyes and shared, "I think the best thing for me to do is to write Snowflake a letter in my journal that I can read at his funeral. I think it makes sense because I will make sure he knows that I loved him and will miss him."

Sydney automatically asked and answered this SELf-question as she continued to plan and act, "First, I will write Snowflake the letter. Then, if I have time, I might even be able to write a poem for the funeral too." The teacher nodded and hugged Sydney to show her emotional support. Further, she complimented Sydney for her plan to help herself address both her sadness and her struggle with her journal entry assignment.

At the end of the ten-minute journal writing time, the teacher allowed a few volunteers to share their writing if they so wished. She was surprised to see Sydney's hand raised and provided her with the opportunity to share. It was incredibly powerful as Sydney confirmed her success using the SELf-questioning set. She stated, "Today, I wrote in my journal to my hamster Snowflake who died this weekend, and it really made me feel better." She read the rest of her essay and concluded, "I used our problem-solving questions, and when I asked myself the last one, 'Did it work?' I answered, 'I know it did because I do feel a little better, and this was the most I ever wrote in my journal."

Writing is one of the most complex and personal tasks teachers require of students. Research writing can be especially overwhelming and frustrating as burgeoning writers are guaranteed to experience numerous challenges that will impact their view of themselves as writers and researchers. Teachers need to build confidence in their students by teaching them a strategy that helps them feel confident using their own critical-thinking and problem-solving skills when writing. Thus, many students will benefit from a metacognitive structured SELf-questioning approach that empowers them to feel confident going forward into the uncertainties, trials, and tribulations of writing. This is not a luxury or an extra tool that you might share with your students if you ever find extra time. It's not a nice-to-have skill. Make it essential, so that your students develop the self-confidence they need to take on the challenges of writing, of inquiry, and of life!

Structured SELf-Questioning for Emotional Recognition

7

If your emotional abilities aren't in hand, if you don't have self-awareness, if you are not able to manage your distressing emotions, if you can't have empathy and have effective relationships, then no matter how smart you are, you are not going to get very far.

—Daniel Goleman

An overarching goal of this book is to show how it is possible to teach all students the coping skills they need for success at school and in life, which includes coping flexibility and positive self-talk. Up to this point, we have written about using SELf-questioning to develop cognitive flexibility and guided self-talk through academic (mathematics, reading, and writing) and social problem solving. In so doing, structured SELf-questioning supports students' development of the SEL competency of responsible decision making (CASEL, n.d.). In this chapter and the ensuing chapters, we demonstrate how the metacognitive strategy of structured SELf-questioning helps develop the other three SEL competencies inherent in coping skills: (1) self-awareness (the ability to recognize one's emotions), (2) self-management (the ability to successfully regulate one's emotions), and (3) social awareness (the ability to take the perspective of and empathize with the emotions of others).

You may be thinking, "What? We need to embed and teach three additional SEL competencies?!" The short answer, which we explain further in this and subsequent chapters, is *yes*. The good news is, with structured SELf-questioning, you do not need to teach a new strategy, and you do not need additional instructional time to teach self-awareness or self-management. This is because our metacognitive strategy is perfect for any SEL competency that involves awareness and management.

When teachers help students develop their self-awareness and self-management of their emotions while also increasing their awareness of and empathy for the emotions of their classmates, friends, and teachers, students also improve their academic performance (Durlak et al., 2011). For now, let's focus specifically on self-awareness and self-management. (We'll return to social awareness in chapter 10, page 153.)

The emotional SELf-questioning set we cover in this chapter and chapter 8 (page 125) utilizes the same strategy to help students be aware of and manage their own emotions. The overall strategy is precisely the same—we've just adapted the SELf-questions for the emotional set to better support emotional contexts. To show the similarities and correlations between the two SELf-question sets, refer to figure 1.1 (page 23), which lists the academic and social and emotional SELf-question sets together.

This chapter demonstrates the importance of the emotional SELf-questioning set in teaching students self-awareness. It also provides an explanation for how any K–12 teacher can develop this SEL competency through common, daily routines and regular practices, such as classroom and behavior-management routines, do-nows, journaling, and restorative circles. Because teachers can apply the scenarios in this chapter successfully across wider developmentally appropriate age spans, the scenarios in this chapter slot into overlapping grade bands of preK–5 and 3–12. We end the chapter with a look at how this work with emotional SELf-questioning enhances students' self-control.

In the next chapter, we explain and demonstrate with examples how any teacher can use the emotional SELf-question set within existing classroom management strategies to teach self-management. Combined, these two chapters show how effective, powerful, and easy it can be to teach students how to guide their self-talk through their own emotional challenges, helping them develop the ability to identify and regulate their own emotions independently. In doing so, students are truly in an emotional state that is conducive to maximizing their mental capacities—specifically, the critical-thinking and problem-solving skills that will guide them toward coping successfully and flexibly when faced with stressful situations and making responsible decisions.

The Importance of Teaching a Metacognitive Strategy for Emotional Recognition

For students to independently apply all the critical-thinking and problem-solving skills teachers work so hard to teach them, they need to be in a state of emotional control. According to psychologists and neuroscientists Hadas Okon-Singer, Talma Hendler, Luiz Pessoa, and Alexander J. Shackman (2015), "stress, anxiety, and other kinds of emotion can profoundly influence key elements of cognition, including selective attention, working memory, and cognitive control." In other words, students who lack or struggle with emotional control will struggle with cognitive control.

Have you ever gotten really mad and—due to a combination of stress, anxiety, frustration, and anger—made a destructive (and self-destructive) choice in the heat of the moment? You have. We all have. Becoming calm, staying calm, and performing at our best through a heated discussion with a loved one, such as a spouse or sibling, isn't easy for adults. We have all said or done things that weren't the most constructive choices at the time, often because our emotions were high and our heart rates were revving up. The same holds true for students, especially since their brains and coping skills are not yet fully developed.

Consider the following example. Student volunteers from Loma Linda School participating in a violence prevention and intervention program (sponsored by Creighton School District 14 in inner-city Phoenix, Arizona, the Phoenix Police Department, the Phoenix City Council, and the Rainwater Charitable Foundation) were on a homeward-bound bus after a teaching session at a neighboring elementary school. Stephanie, an eighth-grade student, first-year volunteer, and a member of Rick's elective class to train middle school students in violence prevention and intervention, worriedly said to him, "Mr. Cohen, Veronica is waiting for me at the corner." Veronica, who Stephanie had past conflicts with, was a freshman in high school who had graduated from Loma Linda School, a K–8 school, and was a former student of Rick's.

Rick asked Stephanie while both were getting off the bus, "How do you want to handle this, Stephanie?" She answered, "I want to talk to her. Otherwise, she'll just be there tomorrow morning."

As they headed to the corner together, Rick hoped Stephanie could remember the steps of the social conflict–resolution skills training she had just passed to become a peer mediator. He was confident Stephanie was equipped with the skills needed to solve the problem without the use of violence. Besides, he was right there by her side.

Veronica was standing on the corner. When Stephanie crossed the street, two of Veronica's friends emerged from behind the house on the corner. The girls sauntered over, flashed gang signs with their fingers, and then began removing their earrings in preparation for a fight. One girl stepped right up into Stephanie's face. Veronica, who was pregnant, took a step back and asked Stephanie why she was saying stuff about her. Stephanie responded immediately with two solid punches to the face of Veronica's friend. As Rick tried pulling Stephanie away, he implored her to go home. She did and went inside her house.

After Veronica and the other girls stormed off, Stephanie came back out of her house and sat on the curb. Stephanie put her head in her hands and cried. She said, "I had no reason to fight that girl, Mr. Cohen. I just have all this anger, and my dad always taught me to fight."

In Stephanie's case, like in so many other of our students' cases, we see the need for students to learn emotional control before they can apply their cognitive and metacognitive control. Despite all the training Stephanie had received on how to thoughtfully and strategically resolve almost any social conflict without the use of violence, all of it went out the bus window when she saw Veronica and started getting angry. Even though Stephanie had learned how to think through a social problem, she had not yet been taught how to think through her anger. She also had not yet learned it is best to take a calming step back before trying to think about how to handle the situation best. Instead, Stephanie determined how to handle the situation while under extreme emotional distress. Rick still regrets asking her first, "How do you want to handle this?" Looking back on it, Rick would have started by asking Stephanie, "How do you feel?" Or better yet, he could have assumed Stephanie was furious if he had been more socially aware and gotten right to the key question, "What strategies can you use right now, Stephanie, to calm yourself down?"

These would have been important questions, in the moment, because self-awareness is a separate skill set from responsible decision making. It's also instrumental to success in both responsible decision making and academic problem solving (Butler et al., 2011; CASEL, n.d.). In Butler and colleagues (2011), *identifying feelings* is the first step in the social-decision-making and social-problem-solving process.

Students must learn both emotional control (think of a comprehensive set of coping skills including coping strategies and coping flexibility) as well as cognitive control (think of all the higher-order cognitive processes inherent in responsible decision making, such as *analyzing, evaluating,* and *reflecting*). This learning ensures they are capable of applying such control while under distress, in the heat of the moment, when teachers aren't there by their side.

Since teaching emotional and cognitive control takes time, and instructional time is not abundant, the most efficient way to teach emotional control is by using the same strategy students are learning and honing for cognitive control. This makes the metacognitive strategy of structured SELf-questioning ideal for a variety of reasons. First, students are already familiar with the strategy and have almost limitless opportunities to practice the strategy in their state standards–aligned academic curricula and instructional experiences. Second, teachers and peers alike already ask students to demonstrate emotional control throughout every class in every day of every school year, in the hallways and at recess, and in every moment of their school life. So, authentic opportunities to practice the strategy to identify one's own feelings in every aspect of school life are plentiful. In addition, giving students the opportunity to transfer the strategy of structured SELf-questioning from academic and social contexts to a new and different emotional context is a highly effective teaching, learning, and assessment practice.

How to Teach a Metacognitive Strategy for Emotional Recognition

Generally, teaching emotional recognition as a component of emotional problem solving is different from teaching academic and social problem solving. For students to think about their feelings, they should focus only on themselves and look inward, not outward. Identifying one's own feelings is very different from identifying academic or social problems, which involve fact finding and gathering information. Even identifying the feelings of others (to engage in social problem solving) is a completely separate SEL competency—social awareness (CASEL, n.d.) because it involves the thoughtful collection of facts, perspectives, and feelings from sources outside oneself. Gathering information to identify the feelings of someone else is visual (observing facial expressions and body language), auditory (listening to tone of voice and volume), and is often done through text or discussion (the words people use and the way they use them). By contrast, identifying one's own feelings means reading one's own body, noticing how one feels physically as well as noticing one's own thought patterns. The process of identifying one's own emotions is not accomplished by looking outside of oneself. In fact, the competency of self-awareness is often best accomplished when one's awareness is clear of focus on others or when one's awareness is free from the thoughts, perspectives, or feelings of others. This is why identifying one's own feelings while under distress, in the heat of the moment, is so difficult and takes a great deal of practice.

To this end, the emotional SELf-question set involves a series of open-ended questions we have adapted to better fit emotional situations. This chapter focuses exclusively on the first step and associated questions, but take a moment to consider the full emotional SELf-question set.

Self-empathy: What am I feeling? How do I feel?

 Gather information: What is causing this feeling?

 Brainstorm: What strategies can I use to make myself feel better?

 Evaluate: Has this strategy helped me in the past? How did it help? How did I feel after?

 Plan and act: What do I do first, second, and so on? Does this work? Is this working?

 Reflect: Did it work? How do I know? Do I need to go back and try again?

A big reason for this shift in questions from the academic and social set is that it's easy to misunderstand the academic and social SELf-questions for emotional situations. For example, when students are dealing with a social problem in the classroom and are very upset with a classmate, a teacher might ask, "What is the problem?" Students may respond by saying the problem is something someone else did. Worse, when upset and asked, "What is the problem?" students may say the other person or people involved are the problem. Such statements are not conducive to gaining emotional control and do not help in problem solving. This is why the emotional SELf-question set focuses internally.

In short, we designed the emotional SELf-question set to encourage students to think about what they can do for themselves when they are feeling low-level anxiety, depression, anger, frustration, and distress. It is also important to emphasize *low-level*. As we discuss later in this section, high-level emotional stressors in these categories require more dedicated intervention than a teacher should attempt to address.

Teaching emotional recognition can be as easy as modeling the act of asking and answering oneself out loud, "What am *I* feeling?" After a teacher conducts such think-alouds for students, he or she then asks students, "What are *you* feeling?" Teaching students self-awareness through structured SELf-questioning does not require a new instructional technique or pedagogy. The only difference between teaching structured SELf-questioning for academic and social problem solving compared to emotional problem solving is the SELf-questions.

Despite this alignment in SELf-question steps, actually teaching self-awareness is different than teaching social problem solving. For teaching social problem solving, pedagogy is for the teacher to start by asking open-ended questions and then suggest options for students to choose from, telling students which option to choose only when necessary (Butler et al., 2011). For teaching self-awareness, we do not recommend teacher suggestions, teacher decision making, or teachers telling students what their students' emotions "really" are or how to deal with their emotions. If necessary, as when students express emotions that give any reason whatsoever for concern or are not successful at identifying their emotions accurately, teachers should immediately recognize that there may be a need for higher-level care and refer those concerns or questions to the school counselor or social worker.

When prompting teachers to ask students on a regular basis to identify and express how they are feeling, they often respond that they fear students will tell them things they won't know how to handle. Remember, the purpose of asking students to identify and express how they are feeling is threefold.

1. Develop students' SEL competency of self-awareness.

2. Help reduce the number of students with mental health concerns that may typically go unnoticed or unidentified.

3. Help the student, parent, and school seek the appropriate professional help and treatment.

Since teachers are not trained to make assessments or determine necessary treatment, they should always alert their school counselor if students express any feelings that arouse concern. Such concerns can vary but include when students are unable to identify or express how they feel, repeatedly express feelings of sadness or anger and frustration, or indicate in any form thoughts of self-harm or lack of self-worth. By following this approach, schools can systematically achieve all three purposes of asking students to express their feelings. For responses that do not cause concern, the goal of asking students, "What are you feeling?" becomes one of prompting self-awareness. Teacher-provided judgments, suggestions, or solutions are the opposite of what we recommend. For example, teachers should refrain from think-aloud statements about their students' feelings, such as saying, "I think you are feeling pretty sad right now," or "It seems to me that you are feeling a lot of anger." Think-alouds for teachers to model self-awareness should be restricted to the teacher expressing his or her own emotions.

Another difference that merits deeper exploration is between the academic and social set's *select a focus* and the emotional set's *self-empathy*. In academic and social problem solving, the first step often involves some level of choice—which problem, question, or task one should choose to pursue further. How students feel (or how anyone feels) is often not a choice. Therefore, for emotional contexts, the first step is to notice and identify what one is feeling by asking "What am I feeling?" or "How do I feel?" This is why the self-empathy step is the only action not to have a verb associated with it. The key with self-empathy is really to do nothing and see what emotions present themselves.

For example, ELA teachers can model self-empathy and how to use this SELf-question when teaching narratives by asking themselves out loud, "What am I feeling?" Then, provide some wait time while posing in a thinking position, demonstrating physically and verbally that an emotion, or emotions, have been recognized. Finally, write down as many feelings and adjectives connected with those feelings as apply for the class to hear and read. This is also an excellent approach for teaching students a more diverse emotional vocabulary. Building on this vocabulary, what psychiatrist Lisa F. Barrett (2018) calls *emotional granularity*, is vital in the development of effective emotional recognition and emotional literacy skills (the ability to express one's own emotions). Barrett (2018) further explains why identifying emotions at a more granular level is helpful:

> If you could distinguish finer meanings within "Awesome" (happy, content, thrilled, relaxed, joyful, hopeful, inspired, prideful, adoring, grateful, blissful . . .), and fifty shades of "Crappy" (angry, aggravated, alarmed, spiteful, grumpy, remorseful, gloomy, mortified, uneasy, dread-ridden, resentful, afraid, envious, woeful, melancholy . . .), your brain would have many more options for predicting, categorizing and perceiving emotions, providing you with the tools for more flexible and useful responses. You could predict and categorize your sensations more efficiently and better suit your actions to your environment.

Not only is asking students to identify and express their emotions to a more specific degree beneficial to their development of self-awareness, it also boosts their likelihood of success with self-management of those emotions.

In the following sections, we provide examples of teaching self-awareness through SELf-questions focused on identifying emotions through practical, easy-to-implement, and regular school-day routines and practices. We refer to these sections as strategies rather than scenarios because we focus them on approaches you might take relative to just the first step—self-empathy. This is the step that most directly involves self-awareness, whereas the remaining steps and SELf-questions for the emotional set are designed to develop and prompt students' self-talk through self-management and coping flexibility.

Strategies for Grades PreK–5

For this section, we look at the two most opportune times in the school day for engaging students in the first step of emotional SELf-questioning by having students ask themselves, "What am I feeling?" or "How do I feel?": (1) morning meetings and (2) door greetings.

Morning Meetings

Morning meetings are common practices in early childhood and elementary classrooms. At Moss Elementary School, early childhood teachers incorporate the SELf-question *What am I feeling?* into their morning routine and have seen the positive impact it has on their students in identifying their emotions, especially students with disabilities who often struggle with impulse control and tantrums. These circle times present the perfect opportunity to teach students how to identify and recognize their emotions and begin making determinations as to whether or not they are ready to learn.

Because preK and kindergarten students have not yet developed the practice of SELf-questioning, Moss teachers ask students each day, "How do you feel?" Students respond directly to the teacher. No matter how the student responds, the teacher asks the student to then identify which *zone of regulations* that feeling falls under. These zones encompass four ranges: (1) red, a heightened state of alertness and intense emotions, (2) yellow, a heightened state but with a sense of self-control, (3) green, a calm, alert state, and (4) blue, a low-alert state that typically occurs when feeling down in some way (Kuypers, 2011). (Visit https://zonesofregulation.com to learn more.) Using these zones, teachers routinely ask students to categorize their stated feeling by asking simply, "What zone is that?" One day, in Ms. M.'s classroom, the morning routine went as follows.

Ms. M.: *"How do you feel?"*

Student 1: *"Sad."*

Ms. M.: *"You feel sad, that means you are in the . . ."*

Student 1: *"Blue zone."*

Ms. M.: *"What do you do when one of our friends is in the blue zone?"*

Student 2: *"Pat him on the back."* The student goes over to the blue student and pats him on the back. *"I hope you feel better."*

Ms. M.: *"Now, how do you feel?"*

Student 1: *"Happy."*

While it may sound overly optimistic to expect these results with each interaction in morning circle time, how students feel after identifying their emotions and helping others with their own isn't the focus of the activity. The main focus or goal of the activity is for students to get practice identifying and expressing their emotions. Notice that the third question the teacher asks here does not prompt self-awareness or self-management. Instead, it prompts social awareness and other regulation.

Door Greetings

We have observed that greeting students before they enter the classroom is a practice that is becoming increasingly prevalent in schools. Greeting students at the door can generally help create a positive environment and tone to start each class. There are a variety of ways teachers may choose to greet their students, such as providing encouraging messages, reminding students of expectations, or shaking hands. To use this daily routine to develop students' emotional-recognition skills, we recommend that you pose the self-question "What am I feeling?" or "How do I feel?" next to the door, before students enter. Underneath the SELf-question, we recommend putting the stem "Today, I feel like I need a _____." and place choices of greetings from the teacher that the student feels best fits his or her need, such as a high five or a hug.

Having students ask themselves, "What am I feeling?" and responding by choosing a high five or hug accomplishes a number of objectives beyond setting a positive tone. First and foremost, students practice asking themselves the SELf-question to foster self-awareness.

Second, it is a helpful practice for students to identify their feelings as a form of a self-check before they engage in learning.

Engaging in an emotional recognition and expression practice before entering class also empowers the teacher to conduct an efficient pulse check of emotional readiness for learning. If a student expresses the need for a hug (either verbally or by tapping on a visual icon or the word *hug* on the poster by the door), the teacher is empowered to provide a timely, low-level intervention that could help the student calm low-level fears or anxieties before class begins.

Strategies for Grades 3–12

For this section, we look at two opportunities for engaging students in grades 3–12 in emotional SELf-questioning: (1) think sheets and (2) journaling. Note that these are very specific tools for engaging self-empathy, but we do not recommend using them to address subsequent steps in the emotional SELf-questioning set as those steps are not designed for whole-group activities or instruction, nor for instructional or assessment purposes. However, think sheets and journaling are ideal tools for building self-awareness, developing an emotional vocabulary, and developing coping strategies for stress and anxiety.

Think Sheets

Individually conferencing with a student when he or she looks upset or when misbehavior occurs can be highly effective but also very time consuming. During class time, when a student acts out, when a student expresses a strong emotion, or when you can just tell something is a bit off, we recommend offering students a think sheet that contains the emotional SELf-questions. The grades 3–5 scenario in chapter 3 (page 52), on social problem solving, included an example of using a think sheet and explained the concept of providing them to students when they have a social conflict (from recess or lunch or something that happened during class). In this case, a teacher might use a think sheet to prompt students to use the first question in the emotional SELf-question set, with the rest of the questions coming from the academic and social SELf-question set. This provides students an opportunity to identify and express emotions before thinking through a specific social problem and the best solution without teacher intervention.

Figure 7.1 (page 122) shows an example of such a think sheet. This think sheet provides steps and SELf-questions that ask students to think about both their feelings first and then engage their academic and social critical-thinking and problem-solving skills but not their emotional problem-solving skills (which are better suited for school counselors and in-school therapists).

By providing students a moment to reflect with the self-empathy, teachers can provide students more than just a practice opportunity. Handing students a think sheet with the self-empathy questions provides them with an emotional and mental time-out, a chance to take a breath and take a step back to have a think about their own emotions before having a think about academic and social thinking and problem-solving options.

Name: _____ Date: _____

1. Self-empathy: What am I feeling? How do I feel?

Embrassesed   Disappointed   Worried   Jealous   Sad

Frustrated   Angry   Confused   Afraid

2. Gather information: What do I know? What do I need to know? What is similar, and what is different?

3. Brainstorm: How can I solve this problem? What are possible solutions? What can I do?

☐ Take three deep breaths   ☐ Talk to a teacher

☐ Move somewhere else   ☐ Count backward

☐ Think calm thoughts   ☐ Do something else

☐ Use self-talk   ☐ Chill (take a break)

4. Evaluate: What is the best way to solve this problem? Does this make sense?

5. Plan and act: What do I do first, second, and so on? Does this work? Is this working?

6. Reflect: Did it work? How do I know? Do I need to go back and try again?

☐ I feel calmer now.

☐ I still feel upset.

Figure 7.1: Think sheet for identifying an emotion to help resolve a social problem.

*Visit **go.SolutionTree.com/instruction** for a free reproducible version of this figure.*

If the think sheet is not helping a student calm down (or if the student needs scaffolded access to the full emotional SELf-question set), consider involving a school counselor or otherwise engaging school support services. Finally, the more often students receive a think sheet from their teacher when their emotions run high, the more they practice identifying their emotions and the better students become at recognizing patterns and identifying their feelings. We find that, over time, many students begin to identify when they are upset and choose to go and get a think sheet of their own accord, which is a great sign of learning and emotional growth.

Journaling

Another powerful practice you can provide students is self-reflective journaling. Grades 3–12 teachers across a wide range of content areas and teaching assignments can always provide students with reflective journal writing as an option when academic journaling is in place or established as an academic activity. Journaling is an excellent *do-now* before the start of any class, with teachers asking students content questions to review, access prior knowledge, and assess learning from the day before. Or, journaling can serve as an excellent exit ticket in which students demonstrate what academic content or skills they have learned or to reflect on how they feel about their learning that day, their effort, or their confidence moving forward with the next day's objective. Teachers can use student journal responses to monitor students' development of self-awareness, as a general screen of their mental health condition, and as a tool for making instructional decisions, such as for determining a student's readiness to move on or who needs reteaching.

We recommend that you incorporate one or more of these practices as an option for your students to select on their own in your classroom on a regular basis. We also recommend always including the option for students to write their answer to "What am I feeling?" instead of writing their answer to the teacher-assigned, content-related do-now questions or exit tickets. While content is important, if a student is upset, the best do-now is the one that helps students self-calm and helps them feel emotionally ready to learn independently. Providing students the choice of opting out of the assigned do-now journal question and instead writing about how they are feeling accomplishes a number of objectives. First, giving students a choice to write about how they feel provides another opportunity for them to practice SELf-questioning, self-awareness, emotional recognition and literacy, self-monitoring, and self-reflecting. Second, and more generally, the more choices teachers can provide students, the more student-centered classrooms they can create. Most important, a student's journal is a pathway for a student to cry out for help. The teacher can read what students say, and if the response is of concern, the teacher should choose to provide a student's written response to the school counselor as another means of proactively engaging school support services to address mental health concerns before they develop into mental health disorders.

Character Corner: Self-Control

When faced with a difficult situation, recognizing how one feels before making any decisions or engaging in action is the first step toward impulse control. As we write in chapter 2 (page 29), structured SELf-questioning is a form of self-monitoring. Making a habit of recognizing feelings before, during, and after decision making provides students with a form of feedback as to how problem-solving efforts and decision making are working, allowing for adjustments as needed. Finally, having students ask themselves how they feel after making a decision is a self-reflective practice that helps them learn about themselves, identify patterns indicating potential triggers, and shape their future decisions and actions that lead them to feel better. All of these are vital to the development of coping flexibility needed for greater self-control. Being more self-aware of feelings and practicing self-monitoring and self-reflection through structured SELf-questioning naturally leads to better control of how students think, act, and feel in the present and future.

Structured SELf-Questioning for Emotional Regulation and Problem Solving

Emotional competencies are not innate talents,
but rather learned capabilities that must be worked on and
can be developed to achieve outstanding performance.

—Daniel Goleman

According to Edward, who is a licensed professional counselor and board-certified school counselor, critical among the mental health-related symptoms or issues students face are anxiety, depression, and adjustment to transition. Mental health needs in schools are at a critical point. One in five youth live with a mental health condition, but less than half of these individuals receive needed services (National Alliance on Mental Illness, n.d.). Compounding this issue is the reality that "undiagnosed, untreated, and inadequately treated mental illnesses significantly interfere with a student's ability to learn, to grow, and to develop" (National Alliance on Mental Illness, n.d.).

Teachers and counselors constantly find themselves in positions in which they must triage social-emotional issues with students. If you're a school counselor, you may deal with an ever-growing caseload and feel overwhelmed by the volume of students in need. As a teacher, you might think, "What in the world can I do about these issues? I have so many students to teach, and I am not a counselor or a psychologist." We have found from experience that the best solution comes from the proverb "Give a student a fish and that student will eat for a day. Teach the student to fish and you feed him or her for a lifetime." Whether you are a mathematics teacher working with a student who feels anxious about mathematics, a physical education teacher who has a student that is resistant to participating, or a school counselor overloaded with cases, we encourage you to utilize the structured emotional SELf-question set as an individual intervention. We ask you to think about structured SELf-questioning as something you can use in eyedropper size doses, bits at a time, to assist students in managing low-level behavioral health issues.

Two words of warning are important here. First, and as we established in chapter 7 (page 113), structured SELf-questioning is an intervention strategy that is *not* appropriate for high-level anxiety, mental health disorders, or chronic depression. If a student appears to be struggling with their mental health or is in distress, inform a school counselor so he or she can support the student and triage the present situation. Second, it is important to note that we did not design structured SELf-questioning to deal with the *causes* of anxiety and depression. In such cases, a licensed mental health professional should administer an assessment of wellness and, if the inventory indicates any signs of suicidal intensity or self-harm thoughts, the student should receive support from a local crisis center or emergency room.

In chapter 7 (page 113), we also wrote about how the first and perhaps most important step of emotional problem solving is to identify one's own emotions (self-empathy). We explained that the SEL competency of self-awareness is a precursor to successfully applying the next two SEL competencies inherent in coping mechanisms: self-management and responsible decision making (CASEL, n.d.). We also explained why it is so important to be *aware of* one's own emotions in order to be able to then *manage* one's emotions and one's thinking through emotional problems.

This chapter demonstrates how structured SELf-questioning serves as a scaffold that develops students as independent managers of their own emotions, thereby enhancing their transfer and performance of problem-solving and decision-making skills. It also shows how teachers can use a common set of structured SELf-questions to collaborate with students, counselors, other teachers, and parents to help students apply this SELf-question set with consistency. We include a series of grade-band-based scenarios to help illustrate this work. Through the application of this one metacognitive strategy, addressing mental health concerns becomes a concerted and cohesive team effort that helps students self-regulate and face life's little challenges and emotional problems while building strong coping mechanisms at the same time.

The Importance of Teaching a Metacognitive Strategy for Coping Skills

To start, let's look at what anxiety is and why it matters to all teachers as well as counselors when it comes to teaching students. *Anxiety* is generally regarded as a feeling of "worry, nervousness, or unease about something with an uncertain outcome" (Lexico, n.d.a). Everyone experiences these feelings of low-level anxiety at different points throughout their lives. For students to be successful in dealing with low-level anxieties, they need to learn how to use metacognitive traits that help them function proactively. The first metacognitive trait is *awareness* of feelings of anxiousness, followed by the second metacognitive trait, *management* of those anxious feelings. Think about these as we more deeply explore the significance and purpose of each step in the emotional SELf-question set.

- The SELf-question for the *self-empathy* action ("How do I feel?") covers emotional awareness. Refer to chapter 7 to learn more about this.

- The *gather information* SELf-question ("What is causing this feeling?") helps students become more aware of possible causes of their feelings of worry or unease.

- Once students have had a chance to gather information, they may be ready to independently *brainstorm* ("What strategies can I use to make myself feel better?") ways to manage or calm their own feelings of anxiousness.

Fortunately, there are many effective strategies anyone can use to help manage low-level worries, fears, and anxieties. The remaining steps are aligned to SELf-questions that further promote coping flexibility.

- The *evaluate* SELf-questions ("Has this helped me in the past? How did it help? How did I feel after?") prompt students to look backward and do some evaluative, strategic thinking about which strategies might be helpful.

- The *plan and act* step SELf-question ("How can I use this strategy?") prompts students to think adaptively before implementing the strategy to best address the nature of the emotion and the situation at hand. For example, sometimes lying down is an effective coping strategy for certain situations but may not be the best fit strategy to calm down during the middle of a quiz. The latter outcome then serves as a prompt to consider alternative strategies.

- The *reflect* step SELf-questions ("Did it work? How do I know? Do I need to go back and try again to solve this?") prompt students after using the full SELf-question set to self-assess their current emotional state and search for evidence of success with using a coping strategy.

As you have likely observed, brainstorming a coping strategy is a particularly vital aspect of this process. Since each person is unique, different strategies work for different people. One time-honored strategy is deep breathing, which lowers the elevated heart rate anxiety causes (Wells & Legg, 2020). Imagine your class arriving after recess upset because of something that happened on the playground. You could simply say, "One thing people do when they are upset is deep breathing. It helps us calm down and enables us to think better. Let's try it." Alternatively, some people find relief from anxiety with music, but even that is highly individualistic. One student may find rap music relaxing, and another may find classical music relaxes them best. A student's individualized education plan may indicate that they need music in times of stress. Drawing and coloring also work to calm many people—thus the increased popularity of adult coloring books. Journaling is still another strategy that works for many people coping with anxiety. Since anxiety lives in the future (someone is afraid of something that might happen), these strategies are all designed to move students from worry about the future into the present to manage academic and social expectations.

Many educators view student anxiety as something mostly seen at the high school level, but middle school and elementary students also experience anxiety, especially as technology-driven social expectations have become more complex. Unfortunately, it feels as if anxiety and depression have become increasingly widespread and pose daily challenges for educators and counselors (Geiger & David, 2019). Edward has observed another trend through his private practice: social media's impact on students' mental health has become an agent of increased depression and anxiety rates in school-aged children and adolescents. They see their peers enjoying social experiences, which can cause feelings of insecurity and questions of self-worth as if their lives are not as valuable or fulfilling as others. When educating parents on the complexities of social media, Edward asks parents to use their own experiences to conceptualize the impact social media can have on their child. Consider this: as an adult, have you ever felt insecure, excluded, jealous, or saddened by the social media post of a friend or neighbor? Imagine how an insecure teenager might feel when attempting to deal with similar social pressures, which can all trigger or exacerbate depressive symptoms.

After anxiety, depression is the second issue often seen in students and patients. It is difficult to pinpoint why depression seems increasingly prevalent in modern society. Are we simply more aware of it than previously? Has technology damaged self-esteem and confidence? *Education Week* staff writer Evie Blad (2019) explains:

> Between 2005 and 2017, the proportion of teens 12–17 who reported the symptoms of a major depressive episode within the last year rose from 8.7 percent to 13.2 percent. . . . Adults ages 18–25 showed similar trends, while rates remained relatively stable for older generations. A respondent was deemed to have had a major depressive episode if they confirmed they had experienced at least 5 of 9 criteria defined by the American Psychiatric Association, including a "depressed mood" or "loss of interest or pleasure in daily activities."

Finally, another emotional issue students face is transition difficulties at school. This can be the transition from elementary school to middle school, middle school to high school, high school to college, or one school to another. It is critical for schools to deploy programming to help students during these transitional times. Teaching the emotional SELf-question set during these transition times helps students find healthy ways of coping with this stress and provides a cohesive, community-building start for students. Proactive support for students during transition can assist with reducing various adjustment-related difficulties.

How to Teach the Structured SELf-Question Set for Coping Skills

When a teacher, counselor, or parent observes that a student may be experiencing some feelings of anxiety, displaying depressive symptoms, or going through a difficult time with transition, asking the initial, structured, open-ended questions of the emotional SELf-question set (refer to figure 1.1, page 23) serves as a low-level intervention that can help students address these challenges.

The questions can help lead students, as well as the adults trying to help them, to be aware of and manage low levels of worry, unease, discomfort, concern, and sadness, as well as initiate problem solving. It's best to use the emotional SELf-question set one-to-one with students in a setting that is appropriate for an adult and student to discuss, such as a private space in a hallway or office. For example, if you observe a student who appears to be crying at his or her desk after recess, quietly ask the student to join you out in the hallway. Once in the private space, you can explore the cause of the student's emotional distress and initiate the emotional SELf-question set. Students can also utilize it themselves in their own time and space (such as in a calming corner in the classroom) to engage in self-talk to guide themselves through emotional literacy, regulation, and problem solving.

As stated throughout chapter 7 (page 113), we only recommend embedding the first step of the emotional SELf-question set (self-empathy) into academic instruction; all other steps in this question set should only take place one-to-one with the student and in private. At that point, teachers may use it to help determine if the level of care the student needs is appropriate for the school counselor, a social worker, or another specialized professional. For example, if, for any reason, you worry that a student needs immediate professional intervention for which the school lacks adequate or available resources, we strongly recommend that you call the Substance Abuse and Mental Health Services (SAMHSA) national helpline (visit www.samhsa.gov/find-help/national-helpline). This service is free, available at all hours, and offers support in English and Spanish.

Let's look a little more deeply at how you might work with a student when implementing each step in the emotional SELf-question set.

Self-empathy: What am I feeling? How do I feel?

Begin with this step when a student has trouble identifying their feelings or emotions. See How to Teach a Metacognitive Strategy for Emotional Recognition (page 116).

Gather information: What is causing this feeling?

One way to help students gather information is through self-reporting or scaling. *Scaling* is an effective way to determine a student's emotional baseline in a given moment and as a measure for progress or regression. For example, students can track their feelings for a day to help determine situations that make them anxious. Or, perhaps you could ask students to identify other times they have experienced that particular feeling to help them identify the root of the problem. Students could also take part in role-playing exercises to reproduce similar solutions to better understand their feelings.

Brainstorm: What strategies can I use to make myself feel better?

There are a variety of strategies students might consider while brainstorming. Consider suggesting the following.

- *Engage in deep breathing*—Have students use a breathe bubble on their phones to help. (Visit www.calm.com/breathe to learn more about this technique.)

- *Exercise or move around during brain breaks*—Brain breaks are when students take a moment to do a different activity, such as dancing, drawing, or engaging in physical exercise. This technique is helpful for depression and anxiety as it helps relieve tension and releases dopamine, which fights the chemical imbalances of depression (Collins & Legg, 2017). To achieve this in short spurts in class, conduct an internet search to locate video clips or apps that can lead students through short exercises, crossing midlines, and movements.

- *Draw*—Drawing involves repetitive motions that help relax minds and bodies.

- *Journal*—Journaling can help reduce stress through a release of thoughts and feelings.

- *Play music in the student's preferred genre*—Allowing students the opportunity to listen to music of their choice can help them soothe their own moods.

- *Reduce social media or take a social media fast*—Reducing (not eliminating) social media consumption is an achievable goal. If a student's social media usage is causing negative emotions, suggest to him or her (and his or her parents) using a smartphone-based app to help monitor and limit social media time. These can include Google's Digital Wellbeing feature or Apple's Screen Time application. You may find other such applications in each platform's respective app stores.

- *Brainstorm using literature*—Asking, "What are strategies you would recommend to _____ to make him- or herself feel better?" helps students focus their thinking. If your class includes the use of literature circles or restorative circles, ask students to reflect on the strategies characters in literature use, such as, "What strategies does Claudia use to make herself feel better? What else could she do?" If a student has a personal attachment to some other text or form of media (movies, tv shows, songs), consider tapping into that. For example, you might ask a Harry Potter fan, "What do you think Hermione would do in this situation?"

Evaluate: Has this helped me in the past? How did it help? How did I feel after?

When evaluating to determine which of the brainstormed strategies to try first, we encourage students to look at how a strategy might have helped in the past. For example, if a student says, "I used deep breathing before my piano recital, and it helped me calm down," then we ask him or her to add an impact statement such as, "It relaxed me and I felt more confident." If you're using literature with the student, evaluate a character's response to difficulty or challenges by asking, "How did the character's response help? How did the character feel after? What do you think might have been a better solution?"

Plan and act: How can I use this strategy?

This is where the student has a go and sees how the strategy he or she selected works. At this point, practice is key. For example, frequently practicing deep breathing will assist in reinforcing proper technique, which in turn will create effective breathing during times of distress.

Reflect: Did it work? How do I know? Do I need to go back and try again to solve this?

At this point, you might want to have the student scale his or her feelings. For example, you can ask the student, "On a scale of one to ten, where ten is the highest, how angry are you feeling?" Scaling is especially helpful when used both during the evaluate and reflect steps to measure progress after utilizing a strategy. On reflection, a student might say they're a *7* or an *8*, but if they started from a *10*, then that's progress. If there isn't progress or the progress is too limited, the student might want to repeat the same steps or try another strategy.

Note that although we focus on the use of literature and restorative circles in this section, if you teach in other content areas, we're sure you can see the applications for this SELf-question set in other situations, such as during Socratic seminars, responsive classroom, and many other areas, especially in the guidance office or with a school counselor.

Let's look at some examples of the strategy across the four different grade bands. Because these scenarios do not focus on academic lessons or standards, we do not include class information as part of the scenarios. Each of these scenarios is based on experiences Edward witnessed firsthand or had a colleague describe to him.

Scenario: Grades K–2

Travis is a second-grade student diagnosed with selective mutism and who struggles with his communication with teachers. As the school counselor, Edward also knows that Travis is easily frustrated and sometimes throws tantrums during structured times of class. Edward is working within the classroom (often called *pushing* into the classroom) to conduct behavioral observations and initiate behavior modification strategies. Edward has asked Travis to join him in the hallway to create more privacy. He then engages Travis in the emotional SELf- question set.

SELF-EMPATHY

Question: What am I feeling? How do I feel?

Travis says, "I don't know how I feel."

Edward motions toward a SELf-question chart strategically located in the hallway and says, "Let's look at our feelings chart. Can you show me which of these emojis shows how you're feeling right now?" (See figure 8.1, page 132, for an example.) This isn't an unfamiliar intervention for Travis, who Edward has already introduced to this strategy. Travis points at the *mean* emoji.

GATHER INFORMATION

Question: What is causing this feeling?

Travis considers the next question and says, "The teacher is being mean." Even though Travis hasn't said what he is feeling, Edward still gathers valuable information about the situation. He asks Travis why he thinks this, and Travis answers, "I still want to play, but she wants me to do math."

BRAINSTORM

Question: What strategies can I use to make myself feel better?

Edward, knowing that he isn't going to change the second grader's mind about his perceived reality, prompts Travis into brainstorming by asking, "What could help you be a good listener right now?" When Travis struggles to come up with an idea, Edward

Emotions

Happy	Sad	Surprised	Sleepy	Mean
Silly	Scared	Angry	Shy	Jealous

Figure 8.1: An emoji-based feelings chart.

*Visit **go.SolutionTree.com/instruction** for a free reproducible version of this figure.*

prompts him to use a technique Travis is already familiar with (*first this, then that*) using a communication board, such as the Picture Exchange Communication System (PECS). (Visit https://pecsusa.com/pecs to learn more about this system.) Travis applies the technique and states, "First math, then recess." This helps Travis understand the idea of time better than saying that recess is in fifteen minutes. This erases the uncertainty, so he knows that the next thing in his schedule is something he enjoys.

EVALUATE

Questions: Has this strategy helped me in the past? How did it help? How did I feel after?

Edward considers that, developmentally, it might be appropriate to skip this step with Travis, since it is beyond his current ability to brainstorm more than one idea (and even that one idea was prompted).

PLAN AND ACT

Question: What do I do first, second, and so on? Does this work? Is this working?

Edward presses forward about the idea of mathematics first and then recess, "Do you think this could work for you?" Travis answers, "Yes." He moves the schedule cards on his first-then board to their new positions.

REFLECT

Questions: Did it work? How do I know? Do I need to go back and try again?

Edward gives Travis a moment to process the change and says, "Let's look at the emoji chart and see you how you feel now." Travis replies, "I feel happy now." The reflection step provides Travis a sense of resolution that can be marked by his ability to identify the change in his emotions. Further, reflection has served as a positive reinforcer for Travis to assist him in initiating the emotional SELf-question set in the future. It also marks the beginning stage of him developing both coping flexibility and autonomy.

Scenario: Grades 3–5

Malik, a fifth-grade student, struggles with executive functioning. Executive-functioning skills such as the following are a struggle for many students at this age.

- Paying attention

- Organizing, planning, and prioritizing

- Starting tasks and staying focused on them to completion

- Understanding different points of view

- Regulating emotions

- Self-monitoring, or keeping track of what they're doing (the Understood Team, n.d.)

During Edward's after school meeting with Malik, Malik is quite upset that he had forgotten to bring his homework home from school and there were repercussions for that mistake: he wouldn't be rewarded with his fifth star and, as a result, he wouldn't be able to participate in the pizza party for those who completed all their homework that week. Edward decides to help Malik work through the problem by leading him through the emotional SELf-question set.

SELF-EMPATHY

Question: What am I feeling? How do I feel?

Malik says, "I'm feeling upset and angry at myself."

GATHER INFORMATION

Question: What is causing this feeling?

Malik immediately responds, "I know remembering to bring my homework home is important, but I forgot, and I won't get my fifth star and be able to go to the pizza party."

BRAINSTORM

Question: What strategies can I use to make myself feel better?

Malik answers, "Last time I forgot something at school, I checked my assignment book. I checked today, and I don't have the worksheet with me. Maybe I could also go to Google Classroom and print out a copy of my homework."

EVALUATE

Questions: Has this strategy helped me in the past? How did it help? How did I feel after?

Malik considers these questions and says, "My homework notebook won't help this time, but since all my assignments are on Google Classroom, I can print out a copy of my homework and still turn it in on time."

PLAN AND ACT

Question: What do I do first, second, and so on? Does this work? Is this working?

Malik says, "I got it printed, and I'll be able to do it on time by finishing during recess."

REFLECT

Questions: Did it work? How do I know? Do I need to go back and try again?

Malik says, "I feel relieved and happy that I can go to the pizza party." In this case, Malik is happy with the outcome because he was able to effect a solution to a time-restricted issue. In another situation, this may not be possible, and the student may need more forward-thinking support for a solution that will help them the next time the situation arises.

Scenario: Grades 6–8

This scenario presents a combination of emotional and social problem solving. Lots of problems don't fall into neat categories. Sal is a seventh grader who got upset during a Wiffle ball game at recess. As the game began, he had run toward center field with his friends. But one of Sal's friends told him, "You're not good enough to play center field; you don't have a strong enough arm. Go take left field." Sal didn't say anything and did as his friend told him. Standing in left field, he experienced a mixture of emotions and later talked it through with Edward. Note that this type of problem could take a while to work through since there are so many emotions, and it takes time to see what the emotions are attached to.

SELF-EMPATHY

Question: What am I feeling? How do I feel?

Sal says, "I'm feeling hurt, embarrassed, angry, disrespected, and I'm afraid I'm just not a good enough player."

GATHER INFORMATION

Question: What is causing this feeling?

Sal says, "My best friend just yelled at me in front of everyone. That makes me feel hurt, angry, and disrespected! I don't know why he had to talk to me like that in front of everyone. I'm so embarrassed. And what if I'm not good enough?" Edward explains that this feeling is called insecurity, and it comes from a lack of confidence in himself. Note that there is no one cause of insecurity, but it sometimes stems from a traumatic event, crisis, or loss. "People who have recurring insecurities may also have low self-esteem, experience body image issues, lack direction in life, or feel overlooked by others" (GoodTherapy, 2019).

BRAINSTORM

Question: What strategies can I use to make myself feel better?

Sal doesn't know how to approach the situation, so Edward helps him to separate out the emotions and possible strategies. He suggests that what would help Sal with the insecurity would be looking at his past history of success—just flooding his mind with times when he was successful with a throw or a catch made from center field. Edward asks, "What did you do the last time you were angry with your best friend?" Sal replies, "Last time I was mad, I talked with him when we were alone, and we made up. You told me last time to use *I* statements, and that worked."

Edward prompts Sal further, "What do you think you could do about the embarrassment?" Sal answers, "I know during recess everyone wants to play center field and win. I have said similar things in the past as well, but we're all good friends, and we have lots of good memories. I think I just need to talk to Elijah about it."

EVALUATE

Questions: Has this strategy helped me in the past? How did it help? How did I feel after?

Sal says, "I have made some good plays from centerfield! I remember the time I got Donnie out with a great catch. Talking worked OK the last time, so I think I'll try it again." It is important to note that the evaluation questions prompt Sal to explore similar situations, behavioral responses, and outcomes. During the evaluation process, Travis is able to identify a social skill that was successful in the past and can be applied in this situation.

PLAN AND ACT

Question: What do I do first, second, and so on? Does this work? Is this working?

Sal continues, "I'll talk to Elijah on our way home from school."

REFLECT

Questions: Did it work? How do I know? Do I need to go back and try again?

Sal reflects, "I feel better now that I have a plan. I'll let you know how my talk with Elijah goes this afternoon." The next day, Edward spoke with Sal to discuss the outcome of the situation. Sal said, "I talked to Elijah before we went outside for recess and told him that what he said hurt my feelings. He said he was sorry, and he would not yell at me like that again."

Scenario: Grades 9–12

Emma, an eleventh-grade student, is struggling with panic attacks but isn't using the strategies Edward had given her to use during times of distress. A colleague of Edward's suggests that he do something to simulate one of Emma's low-level panic attacks. The goal of the intervention is to induce one of the symptoms, such as shortness of breath or accelerated heart rate, Emma experiences during her panic episodes. To accelerate her heart rate and shorten her breath, she blows through a straw for as long as she can and then practices one of the strategies she's learned to use when she has panic attacks: deep breathing using a breathe bubble on her phone. (Visit www.calm.com/breathe to learn about this support app.)

The app Emma uses can guide her through several types of deep-breathing exercises—belly breathing, four-square breathing, box breathing, diaphragmatic breathing, and more. Any or all of these can help overcome the symptoms of anxiety and panic attacks. Ana Gotter and Deborah Weatherspoon (2020), writing for *Healthline*, describe *box breathing*, also known as *square breathing* or *four-square breathing*, as "a technique used when taking slow, deep breaths" that can "heighten performance and concentration while also being a powerful stress reliever" and improve one's mood. Figure 8.2 shows a visual explanation of box breathing.

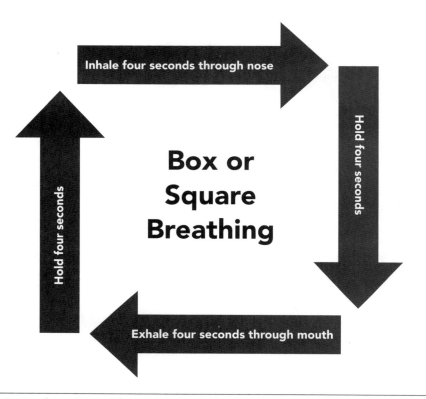

Figure 8.2: Explanation of box breathing.

While sitting in class, Emma starts to experience intense symptoms of anxiety as she realizes she might be called on to speak in front of her peers. Emma's symptoms include shortness of breath and an elevated heart rate. The classroom teacher notices her discomfort and suggests she meet with Edward. By the time she does, her panic attack has passed, so Edward gives her the straw to blow into and engages her in using the emotional SELf-question set.

SELF-EMPATHY

Question: What am I feeling? How do I feel?

Emma says, "The tips of my fingers are tingling. I'm short of breath. My heart is beating rapidly."

GATHER INFORMATION

Question: What is causing this feeling?

Because, in this case, the feelings are simulated and derive from Emma blowing through a straw, Edward encourages her to think about what happened in class and talk about what triggered her attack. Emma replies, "It happens when I'm called on in class, and I don't know the answer or when I don't know something in front of my classmates."

BRAINSTORM

Question: What strategies can I use to make myself feel better?

Emma thinks for a moment and says, "I could open a deep-breathing app on my phone. In the classroom, I could determine if I should ask the teacher if I can leave the room." She adds, "I could also use the check-in of my five senses," which is a technique, also known as *5-4-3-2-1*, in which the student names one thing he or she can touch, hear, smell, see, and taste. Edward agrees and notes that all these strategies are designed to bring one's attention back to the present moment and help reduce the uncertainty and fear of the future. Sarah Smith (2018) of the University of Rochester Medical Center offers more details about the 5-4-3-2-1 coping technique if you want to learn more about checking in on one's five senses.

EVALUATE

Questions: Has this strategy helped me in the past? How did it help? How did I feel after?

Emma says, "I haven't been using the strategies you've given me, but I'll try the breathe bubble now." Emma says she is receptive to using the breathing bubble since she can use the strategy in class. Emma also notes that she has realized that her initial symptom of anxiety was disrupted breathing.

PLAN AND ACT

Question: What do I do first, second, and so on? Does this work? Is this working?

Emma says, "In class, I could look at the clock and deep breathe for two minutes, but for now, I'll use the app to guide my breathing." Using the app for practice breathing sessions helps Emma visualize the breathe bubble so that when a real panic attack occurs, she can draw on the technique even if the app is not available or appropriate for her to use at that moment.

REFLECT

Question: Did it work? How do I know? Do I need to go back and try again?

After a few minutes of practice, Emma says, "I feel more relaxed. I feel like I'm OK right now. I'll try to use this while I'm in class. Can we practice one more time?"

With the development of a breathing coping strategy, Emma is better equipped to manage the onset of symptoms when they occur. Edward later observed her in the classroom during an attack, and she autonomously chose to use deep breathing over other strategies. That she selected for herself among several strategies is key, as these techniques are not a one-size-fits-all solution. Providing students with several interventions may yield more consistency in improving outcomes and allow students to identify which tool they are most comfortable using.

Character Corner: Self-Regulation

In chapter 7 (page 113), we concluded that teaching students to identify and recognize their feelings and take a step back and have a think about those feelings was characteristic of the value of self-control. In this chapter, where we have combined identifying emotions with regulating emotions, we can safely conclude that identifying and regulating emotions are characteristic of self-regulation. Mental health writer Arlin Cuncic (2020) defines *self-regulation* as "controlling one's behavior, emotions, and thoughts in the pursuit of long-term goals. More specifically, emotional self-regulation refers to the ability to manage disruptive emotions and impulses."

As students develop the SEL competencies of self-awareness, self-management, and responsible decision making through structured SELf-questioning, they develop the coping mechanisms they need to control impulses and manage their own emotions. Through consistent practice of the emotional SELf-question set, along with support and feedback from a caring adult, teachers can expect students to feel empowered with the skill set they need to respond to distress. In so doing, students have internalized a strategy for coping, empowering them to better manage and regulate their emotions, which leads to better management and regulation of self.

Transfer Theory and SELf-Questioning

*Transfer is our collective goal. We don't strive to produce students
who are teacher dependent, but rather students who can take
the knowledge and skills they have developed and apply
that to a wide range of problems and situations.*

—Douglas Fisher and Nancy Frey (in Ferlazzo, 2018)

As you have seen throughout this book, the ability for students to apply learning from one aspect of their life to another is essential for success in school and life. In "Students Can Transfer Knowledge if Taught How," *Chronicle of Higher Education* editor Dan Berrett (2014) cites psychologists referring to transfer as "education's holy grail" and "the very measure of learning itself." There are many definitions of *transfer*, but the one that we like best is applying skills, knowledge or attitudes learned in one context or situation to another (Perkins & Salomon, 1992b).

Transfer can take place between situations that are quite similar (near- or low-road transfer) and also between situations that share some qualities but are dissimilar (far- or high-road transfer). Transfer can also take place from problem to problem, class to class, home to school, or school to work. When teachers refer to students utilizing prior knowledge to complete or further a task, they're referring to transfer. It is a key ability for learning and developing competencies for life.

Despite the wealth of knowledge about transfer, it remains a slippery concept. Teachers often bemoan the lack of transfer in schools: "I know they learned metrics in mathematics, but when I give them metrics work in the science classroom, they stare at me like deer in the headlights." Or, "We just learned revision with our newspaper articles; why can't they seem to apply that to revising our narratives?" Wiggins (2012b) writes, "Many teachers just expect transfer to happen if content is well taught. No research supports this view."

It is not that difficult to add a transfer component to teaching; it is just a matter of making it explicit. For example, a teacher might say, "Today, we worked on elaborating your paragraphs using *who, what, when, where, why*, and *how* questions. From now on, anytime you need to elaborate on what you have written, you can use these same questions to help you think it through." This is a regular component of workshop-style teaching, so many teachers already have this in their repertoires.

In the same vein, transfer isn't automatic; it requires teaching (Burke, 2009). Teachers need to help students fill in the gaps between learning goals by explicitly identifying and building connections. As an example, let's have a think about the complex task of content writing, which has a natural component of transfer built into it. Writers write for a particular purpose, to a particular audience, and in a particular genre. The writing tasks in science, for example, are quite different from those in subjects such as social studies. In science, a student might write a lab report geared toward group members or a teacher with the goal of explaining an experiment. In social studies, however, a student might profile a historical figure to analyze that person's contributions to society. While students may need similar skills, such as summary, to complete both of these assignments, they may not notice this connection on their own. Further, standardized mathematics tests often require students to demonstrate their understanding of mathematics concepts through writing, which might be extremely difficult for students who have strong mathematics skills but who struggle to demonstrate and explain their thinking through writing. Kathleen B. Burke (2009), an expert on transfer theory, writes:

> Some educators believe that students automatically apply or transfer the skills learned in their classes to other classes or situations outside of school. Yet, students do NOT connect what they learn in English class to social studies class, or what they learn in math class to a mathematical problem they encounter at work or in life. Transfer of knowledge plays a key role in metacognition. (p. 109)

This chapter explains the importance of transfer in a school environment, in particular how to differentiate between negative and positive transfer with a focus on the latter. We offer guidance for how to teach positive transfer and establish how SELf-questioning supports that teaching and learning. We conclude with some thoughts about how adept usage of transfer skills help students find a sense of inner peace.

The Importance of Teaching for Transfer

Transfer can be positive or negative. If you learn to color with crayons, you can positively transfer much of that learning to coloring with markers. However, if you have driven on the right side of the road in the United States all your life and then move to the United Kingdom, the impulse to return to established driving habits (an example of negative transfer) would definitely affect your reflexes and driving. In another example, Sue had a student who transferred from the United States to an international school in Guayaquil, Ecuador. In this student's former school, students had been encouraged to use three adjectives to describe each and every noun in their writing, as the use of many adjectives greatly increased students' score on the state tests. This student (and her mother) had to unlearn this practice and instead understand that three adjectives per noun made for terribly uninspired writing. The is also negative transfer.

Students can also transfer attitudes—both positive and negative to their work. Positive transfer is indicative of a growth mindset: "I can't do this *yet*." Negative, "I'm not good at this," indicates a fixed mindset.

Transfer also exists on a continuum of near and far. Some researchers refer to this as low-road and high-road transfer. We think Todd Finley, a blogger and assistant editor at Edutopia, explains these concepts best. In an article by teacher and columnist Larry Ferlazzo (2017), Finley defines *near transfer* as "transfer between very similar but not identical contexts" and illustrates with the following:

> An example is learning to drive a Toyota stick shift and then later driving a Honda stick shift. To teach near transfer, provide lots of practice until students can perform the skill without much thought. This is called low road transfer.

Finley (as cited in Ferlazzo, 2017) then defines *far transfer* as "applying learning to situations that are quite dissimilar to the original learning" and provides further clarification:

> An example is learning to write a persuasive essay on gun control and then giving a persuasive PowerPoint presentation on the benefits of solar power. To teach far transfer, use high road transfer: have students deliberately analyze strategies and carefully apply them in different contexts.

Teachers can help students understand these concepts in such a way that they begin to grasp the connectivity of learning, so they don't continue to have a silo mentality about different academic content areas.

Over and over, research links metacognitive learning and transfer. Education scholar Heather N. Hill (2016) cites the sizeable amount of research that supports using metacognition to help support knowledge transfer: "The Influence of Perceptions of Task Similarity/Difference on Learning Transfer in Second Language Writing" (James, 2008), *The Science and Art of Transfer* (Perkins & Salomon, 1992a), *Reflection in The Writing Classroom* (Yancey, 1998), and *Writing Across Contexts* (Yancey, Robertson, & Taczak, 2014).

In *How People Learn*, the National Research Council explains that a metacognitive approach to education helps teach transfer because students learn to understand themselves as learners and also to "monitor and regulate their own understanding in ways that allow them to keep learning adaptive expertise" (p. 78).

Since our SELf-question sets are based on a metacognitive approach of SELf-questioning that promotes reflection and regulation, they lend themselves to transfer. Transfer theory is the bedrock of our strategy. We believe that if students learn our question set in one area, and then teachers point out the possibilities of transfer, students will begin to transfer this problem-solving technique to other areas of their lives.

How To Teach Toward Transfer

Even without naming it, teachers have wanted to teach toward transfer since the beginning of time. The whole point of this book is that we can teach students a very simple process for problem solving that can transfer into every other area of their lives. Both of our SELf-question sets are designed with transfer in mind; for example, the gather information question "What is similar, and what is different?" is directly linked to transfer. The only question is how to teach it most effectively.

Writing for *Education Week*, teacher and columnist Ferlazzo (2017) reviews and synthesizes much of the literature around transfer—both near and far—and recommends the following pedagogical techniques that foster it.

- **Maximize the initial learning experience for transfer using explicit teaching:** For example, after modeling a written argument essay in class, show students how to apply what they learned to persuade a future boss to give them a raise. Or, consider how a student using SELf-questions with prior knowledge about argument writing might utilize that understanding to make a presentation for why her parents should let her have a phone.

- **Push students to generalize broader principles from specific situations:** For example, after studying the early women's rights movement, ask students what elements are necessary to initiate a new form of successful social change. Or, use SELf-questions to ask students to brainstorm practical situations in which they apply what they learned about fractions in mathematics that day.

- **Engage in group learning:** For example, allowing students to work together in groups mirrors the kinds of experiences they are likely to have outside of the classroom. The SELf-questions are a wonderful structure for group work and encourage myriad responses.

- **Use analogies and metaphors to teach students to take what they already know and apply it to a new situation:** For example, when helping students to understand how the human heart works, make a comparison to a pump and how it works. During a unit about pacing, a teacher might say, "It's like you're driving down the road taking your time, and then you hop on the interstate to more quickly get where you're going."

- **Challenge students to reflect on which learning experiences personally work best for them:** For example, if taking notes in science helped students learn key concepts, consider if it can be helpful in other classes? See the grades 6–8 scenario in this chapter (page 149), where a student, Rheyma, uses SELf-questions to determine how best to improve her summaries.

Along with the preceding suggestions, Butler and colleagues (2011) recommend naming a skill to facilitate internalization, which comes before students can adeptly transfer skills. Deliberate practice (spaced practice) is also important for developing initial competency in a subject. Deliberate practice is the opposite of cramming for a test; it is when concepts are reviewed on a regular basis to form strong connections in the brain.

Research reports that the act of prompting or cueing (as when teachers use SELf-question sets with students) and modeling also dramatically increases the amount of transfer (Hill, 2016; National Research Council, 2000; Wiggins, 2012b). Our SELf-question sets and icons (refer to Figure 1.1, page 23) and other visuals that represent the SELf-question categories (see the appendix, page 215) provide that cueing, priming, and guidance.

When parents, teachers, and counselors pair gradual release of responsibility (see Gradual Release of Responsibility, page 26) alongside SELf-questioning techniques, they can look forward to seeing a fair amount of transfer as students commit the SELf-questions to memory and use them innately. However, this raises the question of how long teachers should provide prompting while seeking to release responsibility to students to apply the strategy independently. Our experiences tell us you should continue to provide prompts until students can demonstrate they have internalized the strategy by stepping through each step without the need for such prompts. This internalization leads to student autonomy in problem solving, which we write about in chapter 12 (page 195).

Finally, in addition to these suggestions, educational consultant Adeyemi Stembridge (as cited in Ferlazzo, 2017) asserts:

> When planning with transfer of learning in mind, there is one enormously [sic], consequential question teachers are wise to consider—and that is, What do I want my students to feel? What students understand deeply enough to apply in a range of contexts is always that which has been embedded in a rich, emotional narrative.

This affective addition is an interesting area to consider when planning a unit. As an illustration, one of the reasons people read is to understand themselves and others through the characters in the books they choose. When students read *Thank-You, Mr. Falker* (Polacco, 1998), they can understand how the character Trish feels about not being able to read in the fifth grade—perhaps also why someone might sometimes not feel smart enough. When students (or adults) read *Jane Eyre* (Bronte, 2014), they learn about the cost of deep personal integrity and commitment to faith.

Another place we can see the importance of "What do I want my students to feel?" is in their attitudes toward a subject or their abilities in that subject. We all know students who are hindered by their emotional responses to academic and social issues: "I hate math." "I'm not a reader." "I'll never have friends." "I'm just stupid." Teachers, counselors, and parents are not always able to be with a student facing an emotional problem or needing to regulate an emotional response. This is why it is vital for students to internalize and know how to independently use the emotional coping strategies SELf-questioning provides. We recommend transitioning them from guided self-talk through problem solving using the SELf-questions as a stepping stone to totally independent problem solving.

The following scenarios illustrate examples of transfer occurring at a variety of grade bands.

Scenario: Grades K–2

Class: First-grade classroom (Ms. H.; teacher)

Objective:

- Identify emotions felt by characters in a text and support this with evidence.

Standards:

- Ask and answer questions about key details in a text. (RL.1.1; NGA & CCSSO, 2010a)
- Use illustrations and details in a story to describe its characters, setting, or events. (RL.1.7; NGA & CCSSO, 2010a)

A first-grade class utilizes structured SELf-questioning sets to address academic, social, and emotional problems they encounter on a daily basis. The students are quite comfortable and confident in using the SELf-questions across multiple contexts. With this in mind, the teacher, Ms. H., purposefully plans for the integration of reading comprehension while addressing a typical problem with jealousy that students might feel if they find that their best friend has befriended another classmate. At the ripe old age of six, it's common for students to want to keep their best friends all to themselves, which, in our experience, doesn't make them much different from many adolescents or adults. In this scenario, Ms. H. is opening the door for students to identify with a book's characters and facilitate high-road transfer using both cognitive flexibility and coping flexibility, which, in this case, transfers from academic problem solving to social problem solving.

Ms. H. determines that students will read *Junie B. Jones, First Grader (at Last!)* (Park, 2001), and the objective of the minilesson is to deepen comprehension by analyzing the plot—more specifically, the problem-solution structure it presents. Essentially, Junie B. Jones is jealous that her best friend, Grace, sits with someone else on the bus during her first day of school. Ms. H. had already used a sequence of minilessons to model for students how to use the SELf-question set to build comprehension by inferring character traits using the characters' words and actions. During these lessons, to concretely teach metacognition through SELf-questioning, Ms. H. holds up a thinking cloud to show when she asks herself questions. She stands in one spot when reading words directly from the text. She stands in another spot when thinking aloud, and she asks herself questions as she holds up a poster board cut in the shape of a cloud with the words *I am thinking* written boldly in a colorful sharpie.

For the next part of the lesson, Ms. H. instructs students to work with a partner to identify the characters' problem in the second chapter and draw an illustration of the problem they identify on a graphic organizer. As students engage in the lesson, Ms. H. confers with two students, Briana and Carrie, who appear to be experiencing some difficulties working together to accomplish the task. She decides to engage them in the academic and social SELf-question set.

SELECT A FOCUS

Questions: What is the problem? What is the question? What is the task?

Briana begins reporting immediately before the teacher can even bend down next to them. She says, "We are trying to figure out if the problem is with Junie B. or Grace. We are actually fighting about it because I think the problem is with Grace because she is being mean by being a flat leaver. Junie B. is supposed to be her best friend, but Carrie thinks the problem is with Junie B. because she is jelly." (Who knew that first-graders had shorthand for *jealous*?) Note that the girls have jumped into their academic task of analyzing the problem-solution structure in the book. They are using near transfer because they have done similar tasks before. Although the students are using the academic and social SELf-question set, also note the crossover with the emotional set in that Briana and Carrie are also focused on how characters are feeling and revealing their own feelings in the process.

GATHER INFORMATION

Questions: What do I know? What do I need to know? What is similar, and what is different?

Carrie immediately interrupts, "I told Briana that since we disagree, we should use the problem-solving questions you showed us. So we are up to asking, 'What do I know?'"

Ms. H., who had previously introduced the academic and social and emotional SELf-question sets to students and explained that they are questions students can ask themselves to solve any type of problem, is thrilled and compliments the girls on using them. Briana slightly smiles and joins in, "I know that Grace and Junie B. are best friends because they sat together every day in kindergarten, and it says so right there." She points to the illustration and text where Junie B. is looking angrily at Grace and a new girl sitting together on the bus. As it relates to building comprehension, this was exceptional in that a first-grade student demonstrated her use of text evidence by thinking and asking, "What did the character do or say?" as this was part of the previous day's lesson on reading comprehension. Briana continues, "Since they sat together every day, I know Junie B. will be sad that Grace chose to sit with someone else on the first day of school. Junie B. even said, 'Today is not off to a good start.'"

At this point, Ms. H. documents Briana's use of the previously taught comprehension strategies to remind her to celebrate Briana's application of them. As she writes, Carrie looks Briana right in the eyes and responds, "But I know that Junie B. being jelly is really the problem because you can sit or play with other people that aren't just your best friends. My mom always says to play with everyone, and it is not nice to say someone is your best friend." She rolls her eyes as she continues, "It's like you and Adrian. You always say you are best friends, so you have to be partners in gym and music and sit together at lunch and always have playdates. Then, today, when I wanted to be Adrian's partner in centers, you got mad—just jelly!" Note that Carrie pivots from the near transfer of the academic task to the far transfer of a real-life situation.

As much as Ms. H. wants to intervene and support the students in solving the problem, instead, she prompts them to continue to the next problem-solving question.

BRAINSTORM

Questions: How can I solve this problem? What are possible solutions? What can I do?

Briana starts by asking, "'How can I solve the problem?' I wish we could all be partners for centers and be a group of three." Carrie then adds, "Maybe Junie B. and Grace and the new girl can all sit on the bus together. You know, it might not work because it is dangerous to have three across because they won't have enough buckles." Notice how Brianna and Carrie automatically switch between their social problem and the academic focus on analyzing the characters' problem in the text. They also move immediately onto the next SELf-question, which is to evaluate their possible solutions as they determine that groups of three might not work in either case. This flow of brainstorming indicates the girls' fluency with the SELf-question set.

To support their process, Ms. H. asks, "Might you work together to brainstorm more solutions?" Carrie suggests that they all sit together at lunch because three can fit at a table, and Briana offers that they all have a playdate after school together. Carrie responds, "My mom only allows one friend over at a time, so we need to take turns being partners and going over to each other's houses."

As this plays out, it's clear that the girls are beginning to feel more comfortable with their social problem, so Ms. H. turns their attention back to the book as she asks, "So how can you solve your problem, which is about disagreeing about the problem in the book?" As the girls pivot back to the academic task, Carrie laughs and says, "We have a problem about problems!" Briana laughs as well until Carrie gets really quiet and suggests, "Maybe the problem is not Junie or Grace or the new girl. They just need to talk and ask questions and brainstorm choices like we did because I am not even mad anymore."

Although the pair still has some ground to cover, notice how powerful an example this is of first-grade students internalizing the advantages of utilizing SELf-questions and demonstrating both cognitive and coping flexibility while they did it.

EVALUATE

Questions: What is the best way to solve this problem? Does this make sense?

As the students think on the *evaluate* questions, Briana says, "Our best choice is to say the problem is that no one is talking to each other or telling their feelings in the story. Maybe Grace doesn't even know Junie B. is that mad, just like I didn't even know that other people were mad that I always want to be Adrian's partner."

PLAN AND ACT

Questions: What do I do first, second, and so on? Is this working?

Briana adds, "So, first we need to tell Adrian our plan to play together, so no one is jelly." Ms. H. interjects at this point and compliments the partners for using the problem-solving questions, but to help them continue to the reflect step, she modifies the SELf-question more appropriately for the situation by asking them, "How will you check if your plan works?"

REFLECT

Questions: Did it work? How do I know? Do I need to go back and try again?

Carrie and Briana look at each other blankly for a minute. Carrie finally offers, "Well, if we all sit together at lunch and all play together at recess for a whole week, it probably works!" Briana continues, "I think it will work because my mom lets three people over at the same time."

Although this outcome may seem simplistic, it also clearly demonstrates that Briana is aware that she and Adrian hurt other students' feelings when they are exclusive in their friendship. Not only were the girls able to have a deep conversation about the plot in the book, they were able to transfer that learning to their personal situation. While authors often construct text where characters face problems that children may encounter in everyday life, students typically depend on teachers to notice these parallels to learn from the similar challenges the character in the text is confronting. However, as evidenced by Carrie and Briana's example, when empowered with SELf-questioning as a tool to build metacognition, students can independently engage in this high-level critical thinking and reflection to learn alongside the characters in their text. The transfer of examining the characters to their own lives helped the girls resolve a common social conflict that would typically escalate or cause a teacher-parent intervention.

Scenario: Grades 3–5

Class: Fifth-grade student (Mr. M.; teacher)

Objective:

- Infer the main character's feelings from a text.

Standards:

- Quote accurately from a text when explaining what the text says explicitly and when drawing inferences from the text. (RL.5.1; NGA & CCSSO, 2010a)

Consider a scenario in which Mr. M. and Maria, a fifth-grade student, are reading *From the Mixed-Up Files of Mrs. Basil E. Frankweiler* (Konigsburg, 2007). They have reached the section where, instead of simply washing her hands before lunch in Mrs. Frankweiler's mansion, Claudia decides to take a bath in the fancy black marble bathtub. Since Claudia is taking so long, Mrs. Frankweiler and Claudia's brother, Jamie, start lunch without her. When Claudia gets to the table, she feels miffed they hadn't waited for her, and she makes her feelings known.

SELECT A FOCUS AND SELF-EMPATHY

Questions: What is the problem? What is the question? What is the task? What is he or she feeling?

Although this is an academic task, Maria and Mr. M. decide that the problem is academic, social, and emotional, so they agree to mix the SELf-questions up a bit. In and of itself, this shows near transfer. They decide that the best first question would actually be from the emotional question set, and Mr. M. asks, "How does Claudia feel?" Maria answers, "Claudia feels annoyed, mad, and sad. Usually *mad* and *sad* go together."

GATHER INFORMATION

Questions: What do I know? What do I need to know? What is similar, and what is different? What is causing this feeling?

Since Maria is making an inference from a combination of text evidence and background knowledge, Mr. M. asks, "How are you and Claudia similar and different?" Mr. M. also knows that seeing similarities promotes transfer—in this case, from her knowledge of herself applied to her knowledge of her character. Maria replies, "Usually, I'm mad when I'm sad about something, like when we lost the soccer game or when my best friend moved to Utah. Claudia and I are the same in that way. I think I am more mature than Claudia, though. After all, she ran away from home because she had more chores than her brothers!"

BRAINSTORM

Questions: How can I solve this problem? What are possible solutions? What strategies can I use to make myself (or them) feel better? What can I do?

Mr. M. wants Maria to transfer her personal experience to help a character in a book, and so he adapts his question to the situation: "If you were in Claudia's situation, what are some strategies you could use to make yourself feel better?" Maria answers, "I don't know. . . . I wouldn't think about it. I'd watch a movie or talk to a friend about a different topic." She was able to generate three possibilities but still doesn't look happy with any of them.

EVALUATE

Questions: What is the best way to solve this problem? Does this make sense? Has this strategy helped me in the past? How did it help? How did I feel after?

Switching back to the academic and social SELf-question set, Mr. M. asks, "What is the best way to solve this problem?" Maria thinks for a few minutes about which of her ideas would work best. "Oh! Oh!" she says with great excitement. "I know what I'd do to not be mad! I'd introduce a totally different topic at the lunch table: 'What have you been doing today, Mrs. Basil?'" This is a new idea and demonstrates great coping flexibility.

PLAN AND ACT

Questions: What do I do first, second, and so on? Does this work? Is this working?

"So, I would do what I just said, but I've also noticed in this book that Claudia isn't like me. When she gets mad, she likes to stay mad for a while. This strategy would work for me but not for Claudia until she grows up a little. So I guess Claudia could try watching a movie. By the time it's over, she might not be mad anymore."

REFLECT

Questions: Did it work? How do I know? Do I need to go back and try again?

Maria is convinced she has solved Claudia's problem, and in the process, she has tapped into self-awareness and social-awareness with great insight. She used coping flexibility as she looked for strategies that would work and cognitive flexibility as she analyzed similarities and differences between her and Claudia. She transferred knowledge from her experience to infer how Claudia was feeling and why she was feeling that way. And, it was the SELf-question sets that helped her make these moves.

Identifying the emotions of characters and their challenges in books, then problem solving with those characters as they overcome obstacles is great scaffolding upon which students can learn to identify their emotions and think of new ways to approach real-life problems, thus using far transfer to the real world.

Scenario: Grades 6–8

Class: Sixth-grade homeschool (Mrs. S.; teacher)

Objective:

- Learn to summarize a chapter.

Standard:

- Describe how a particular story's or drama's plot unfolds in a series of episodes as well as how the characters respond or change as the plot moves toward a resolution. (RL.6.3; NGA & CCSSO, 2010a)

Rheyma, a home-schooled sixth-grade student, is having problems focusing on what is important in her reading of *Harriet the Spy* (Fitzhugh, 2016) and is struggling to give oral summaries of its chapters. Her teacher, Mrs. S., knows from *Classroom Instruction That Works* (Marzano, Pickering, & Pollock, 2001) that summarizing is a highly effective instructional strategy and thus an important skill to camp on for a while. She also knows that if Rheyma focused more on her reading, she would be more successful. Let's examine the many ways that Rheyma uses transfer to come up with strategies that have worked in the past and far transfer of her work ethic in soccer to her new work ethic in reading. She also uses cognitive flexibility through her metacognitive thinking throughout the SELf-questioning process.

SELECT A FOCUS

Questions: What is the problem? What is the question? What is the task?

Mrs. S. proposes a problem to Rheyma, "You're having difficulty determining what is important to include and what is not important during your summaries. Let's use SELf-questioning to see how you might improve. First, let's gather information about your summarizing process."

GATHER INFORMATION

Questions: What do I know? What do I need to know? What is similar, and what is different?

Mrs. S. asks Rheyma, "What do you know?" Rheyma replies, "I know that I sometimes skip over the journal entries in *Harriet the Spy*, and that they are there for a reason. I also know that I sometimes get carried away with the drama of the situation, and I need to focus on just-the-facts-ma'am for a summary. I also have problems remembering everything that is in the chapter when I go to give a summary."

Mrs. S. asks, "Why do you think you have problems remembering?" Rheyma answers, "Well, sometimes I read too quickly."

BRAINSTORM

Questions: How can I solve this problem? What are possible solutions? What can I do?

Mrs. S. asked Rheyma to brainstorm some ideas that might help her. Rheyma thinks for a while and comes up with the following.

- "I could make sure to read Harriet's journal entries carefully."
- "I could take notes on each chapter in my little notebook as I read it and then refresh my mind with the notes before I give my summary."
- "I could reread anything I don't understand well."

EVALUATE

Questions: What is the best way to solve this problem? Does this make sense?

Mrs. S. asks Rheyma what she thinks is the best solution, and she answers, "I'm going to do all of them. I have just the perfect little notebook here that I can use for taking notes." (It's worth noting that Rheyma *loves* school supplies.) Mrs. S. suggests that doing all three ideas is a lot of work, but Rheyma insists. She says, "I learned that it takes a lot of work to be an excellent soccer player, so I think it makes sense that it would take a lot of work to be a good reader."

PLAN AND ACT

Questions: What do I do first, second, and so on? Does this work? Is this working?

Rheyma begins by taking notes in her notebook and slowly adds in reading carefully, and rereading when she doesn't understand Harriet's journal entries from the book. She then refreshes her brain using her notes before giving the chapter summary with her usual dramatic flair. Mrs. S. observes that the quality of her summaries (and thus, her reading comprehension) is steadily improving.

REFLECT

Questions: Did it work? How do I know? Do I need to go back and try again?

At the end her work reading *Harriet the Spy*, Rheyma is determined that she wants to continue the practice for the next reading, *Ella Enchanted* (Levine, 1997). The part that amazes Mrs. S. is Rheyma's ability to transfer her knowledge that hard work brings results from the sphere of athletics to the sphere of language arts. This is a great example of far transfer: from the athletic field where she excels to her reading where she is not quite as naturally motivated.

Scenario: Grades 9–12

Class: Eleventh-grade ELA (independent student)

Objective:

- Independently solve problems while writing.

Standard:

- Write narratives to develop real or imagined experiences or events using effective technique, well-chosen details, and well-structured event sequences. (W.11-12.3; NGA & CCSSO, 2010a)

For this scenario, we organize things a bit differently. As we wrote in the introduction, and as we've indicated throughout this book, the goal for using our SELf-question sets is for students to find the questions so useful that they internalize them to the point where using them to find solutions to problems is automatic. To that end, we do not show a SELf-question set for this scenario, as our student, Karen, can quickly sort through her mental question set and come up with a solution for her problem.

Karen is a high school junior who her teachers know well for wanting to do the least amount of work possible. She has no structure or responsibilities at home and often spends more time avoiding school work than she would spend actually doing the work. But in the midst of writing a science fiction piece, she stops and thinks, "I feel like I don't know where I'm going with the story. I think I need to create a storyline like I did for my story last fall. I think that will give me direction and even save me time in the long run."

Notice how just three simple statements, all in a row, establish a focus based on gathering information, brainstorming, evaluating a solution, and determining a plan of action. No one has to cue Karen to use the questions, and she doesn't need to speak them aloud in a structured way. She has simply internalized them to the point she can automatically generate a near transfer of something that she's been required to do frequently in the past (make a storyline) and generalize or transfer that knowledge to what she is writing now. This is a great example of transfer's role within autonomy; it is the goal teachers want students to reach when using the SELf-question sets.

The next time they meet, Karen proudly tells her teacher about her realization, shows her teacher the storyline she generated, and says that it was really saving her time because now she knows where the story is headed.

Character Corner: Inner Peace

David Sousa, past president of the National Staff Development Council, claims that "it is almost axiomatic that the more information students can transfer from their schooling to the context of everyday life, the greater the probability that they will be good communicators, informed citizens, critical thinkers, and successful problem solvers" (as cited in Burke, 2009, p. 109). Thus, it is imperative that teachers support students in connecting their learning with the use of the SELf-question set during academic content-area instruction and with problems they might encounter socially and emotionally both within and beyond classroom walls. Burke (2009) further confirms that "The more connections students are able to make between past learning and new learning, school learning, and life learning, the more likely they are to be successful in both school and life" (p. 109).

In this context, we see success in school and life in another way—inner peace. By teaching your students to be adaptive, intelligent critical thinkers and problem solvers, you will help them develop their ability to cope more successfully with the wide range of daily stressors and problems they face. By serving as models of self-awareness, social awareness, self-management, and responsible decision making at work, at school, and in our homes and our communities, teachers can develop future leaders of our world as adaptive, intelligent, and above all, peaceful resolvers of conflict, especially within themselves and among their peers. You can prepare your students to be the designers of their own inner-peace; in doing so, you prepare them to help make the world a more peaceful place.

Structured SELf-Questioning
for Social Studies

*The cumulative goal of education is to offer students
opportunities to develop interrelated academic, personal, and social
competencies that have a long-term impact on their lives . . .
To better achieve the goal of developing interrelated competencies in
children, schools must take steps to shift away from a siloed approach . . .
Instead, the focus should be on an integrated, systemic framework,
in which parallel processes of interrelated competencies for both
educators and students are identified, built, and sustained."*

—Nadja N. Reilly

We are big fans of the epigraph for this chapter, for a variety of reasons. First, it emphasizes the need to design curriculum and instruction that are interdisciplinary, because life's real-world problems do not always come in neatly organized, departmentalized packages. Second, the quote sets the stage for the transfer of structured SELf-questioning as an interrelated competency from academics to students' personal and social lives (Reilly, 2017/2018).

In previous chapters, we demonstrated how educators teach social and emotional competencies, such as self-awareness, self-management, and responsible decision making, within discrete content areas such as mathematics, reading, and writing. In chapter 9, you learned about how transfer occurs and the effectiveness of structured SELf-questioning as an interdisciplinary strategy for transfer. In this chapter and chapter 11, we use the social studies and science content areas to shift toward a focus on teaching SEL competencies from one academic content area *to* another academic content area, as well as real-world social problem solving. We find that educators often teach academic curricula and instruction in isolated academic departments—a mathematics department or an ELA department, for example. Such siloed approaches fail to maximize learning opportunities (Reilly 2017/2018).

The advantages of challenging students to transfer their growing understanding of SELf-questioning as a problem-solving strategy from one academic discipline to another include the following.

- Saving instructional time
- Providing students with opportunities for transfer and practice of interrelated competencies

- Developing students as social problem solvers and responsible decision makers for the common good

This chapter focuses specifically on social studies and providing practical methods of melding the academic and social SELf-question set and the self-empathy step of the emotional SELf-question set for use in social studies. The goal is to promote what Reilly (2017/2018) refers to as the perfect example of an "interrelated academic, personal and social competency" that marries responsible decision making with social awareness and self-awareness. Social awareness and self-awareness are quintessential competencies that all students and staff need to be responsible decision makers at school, in their personal lives, and within a diverse and democratic society.

Again, at first, it may sound overwhelming to contemplate integrating not just one but multiple SEL competencies into a subject area already jam-packed with content. But as you've seen throughout this book, SELf-questioning provides a way to make teaching these academic, social, and emotional competencies simple and efficient through a slight adaptation of the SELf-question sets.

As an example, ELA teachers who use our strategy often use the SELf-questions for self-empathy to teach students to identify their own emotions by asking themselves, "What am I feeling?" or "How do I feel?" We designed this SELf-question to develop self-awareness through self-empathy. In social studies, students need to be as aware of the feelings, thoughts, and perspectives of others as they are of their own. Therefore, instead of asking "What am I feeling?" social studies teachers ask, "What is he or she feeling?" or "How do they feel?" By helping students gather whatever information they can about what others are thinking and feeling—from texts, discussions, videos, social media posts, or a wide range of other sources—teachers support students in understanding and empathizing with others. This is especially important for social studies learning, given the need for students to understand people from diverse backgrounds, cultures, and contexts.

Rather than covering what seems like an insurmountable quantity of information in social studies, then teaching a separate, unrelated lesson in ELA on identifying character traits and plot (and then lamenting that there is no time to teach SEL), SELf-questioning makes it possible to teach all three disciplines simultaneously. Social studies presents a wonderful interdisciplinary sandbox for teachers and students to play with historical content, reading and writing strategies, and the SEL competencies of responsible decision making and social and self-awareness.

This chapter shows what makes this metacognitive strategy so important for social studies instruction and how to turn social studies lessons and projects into interdisciplinary sandboxes for students to dig deeper into social studies content and standards while utilizing interrelated literacy skills and SEL competencies. It closes with an examination of how this metacognitive work enhances students' development of empathy.

The Importance of a Metacognitive Strategy for Social Studies

We cannot overstate the importance of teaching students how to be socially aware, self-aware, and collaborative decision makers and problem solvers. Social studies teachers know well the crippling effect of hyperpartisanship on democracy in countries like the United

States, Canada, and many more in which elected representatives and their voters become so ideologically entrenched that they are unable to hear one another's perspectives, thoughts, or feelings. According to the National Council for the Social Studies (NCSS, n.d.), the largest professional association for social studies educators in the world, "The primary purpose of social studies is to help young people make informed and reasoned decisions for the public good as citizens of a culturally diverse, democratic society in an interdependent world." Therefore, the investments educators make in teaching one overall strategy to guide students' self-talk through informed and reasoned decision making in ELA and mathematics pay huge dividends when adapted to social studies.

However, we must recognize here that teachers who teach problem solving and decision making in siloed academic courses do not always have to worry as much about the consequences of solutions or decisions on others. In social studies and science (chapter 11, page 171), the implications and consequences of decisions and solutions on others is paramount. For example, consider the difference between students reading a persuasive article about President Harry Truman's decision to drop two atomic bombs on Japan during World War II. In an ELA class, where students are learning about persuasive writing, teachers may ask them to analyze and evaluate the author's perspective and the strength of his or her supporting details to determine whether they agree with the author. However, in social studies, students' analysis and evaluation of the decision must take into account multiple perspectives from all involved stakeholders. This doesn't do away with analyzing the author's perspective, but social studies students reading this article would also have to consider the perspectives of President Truman, the U.S. military and its allies, and the consequences of the decision on citizens of both the United States and Japan, past and present.

To that end, and to ensure students are truly informed and reasoned decision makers for the public good, teachers need to understand the scope of CASEL's (n.d.) social awareness competency. Not only must they help students understand and empathize with diverse, backgrounds, cultures, and contexts, they must help students develop their capacity to "feel compassion for others, understand broader historical and social norms for behavior in different settings, and recognize family, school, and community resources and supports" (CASEL, n.d.).

To achieve this goal, consider the modern social studies classroom, in which we often see debates or discussions focused solely (or nearly so) on winning the debate or having a drop-the-mic moment. Classrooms devoted to these disciplines must instead transform into laboratories of collaborative inquiry that extend beyond existing perspectives and thinking, promoting the discipline and capacity for deeper understanding of how others think and feel. Teachers must ask themselves, "What if students are actually graded not only on what they think and feel, but also on their understanding of what other people think and feel?" This chapter not only asks that question via our structured SELf-questioning strategy, it also demonstrates how to foster that thinking in students.

When teachers don't teach students how to recognize and consider the feelings of others, as well as their own feelings, they fail to set students up for success as social decision makers and social problem solvers. One example of the importance of teaching students social awareness and self-awareness as core competencies of social problem solving derives from an example we first highlighted in chapter 7 (page 113) about a fight that occurred between two students, Stephanie and Veronica, outside of Loma Linda School.

Recall that Rick never had Stephanie, an eighth grader, in any core content classes he taught, but he had taught her how to use problem-solving processes for peer mediation as part of an elective class. At this point, Veronica was a high school freshman, but Rick previously had her as a student for seventh-grade reading and social studies classes. During that time, he'd taught Veronica how to use one problem-solving process to analyze the plot of a story and how to use that same problem-solving process to resolve social conflict in social studies. Rick had not explicitly taught either Veronica or Stephanie how to, or why to, identify the feelings and perspectives of themselves or others at any time during any of these processes.

Having heard rumors that Stephanie was saying things about her, Veronica decided she was going to use violence to teach Stephanie a lesson. Since Veronica was pregnant, she did not want to jeopardize her baby's health by getting in the fight herself. So, Veronica convinced two of her friends to come with her to Stephanie's bus stop and beat her up.

After the fight occurred between Stephanie and Veronica's friend at Stephanie's bus stop, Rick asked Veronica how and why the fight happened. He asked her what in the world Stephanie could have done to make her so mad that she would get two of her friends to come to Stephanie's bus stop and beat her up on her walk home from, ironically, tutoring younger kids on how to stay out of fights. The following conversation ensued.

> **Rick:** *Veronica, what is the problem with Stephanie?*
>
> **Veronica:** *She's talking stuff about me. She talks too much stuff all the time, and you know it, Mr. Cohen.*
>
> **Rick:** *Haven't you and Stephanie fought a bunch of times before?*
>
> **Veronica:** *Yes.*
>
> **Rick:** *Has fighting stopped her from talking stuff?*
>
> **Veronica:** *She better not keep talking stuff.*

At that point, Veronica and her friends left.

Although Stephanie had a great deal of social intelligence for age twelve, she hadn't yet developed the habit of mind to take a step back and have herself a quick think about her thinking or feelings. If she had, Stephanie could have easily figured out what Veronica was up to. If Stephanie had been thoroughly trained to gather information by asking herself, "What is she feeling?" before taking action, she could have easily recognized that Veronica was setting a trap for her, and it was best not to fall into it (again). Or, if Stephanie had been thoroughly trained to gather information by asking herself, "What am I feeling?" before taking action, she could have easily recognized her own rage and decided not to fall into the trap she falls into every time she lets her anger get the best of her. If Rick could go back in time, he would teach both Veronica and Stephanie how to take a step back and have a real think about their own feelings, as well as the feelings and perspectives of the other person or people involved in the conflict.

Obviously, going back in time is impossible. But it is possible to use hindsight to teach all students and adults how to identify the feelings of others by simply making it part of the process to ask, "What is he or she feeling?" Let's reconsider the assignment to analyze and evaluate the decision to drop atomic bombs on Japan. What if students had been trained over and over in that unit to ask themselves, "How did he [President Truman] feel?" as well as "How did they [Japanese survivors who lost everything] feel?" and "How do I feel [about the massive civilian death toll]?" By incorporating this pattern of SELf-questioning into students' regular social studies learning experiences, students develop the habit of mind to take a step back and have a think about their own feelings and thinking as well as the thinking and feelings of others. In so doing, teachers further empower students to be even more informed, reasoned, and *response-able* decision makers in both interpersonal and social problem-solving situations.

How to Teach a Metacognitive Strategy for Social Studies

The following SELf-question set is a bit of a melding of academic and social SELf-questions along with the emotional SELf-questions, which includes questions we added explicitly to the *gather information* step to promote social awareness. In this way, the academic and social SELf-questions incorporate an empathetic component as featured in the emotional SELf-question set.

 Select a Focus: What is the problem? What is the question? What is the task?

 Gather information: What do I know? What do I need to know? What is similar, and what is different? What is he or she feeling? What do they feel? How do I know?

 Brainstorm: How can I solve this problem? What are possible solutions? What can I do?

 Evaluate: What is the best way to solve this problem? Does this make sense?

 Plan and act: What do I do first, second, and so on? Is this working?

 Reflect: Did it work? How do I know? Do I need to go back and try again?

Why add these questions to the gather information step? In chapter 7 (page 113), we established that the ways to identify one's own feelings (self-awareness) are different from the ways to identify other people's feelings (social awareness). Both involve the cognitive processes of recognizing and identifying, but the sources of information are different, as are the senses people use to gather that information. Emotional recognition requires an inward *focus* for patterns of thought and identifying how one's body feels (self-awareness). Social awareness requires *gathering information* about someone else's feelings, thoughts, and perspectives, which necessitates looking outward by gathering visual information (facial expressions or body language), auditory information (what the other person says, the tones we hear), and direct communication (the words a person chooses to use, verbally or in text messages, social media posts, emails, and so on). The rest of this section (plus the grade-band scenarios we provide in this chapter) details models of social awareness via SELf-questioning and illustrates what looking outward sounds and looks like.

Through the work of the Rutgers Social-Emotional and Character Development (SECD) Lab, Elias and other staff and students have developed "a social action pedagogy" called Students Taking Action Together (STAT) so teachers can integrate social-emotional learning skills and civil discourse with curricula (SECD Lab, n.d.). The SECD Lab (n.d.) website further explains that STAT provides strategies and tools for teachers that "increase students' perspective-taking, empathy, problem solving, communication, and civic engagement." They specifically designed these strategies and tools to align with teaching history, current events, and school and community issues.

In 2018, the Metuchen School District began piloting STAT within its social studies department as well as in elementary and ELA classrooms through an infusion of STAT and SELf-questioning strategies to teach students perspective taking, empathy, and problem solving. Teachers use the SELf-questions, *What is he or she feeling?* and *How do they feel?* to prompt students to think about the feelings and perspectives of others. Teachers model these questions via think-alouds, having previously gauged their effectiveness as guiding questions for respectful debates, Socratic Circles, self-assessment, and promotion of empathy. They then use the academic and social SELf-question set as the framework for social problem solving.

To help promote your students' near transfer (see chapter 9, page 139) of structured SELf-questioning from ELA to social studies to real world social problem solving and decision making, we recommend that you first identify a real-world social problem, current event, or historical conflict that you are particularly passionate about (and that is within your content standards, of course). Pose that problem to your students. Next, let them utilize with high degrees of independence the academic and social SELf-question set for a specific task, such as an inquiry-based research paper, document-based question (DBQ), problem-based or project-based learning, or even a service-learning project. As early as the third grade and all the way through college, we've observed success with posing problems and students then independently applying transfer and using the SELf-question set in social studies. We've even seen success with it in the workplace as teachers and administrators facilitate shared decisions around school-improvement efforts.

By giving students the opportunity to try near transfer and independent application of the synthesized academic, social, and emotional SELf-question set in social studies, some big things happen.

- Social studies teachers no longer have to feel the pressure of becoming ELA teachers because they can challenge their students to apply near transfer of the SELf-questioning strategy in reading and writing in their class without the need for additional teacher training, resources, or instructional time.

- Having students transfer the SELf-questioning strategy from ELA to social studies not only provides students opportunities for practice with transfer across academic content areas but also provides students the opportunity to practice near transfer from academic contexts to social contexts, which are inherent in social studies.

- When social studies teachers model the SELf-questioning strategy through think-alouds in the classroom, they identify, build, and sustain parallel processes of interrelated competencies (Reilly, 2017/2018).

A major outcome of student transfer and practice of SELf-questioning in social studies classrooms is that students begin to feel more confident with the strategy and more comfortable within themselves as they face the challenges of a complex, diverse society. Students begin to feel more comfortable and confident when confronting conflict because they have had a great deal of experience and practice dealing with conflict in class at school, where it is safe. After all, societal problems are not always so black and white, so giving students opportunities to practice working through conflict with greater independence, allowing them to sift calmly and thoughtfully through a world of information and disinformation, is essential for their learning. If we expect students to make responsible choices on their own, when no teacher or other adult is present to guide their decision making, it is especially important to teach students what to do when they are uncertain about their course of action.

As a final note before diving into the following grade-band scenarios, all the K–12 examples in previous chapters have demonstrated implementation in an isolated content area. For this chapter and chapter 11 (page 171), we shift away from siloed content and move toward transfer with social studies and then science as the focal points. This chapter's scenarios emphasize interdisciplinary learning in social studies and ELA.

Scenario: Grade K–2

Class: Kindergarten classroom (Mrs. K.; teacher)

Objective:

- Gather information to understand how characters feel in a teacher-assigned reading (a picture book) and identify the characters' body language and facial expressions to recognize their moods and feelings.

continued ▶

Standards:

- With prompting and support, ask and answer questions about key details in a text. (RI.K.1; NGA & CCSSO, 2010a)

- With adult guidance and support, bring awareness of a local issue to school and/or community members and make recommendations for change. (6.3.2.CivicsPD1; New Jersey Department of Education, 2020)

- Recognize and identify the thoughts, feelings, and perspectives of others. (SEL competency and skill; New Jersey State Board of Education, 2017)

At Moss Elementary School, the half-day kindergarten teachers have no time to waste and high standards to reach. To maximize instructional time, Mrs. K. embeds the SEL competency of social awareness into social studies standards-based instruction and reading instruction. To accomplish this integration, she wants students to focus specifically on the *gather information* step of the SELf-question set, so she utilizes the SELf-questions *What is he or she feeling?* and *How do you know?* along with her own SELf-question, *What do you notice?*

Mrs. K. wants to model for students how to use the questions as a reading-comprehension strategy aligned to state standards for both ELA and social studies as well as a real-world social and emotional skill. She intends to prompt students to gather information from visual cues, both in pictures while reading a picture book about Rosa Parks and then transfer the academic skill to people's (their classmates) faces in the classroom. She starts by telling students the learning goal for the lesson: "We are going to gather information to understand how the characters in this story feel. To do this, we will read their faces and bodies."

Mrs. K. accesses and assesses students' background knowledge by asking, "When someone tells you something with their face, what are they telling you?" Students call out, "Their feelings." She then asks, "When someone tells you something with their bodies, what are they telling us?" Students again call out, "Feelings."

Mrs. K. then asks a student volunteer to show with his body what he is feeling. The student stands up with fists clenched and arms straight. Mrs. K. asks the class, "What is he feeling?" Students respond with words like *angry*, *mad*, and *frustrated*. She then explains they are going to read a book and identify how the characters are feeling by noticing their faces. She conducts a read-aloud of a picture book with a variety of faces in the pictures. At a specific point, she stops reading aloud and says, "Look at the expressions on the faces of the people. What do you notice? What do you notice about the man's eyes? What do you think he is feeling?" A student answers, "He is frustrated because she is not sitting in the back." Mrs. K. asks, "How do you know he is frustrated?" and the student says he can see his eyebrows are pointing downward.

After reading a few more pages and modeling by asking herself, "What is he feeling? What do I notice?" and answering based upon the picture clues in characters' faces, Mrs. K. says, "We just read the words, and we also read the characters' faces and bodies to see their feelings. We can do this same thing in real life. How can we read other people's feelings? We can't read their minds." A student says, "Faces" and Mrs. K. replies, "Yes, we can read their faces and their bodies."

To check for understanding, teach transfer, and promote empathy, at the end of the read-aloud, Mrs. K. asks a series of questions including, "What is this person feeling? What do you think his or her facial expression would be if . . . ? Why do you think . . . ? What do you think he or she is feeling? How do you know?" She then tries to have students use the same questions to make connections and empathize by asking about events from the book, "How would you feel if you were Rosa Parks? What would you do with your mouth if you were sad? Use your arms to show me you are feeling sad?"

Students respond to each of these prompts, absorbing the information Mrs. K. provides. She then has students sit in a circle and provides each with a drawing board with three sticky notes. She asks students to draw the face of a person who is frustrated, which they do. She then asks students to draw someone angry and then someone surprised. While monitoring students' efforts, she assesses and reinforces their drawings. She also uses the opportunity to promote students' development of their emotions vocabulary so students not only develop awareness of feelings, but enhance their ability to accurately express their own feelings and empathize with the feelings of others.

Scenario: Grades 3–5

Class: Fourth-grade inclusion classroom (Ms. L. and Ms. P.; coteachers)

Objective:

- Recognize the perspective of U.S. patriots, identify the perspective of British loyalists, and then come to a solution for solving the debt from the Revolutionary War.

Standards:

- Refer to details and examples in a text and make relevant connections when explaining what the text says explicitly and when drawing inferences from the text. (RI.4.1; NGA & CCSSO, 2010a)

- Compare and contrast historians' interpretations of important historical ideas, resources and events. (6.1.5.HistoryUP.5; New Jersey Department of Education, 2020)

- Evaluate the impact of different interpretations of experiences and events by people with different cultural or individual perspectives. (6.1.5.HistoryUP.6; New Jersey Department of Education, 2020)

- Recognize and identify the thoughts, feelings, and perspectives of others. (SEL competency and skill; New Jersey State Board of Education, 2017)

- Develop, implement and model effective problem-solving and critical-thinking skills. (SEL competency and skill; New Jersey State Board of Education, 2017)

Ms. L. and Ms. P. coteach a fourth-grade inclusion class. Throughout the year and across curricula, they embed the SEL competency of responsible decision making via structured SELf-questioning, and they conduct multiple service-learning projects by modeling and facilitating their students' structured SELf-questioning. Their IBL unit is a model of integration of SEL, social studies, and ELA that challenges students to apply, at a developmentally appropriate level of independence, the academic and social SELf-questioning set to guide their research, reading of informational text, writing of research papers, and a service project.

To take a gradual-release approach toward developing their students' metacognitive skills, Ms. L. and Ms. P. embed modeling and guided practice of the strategy into daily instruction over the course of the fall and winter. The scenario presents a snapshot of one kind of daily lesson they teach in social studies that also teaches social awareness as well as transfers students' application of the academic and social SELf-question set. To reinforce students' development of social awareness through the use of SELf-questions (*What is he or she feeling?* and *How do they feel?*), Ms. L. and Ms. P. design a lesson about the tea tax Britain imposed on colonists that led to the Boston Tea Party. This forty-five-minute lesson not only asks students to demonstrate deep understanding of content but also social awareness and responsible decision making. The following sections illustrate how the lesson challenges students to transfer their social awareness and problem-solving and decision-making skills to resolve a political conflict and promote the common good using SELf-questioning.

SELECT A FOCUS

Question: What is the problem? What is the question? What is the task?

Ms. L. starts by asking students content-related questions to set the focus and access prior knowledge from previous lessons. She says, "The day we have all been waiting for . . . the patriots versus the loyalists. What was happening? Why were people so mad about this? Why were they shouting, 'No taxation without representation'?" What does taxation without representation *mean*?

A student raises her hand and says, "They shouted that because . . . ." She pauses in thought and continues, "So they wouldn't get taxed on things."

Ms. P. chimes in, "They were getting taxed on stamps, tea, lots of things. Taxation was a law. Is that fair? What is the problem with taxation without representation? Let's see which side we empathize with."

GATHER INFORMATION

Questions: What do we know? What do I need to know? What were they feeling?

Ms. P. says, "What do we know? Well, we know some colonists were taxed and had no say about it, and we know that British citizens were taxed but had a say in it because they had representatives in the British government."

The students chanted, "We want war!" Note that, as U.S. citizens in the midst of a unit on U.S. history, these students had already learned much about the patriots' perspective on taxes imposed on colonists by King George and their impact. For this age group, a lack of awareness about the implications inherent in their chant isn't malicious nor unexpected.

Ms. L. cautions, "Remember, there are two sides to every story, and we are missing someone's perspective." She posts a T-chart on the smartboard with two columns, one that is labeled *Patriots' Perspective* and the other *Loyalists' Perspective*. Together, Ms. L. and Ms. P. conduct a read-aloud and think-aloud from a short text about the patriots' perspective to reinforce the reading strategy of SELf-questioning and making inferences. Ms. P. asks, "What were they feeling? What can we infer from this? For example, I can infer the thoughts and feelings of the patriots. They thought it was unfair and felt angry."

Again, the students chant, "We want war!"

The teachers finish reading the text aloud and then give students a one-page text detailing the loyalists' story. Ms. L. asks students to read along as she reads it out loud. She then tells students to get a partner and answer the SELf-question, "What were the loyalists feeling?"

A student answers, "That they were just trying to help the colonists."

Ms. P. asks, "How do you know that? Why do you infer that?"

The student reads from the text, "'Great Britain had spent plenty of money fighting in America for the benefit of the colonies. The king was still supporting a British army to help suppress Native Americans.' They went back to fight for the American Colonies, which caused the debt that they were taxing the colonists to pay for." (Note that Ms. P. and Ms. L. would also address the feelings and motivations of Native Americans experiencing colonization of their lands.)"

Ms. L. asks, "What else were they feeling? Do they feel any other way, or do they have any other feelings?"

Another student answers, "In the text, it says they feel bad."

Another student chimes in, "I think the loyalists feel angry because the patriots can only back up one side of the story, 'We don't have any representatives!' blah, blah, blah . . .' but still I am with the colonists on this one."

 BRAINSTORM

Question: How can I solve this problem? What are possible solutions? What can I do?

Ms. P. says, "Think about this question: After hearing these two different perspectives, how would you have solved the debt from the war? How can we solve this problem in a way that both sides could have felt happy with? We will pair you up, loyalist and patriot, and you must work together and come to an agreement or compromise that works for both sides. If you come up with a solution, but one side says, 'I do not feel happy about this solution.' then you have to keep working on a compromise where both sides agree. We want for both sides to say, 'I feel happy.'"

After providing time for students to brainstorm via small-group discussion, one group of students decides to share their idea. A student says, "You should have to pay taxes on half of what you spend . . . spend your money wisely."

Ms. L. says, "What are other possible solutions?"

A student that is part of another group replies, "Tax them but have the representatives come to hear what they have to say. Have a huge meeting, and let everyone say how they feel and what they want. They can talk about fair taxes and get representation too."

REFLECT

Questions: Did it work? How do I know? Do I need to go back and try again?

At this point, the bell for recess rings, and time does not permit students to complete all the problem-solving steps of the lesson. Instead, Ms. L. and Ms. P. use the last minute to ask students to reflect on their learning. Ms. P. asks, "What are you learning? Why are you learning this?" A student replies, "We are learning about the perspectives of the loyalists and the patriots. We are learning how to solve problems when both perspectives are reasonable."

This student's response speaks volumes about the power of using SELf-questions as prompts for all students to take a moment and think about the feelings of both sides in a social problem or conflict. Consider the fact that these students just learned how to solve problems when both perspectives are reasonable right before they headed out to recess. As a result, students are more empowered that day and future days (especially as they continue to engage with and practice SELf-questioning) to recognize that problem solving requires understanding both sides' perspectives. In addition, the SELf-questions not only prompt the critical thinking skill of recognizing other's perspectives inside the classroom, but they also empower students to use those same practices in the classroom to guide their self-talk out on the playground and beyond.

Scenario: Grade 6–8

Class: Seventh-grade interdisciplinary ELA and social studies (Mrs. E.; teacher)

Objective:

- Students will analyze a text for pathos.

Standards:

- Determine an author's point of view or purpose in a text and analyze how the author distinguishes his or her position from that of others. (RI.7.6; NGA & CCSSO, 2010a)

- Determine the meaning of words and phrases as they are used in a text, including figurative, connotative, and technical meanings; analyze the impact of a specific word choice on meaning and tone. (RI.7.4; NGA & CCSSO, 2010a)

- Examine sources from a variety of perspectives to describe efforts to reform education, women's rights, slavery, and other issues (6.1.8.CivicsHR.4.a; New Jersey Department of Education, 2020)
- Recognize and identify the thoughts, feelings, and perspectives of others. (SEL competency and skill; New Jersey State Board of Education, 2017)

Mrs. E. has designed a lesson to teach her seventh-grade students social awareness through an interdisciplinary unit that reinforces and develops SELf-questioning as a reading comprehension strategy for informational text, an inquiry-based research writing strategy, and an approach to deeper understanding of social studies content. This all comes as part of an argumentative writing unit, and Mrs. E. has provided students with background knowledge in Aristotle's techniques of persuasion: ethos, pathos, and logos (Purdue Online Writing Lab, n.d.). To teach students how to better connect with the reader by identifying the feelings of their audience (pathos), Mrs. E. teaches her students how to use the SELf-questions *What is he or she feeling?* and *How are they feeling?* as a reading-comprehension strategy, an argumentative writing strategy, and as a focus question for whole-group and small-group discussion.

Note that, prior to this class, Mrs. E. has discussed Malala Yousafza and her book *I Am Malala* (Yousafzai, 2013). Her students were already aware of how Malala had been shot for speaking out for the right to an education (particularly for young girls) and how she continues to fight for the rights and well-being of others. Mrs. E. has also explained to her students that Malala's book not only tells Malala's story, but also includes the stories of other people's struggles as well. As in the K–2 scenario for this chapter, Mrs. E.'s focus is specifically on engaging students in gathering information as opposed to the full SELf-question set. She begins by asking the whole group, "What is pathos?" A student answers that it is tapping into an emotion.

Mrs. E. says, "Yes, pathos can mean both putting yourself in someone else's shoes and getting the reader to put themselves in your shoes." She provides an example of how people use pathos in real life and in teaching by talking about her yoga instructor. She says, "I will tell you a short story about one of my yoga teachers who is incredibly strong. Even as strong as she is, she often tells us during class when she is having one of those days when nothing seems to work out and nothing feels good. She reminds us that we all have those days but also asks us to think, 'What if we are able to accept those feelings of negativity, recognize those feelings, let them pass, and be open to doing great things despite those feelings.' Malala, from our unit of study, is an example of that."

Mrs. E. directs her students to read a short excerpt from the speech Malala Yousafzai (2014) wrote and delivered in Oslo, Norway, where she received the 2014 Nobel Peace Prize. Mrs. E. asks students to identify examples of how Malala used pathos.

After giving students a few minutes to read, Mrs. E. asks what examples students found, and a student answers, "She talks about children being forced into childhood marriage and how some are beaten and abused." Mrs. E. then asks, "How does that make the audience feel?" Another student answers that it makes him feel sympathetic.

Mrs. E. asks for other examples, and a student identifies a statement Malala makes within the text: "There are many countries where millions still suffer from the very old problems of war, poverty and injustice" (Yousafzai, 2014). The student says that this is an example of connecting with the audience's emotions because it tells members of the audience, "Even in first-world countries, people make it seem like they don't have problems, but they do." Mrs. E. asks, "How does that make them feel?" The student reflects for a moment and says he feels embarrassed. Mrs. E. follows up by asking, "What does making the audience feel sympathetic and embarrassed do for Malala as an argumentative writer?" Another student says, "It can make you want to take action."

Mrs. E. directs students to read the rest of the speech and, while reading, identify more examples of how Malala uses pathos. To support her students, she provides three SELf-questions and explains that, when they are done reading, they are going to meet in small groups and discuss their answers to the questions. She posts the following two questions on the smartboard.

- What do you think Malala is feeling?

- How do you know?

Mrs. E. reminds students that the "How do you know?" question requires them to identify textual evidence. Although this question is most often utilized in the reflect step, using it while gathering information holds students accountable to the text when identifying the feelings of characters within the text instead of just reciting, "He said . . . ." or "She said . . . ."

When students are done reading, Mrs. E. reminds them before they get into their groups to continue utilizing the questions to help them work better as a group. She emphasizes that sometimes working in groups can make them feel like nothing is going right, and she encourages them to gather information about that challenge by asking themselves the questions, "What is he or she feeling?" or "What are they feeling?" when they feel that way. She explains that asking themselves these questions will help them to empathize, to not feel disrespected, and to get past those negative feelings. She also encourages students to use eye contact and smile. A student stands up, makes a big smile, and all the students laugh.

Scenario: Grades 9–12

Class: Ninth-grade interdisciplinary ELA and social studies (Ms. B.; teacher)

Objective:

- Through a Socratic seminar, students will answer both interpretive and evaluative questions concerning important issues in a teacher-assigned text and in real life.

Standards:

- Determine an author's point of view or purpose in a text and analyze how an author uses rhetoric to advance that point of view or purpose. (RI.9-10.6; NGA & CCSSO, 2010a)

- Determine the meaning of words and phrases as they are used in a text, including vocabulary describing political, social, or economic aspects of history/social science. (RH.9-10.4; NGA & CCSSO, 2010a)

- Recognize and identify the thoughts, feelings, and perspectives of others. (SEL competency and skill; New Jersey State Board of Education, 2017)

Ms. B. wants to engage her ninth-grade students in a respectful debate focused on nature versus nurture. It's a precursor to a unit on *Lord of the Flies* (Golding, 1954), with readings to build background knowledge about why people choose to do "bad" things and practice considering the perspectives of others. For this activity, she arranges students in two concentric circles. All the students face inward so that the inner circle can have a fishbowl conversation while the outer circle observes.

This will be a multiday exercise, but for the first day, Ms. B. focuses students on the guiding question, Do you think society prevents evil or helps people get away with doing evil things?

For discussions that involve concentric circles, Ms. B. always establishes a student facilitator for the inner-circle students. Students in the inner circle take turns discussing their ideas with each other one point at a time, and the student facilitator makes sure everyone has the chance to be heard. The facilitator also ensures that the person who is speaking calls on the next person who wants to speak; there is no talking out of turn. Those in the outer circle participate in an online discussion using Google Classroom. These students observe the fishbowl conversation and digitally take notes on any main points as well as any questions that they have about the information they have heard. To receive credit, students must respond to at least four classmates via the online discussion thread, which Ms. B. monitors.

For inner-circle discussions, Ms. B. incorporates the SELf-questions for only the select a focus, gather information, and reflect steps. The facilitator is responsible for asking the SELf-questions from these steps in order to elicit students' thinking and guide the discussion. Ms. B. set the initial questions for this discussion, including an information-gathering *How do I feel?* component, although she encourages students to think of their own questions. The student facilitator is first responsible for clarifying the focus by reading off a specific focus question Ms. B. has provided. Next, the facilitator asks gather information questions. In so doing, Ms. B. is able to ensure students are challenged to identify the feelings and perspectives of others as well as their own.

SELECT A FOCUS

Question: What is the question?

The student facilitator asks, "How do you think a child's environment affects whether they do good or bad things?"

GATHER INFORMATION

Questions: How are they feeling? What am I feeling?

Several students take turns responding, with each subsequent speaker chosen by the person preceding them. Two of the responses include the following.

- "In school, we learn to be respectful from a young age, but mostly your family has a bigger impact."

- "I agree with you. I was reading an article about confirmation bias. We are taught to act a certain way, but when humans evolved, they didn't have school, there were tribes, so in the article, it says that people are good to their families but can be bad to people that are not in their families."

The student facilitator picks one student who has not yet participated and asks him specifically, "Do you have anything to add?" The student answers, "When I was in school, I learned all about being good to others, not being mean."

SELECT A FOCUS

Question: What is the question?

The student facilitator asks, "I feel like nowadays, social media can be very influential. How do you feel social media impacts people's decisions?"

GATHER INFORMATION

Questions: How are they feeling? What am I feeling?

Student responses to the focus question include the following.

- "It reinforces strongly the way you think. You would not call someone out in person or in a group setting, but on social media, it is so much easier."

- "On social media, there is always someone who is going to agree with you and always someone who disagrees with you."

- "It is proven that there is cognitive bias called confirmation bias. It is amplified by social media due to animosity."

To ensure that the discussion remains respectful and safe for all students, Ms. B. omits the brainstorming, evaluate, and plan and act steps. This avoid students evaluating others' feelings and perspectives as wrong or right. By keeping the questions focused on the topic and on social and self-awareness via the initial SELf-question steps, the discussion stays focused solely on perspective taking and making until students are ready to reflect.

REFLECT

Questions: Did it work? How do I know?

At the end of this respectful debate, as a class, students reflect on the Socratic circle and their feelings about the activity. Ms. B. asks the whole class, "How do you feel about this respectful debate?" and "How do you know?" Responses include the following.

- "The inner circle was good today. The worst part was I didn't want to interrupt anything."

- "I was so annoyed. I so wanted to be in the inner circle today."

- "I way prefer being on the outside circle to the inside. It was still stressful trying to get everything in, but I prefer it that way."

Notice how Ms. B.'s questions reflect on the effectiveness of the discussion itself rather than on the content. In doing so, she asks students to demonstrate self-awareness by self-assessing the impact the activity had on them as learners. Posing these reflective questions at the end of any learning activity not only challenges students to identify how they feel but also how they learn and the impact that their feelings can have on their learning. Over time, students begin to recognize when strong emotions arise during a discussion of differing views. The more self-efficacy students develop in this type of reflection, the more they are empowered to model respect and civility when discussing issues of race, gender, politics, and other emotionally charged topics.

Character Corner: Self-Empathy and Empathy

We hear from so many teachers that their students lack empathy. This is true of empathy of others, but often, it's also true of how students see themselves. As teachers, rather than asking why students lack empathy or whose fault it is and whose responsibility it is to teach empathy, we must develop self-empathy and empathy in all students throughout their K–12 education. Teachers develop students' self-empathy and empathy by teaching them the habit of mind of asking themselves questions about their own feelings and the feelings of others while reading and during classroom discussion.

Challenging students to gather information about important historical figures' perspectives not only engages students in the social and emotional cognitive processes of empathy but also puts students in another person's shoes and builds their understanding of how feelings, thoughts, and perspectives are powerful influences on social decision making and social problem solving. By instilling the practice of empathy in social studies classes through SELf-questioning, students' understanding of pivotal decisions in history will be much deeper and more meaningful, thereby increasing student retention and motivation.

By developing students' self-empathy and empathy and joining that with classroom interactions, teachers can systematically develop a more thoughtful, more informed, more empathetic and aware generation of leaders and social problem solvers. We are going to need them.

Structured SELf-Questioning and Metacognitive Components in Science

11

"Never before has our world been so complex and scientific literacy is critical to making sense of it all."

—NGSS Lead States

As you've seen in the preceding chapters, structured SELf-questioning offers teachers the opportunity to increase student learning in ways that are straightforward, explicit, and applicable to any age group and content area. We focus this chapter on ways educators can teach to both Next Generation Science Standards (NGSS) and CCSS in the sciences using SELf-questioning. At the same time, we'll dive a little deeper into how teachers can use structured SELf-questioning in a science curriculum to enhance student understanding of the components and subcomponents of metacognition, an important step in helping students use metacognitive strategies effectively.

The NGSS Lead States (2013), establish three domains related to science learning.

1. **Scientific practices:** The actions that scientists and engineers perform

2. **Core ideas:** The key concepts within the sciences

3. **Crosscutting concepts:** The connecting ideas across the branches of science

When combined, these domains create assessable performance expectations (what students should know and be able to do) through which teachers can develop a science curriculum. For example, the second-grade NGSS performance expectation 2-PS1-2 reads: "Analyze data obtained from testing different materials to determine which materials have the properties that are best suited for an intended purpose" (NGSS Lead States, 2013). According to NGSS Lead States (2013), this performance expectation originates from the scientific practice of *analyzing and interpreting data*, the core ideas of *structure and properties and matter*, and the crosscutting concept of *cause and effect*.

Performance expectations in the NGSS often connect with CCSS, particularly in literacy and mathematics. For example, performance expectation 2-PS1-2 relates to the literacy standard R.I.2.8: "Describe how reasons support specific points the author makes in a text" (NGA & CCSSO, 2010a). Figure 11.1 (page 172) provides a Venn diagram that further demonstrates how NGSS and CCSS overlap. Note that the standards marked *MP* derive from CCSS Mathematical Practices, the *EP* standards from the CCSS for ELA, and the *SP* standards from the NGSS Science and Engineering Practices (CCSSO, 2014).

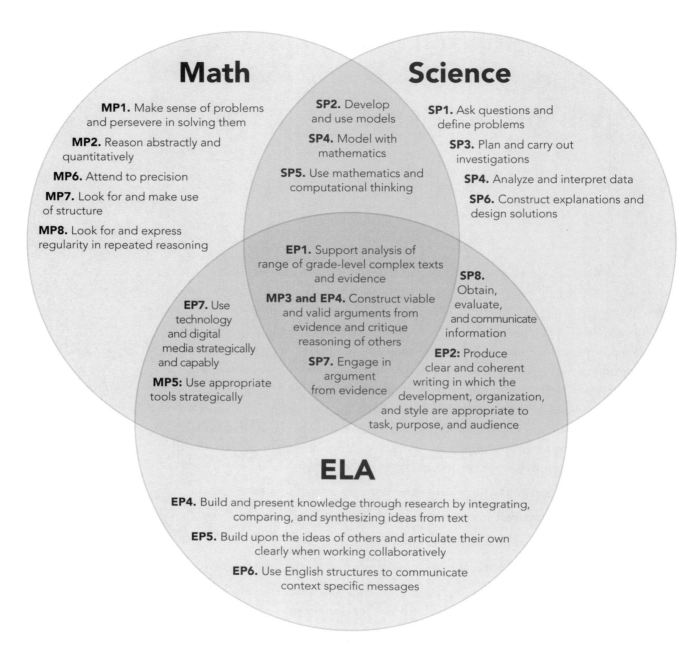

Source: CCSSO, 2014, p. 32.

Figure 11.1: Overlap of NGSS and CCSS.

On the one hand, educators benefit from NGSS's performance expectations because they bring scientific content and scientific practices together, and they show explicit connections with CCSS. On the other hand, since NGSS is not, by itself, a curriculum; the expectations they set leave many open questions about how best to help students achieve them. This chapter, therefore, demonstrates how structured SELf-questioning can act as a guide in helping students meet NGSS's expectations and CCSS's connections to them.

One way this chapter will be different from what you've read so far is that it goes deeper into the components of metacognition. We want to support science teachers in gaining a better understanding of not only what these metacognitive components are but also how they are represented in each step of our problem-solving process. Our decision to dive deeper into these components is based on the findings of education scholars Shirly Avargil, Rea Lavi, and Yehudit Judy Dori (2018), who extensively review the literature on the connection between metacognition, metacognitive strategies, and science education:

> We recommend teachers engage in explicit teaching of the different components [of metacognition] from the theoretical metacognitive construct viewpoint. This would require prior training of teachers in the knowledge and practice of metacognitive learning. They would be able to enhance their teaching strategies using different components of metacognition, while students will better understand their different meanings. Metacognition needs to be intertwined with learning science core ideas and scientific practices as an integral part of science education." (p. 59)

With this recommendation in mind, this chapter builds the case for the importance of teaching metacognition in science by defining the components and subcomponents of metacognition. This chapter's how-to-teach section provides a detailed example that pulls together the use of SELf-questioning to integrate the components of metacognition into instruction aligned with NGSS. With this knowledge, science teachers will be better equipped to make these components explicit to their students and show them explicitly how each step in our process aligns metacognition with core scientific ideas and practices. You will see from our grade-band scenarios how we align use of our metacognitive strategy with both NGSS and CCSS. Finally, we close this chapter with a look at how using our strategy in the sciences helps further students' ability to adapt to new learning and experiences.

The Importance of Teaching Metacognition in the Sciences

Metacognition is an essential component in the development of scientific literacy and the understanding of the concepts inherent in any scientific curriculum (Avargil et al., 2018). Any student, even the very young, can learn metacognitive techniques to develop scientific literacy and understanding of scientific concepts. At the same time, many science teachers do not know quite how to teach metacognition, and many others don't attempt to teach it to elementary-level students (Zohar & Barzilai, 2013).

Up to this point, we have broadly defined metacognition as awareness and management of one's thinking, and we have shown how structured SELf-questioning is designed to help students improve their metacognition. To build on this understanding, let's dig a little deeper into the components of metacognition and see how they align within the sciences.

Many researchers consider metacognition a fuzzy concept, and there has been a push in various fields to define it more specifically (Scott & Levy, 2013). Researchers within the sciences, like researchers in other fields, often break metacognition into two distinct parts: (1) metacognitive knowledge and (2) metacognitive regulation. *Metacognitive knowledge*, which constitutes knowledge about cognition (Avargil et al., 2018), further breaks down into three subcomponents.

1. **Knowledge about people:** This boils down to having knowledge of one's own and other's cognitive processes, although, for our purposes, this subcomponent focuses on the knowledge perceptions students have of themselves as learners. For example, a high school student asked to build a computation model might wonder, "What are my strengths and weaknesses when it comes to building models?"

2. **Knowledge about tasks:** This knowledge includes a student's perception of what a task entails, such as whether it will be difficult or easy or whether the time allowed for it is sufficient. For example, a student reflecting on his or her task knowledge might ask, "Do I have any background knowledge about building models?" Or, "Have I ever built a model before in another context?"

3. **Knowledge about strategies:** This knowledge includes all the strategies at a student's disposal as he or she endeavors to complete the task. For example, a student accessing knowledge of a strategy might ask, "What strategies do I know that could help me build a model?"

Avargil and colleages (2018) also break down the research about metacognitive *regulation*—regulation of one's thinking and learning—into subcomponents, the key parts of which include the following.

1. **Planning:** This occurs before a student completes a task and includes recognizing and defining a problem as well as choosing an appropriate strategy to solve it. Students involved in planning might ask themselves, "What is the problem?"

2. **Monitoring:** This occurs during the learning process and involves a student's perception of his or her own success or failure when thinking about and working on a problem. For example, students monitoring their thinking might ask, "Is this model working?"

3. **Evaluating:** This occurs after the learning process is complete and involves a student's assessment of his or her completed work. A student engaged in evaluation might ask, "Did my model work?"

We present these lists of subcomponents as a starting place for educators to begin a process of defining metacognitive components more clearly for themselves and their students in the context of a science curriculum. Table 11.1 more clearly shows how each maps onto our academic and social SELf-question set. Our goal is not to definitively place these components into categories, nor is it to suggest that these components work in isolation; instead, by suggesting a relationship between a metacognitive component or subcomponent and a step in the SELf-questioning process, we hope to offer teachers the opportunity to become more explicit with their students about the various aspects of metacognition.

Table 11.1: Mapping the Components of Metacognition to SELf-Questioning

Structured SELf-Question Set for the Sciences	Metacognitive Component or Subcomponent
Select a focus: What is the problem? What is the question? What is the task?	Metacognitive knowledge: Knowledge about people and tasks Metacognitive regulation: Planning
Gather information: What do I know? What do I need to know? What is similar, and what is different?	Metacognitive knowledge: Knowledge about all subcomponents
Brainstorm: How can I solve this problem? What are the possible solutions? What can I do?	Metacognitive knowledge: Knowledge about strategies Metacognitive regulation: Planning
Evaluate: What is the best way to solve this problem? Does this make sense?	Metacognitive knowledge: Knowledge about strategies Metacognitive regulation: Planning and monitoring
Plan and act: What do I do first, second, and so on? Is this working?	Metacognitive regulation: Monitoring
Reflect: Did it work? How do I know? Do I need to go back and try again?	Metacognitive regulation: Evaluating

As table 11.1 demonstrates, whenever students work through our SELf-question set to solve a problem or complete a task, they use various metacognitive components and subcomponents, beginning with metacognitive planning and knowledge and ending with evaluation. Science educators have a golden opportunity to recognize the metacognitive components that align with each question in our problem-solving process so they can be explicit with students about how these components can help them learn scientific content and scientific practices.

How to Teach SELf-Questioning to Integrate the Components of Metacognition into NGSS Instruction

Teaching science offers educators countless opportunities to engage learners' curiosities about the world. However, science education often fails to realize its potential. On the science portion of the 2015 PISA (Desilver, 2017), for example, the United States lagged behind twenty-three other countries. NGSS is an attempt to address these problems and tap the full potential of science education. Although we fully support this effort, we argue for the explicit integration of metacognition into the sciences as well, specifically through the use of structured SELf-questioning. Let's take a closer look at how teacher might effect this.

One of the NGSS performance expectations for high school students reads: "Analyze a major global challenge to specify qualitative and quantitative criteria and constraints for solutions that account for societal needs and wants" (HS-ETS1-1; NGSS Lead States, 2013). According to NGSS Lead States (2013), this performance expectation connects with the science and engineering practice of *asking questions and defining problems*, the core idea of *defining and delimiting engineering problems*, and the crosscutting concept of the *influence of science, engineering, and technology on society and the natural world*. It also overlaps with several standards in the literacy and mathematics CCSS, including "Synthesize information from a range of sources (e.g., texts, experiments, simulations) into a coherent understanding of a process, phenomenon, or concept, resolving conflicting information when possible" (RST.11-12.9; NGA & CCSSO, 2010a).

To achieve both the NGSS performance expectation and the literacy CCSS, let's imagine that an instructor, Ms. M., assigns her eleventh-grade class the task of writing a review of the literature about potential solutions to some aspect of the global climate crisis, such as air pollution, rising temperatures, rising sea levels, or migration. Let's also imagine that students have already read some popular and academic sources that have proposed some solutions, and now they are charged with developing a research question for the project. Collectively, they might use the following SELf-question set.

 Select a focus: What is the problem? What is the question? What is the task?

 Gather information: What do I know? What do I need to know? What is similar? What is different?

 Brainstorm: How can I solve this problem or complete this task?

 Evaluate: What is the best way to solve this problem? Does this make sense?

 Plan and Act: What do I do first, second, and so on? Is this working?

 Reflect: Did it work? How do I know? Do I need to go back and try again?

To begin the lesson, Ms. M. asks the first question to *select a focus*, "What is our task?" She answers that question herself by saying, "Today, our task is to draft a research question." She also adds that, by defining and understanding the task, students are using two different types of metacognitive awareness: knowledge and planning. For example:

When thinking about creating a research question for our projects and what that might entail, we are already being metacognitive. And as we know, the more metacognitive we can be, the more likely we are to succeed at this task. So, I want you to begin by thinking about what it means to create a research question for this project. This is a part of metacognitive regulation called planning. Part of our planning may be that you have questions about the assignment. If you do, you can ask them now, or you can write them down, and I'd be happy to try and answer them at a later time. I also want you to think about how difficult or easy you think this is going to be and why. This will help you access your knowledge about yourself before you begin. In other words, based on what you know about yourself, do you think writing a research question will be easy? Why or why not?

Once the students understand the task, Ms. M can move into the second step of the SELf-questioning process, *gather information.* She continues by using research to help support the importance of gathering information—in this case, research by Paul R. Pintrich (2002)—before assigning students a task:

When we gather information about what we know and don't know or look at how the task is similar or different to things we have done before, we are also using our metacognitive knowledge. Researchers, like Paul R. Pintrich, have found that this can help us learn and might help us make better choices. So, let's answer some questions in pairs. You may notice that some of these questions come from step 2 of our problem-solving process, gather information. Get together with your partner and answer the questions I've posted to our smartboard.

1. *What do we know about research questions? Why do scientists and engineers ask or write research questions? (Metacognitive subcomponent: knowledge of people and task)*

2. *Have you ever written a research question before? If so, how do you think this will be similar to that experience? How do you think it will be different? If you haven't written a research question before, how might this be similar or different from other writing assignments you've had in science class? (Metacognitive subcomponent: knowledge of task)*

3. *What information do you already have that might help you write a research question? What information do you still need? (Metacognitive subcomponents: knowledge of task and strategy)*

After students work in pairs to generate answers to the questions, Ms. M. brings the whole class back together, eliciting responses from a few individuals and filling in gaps where necessary. She points out that research questions are often open-ended, but they are also manageable and debatable. She also clarifies that, for the assignment, students will bring together (synthesize) several scholarly resources as they try to answer their questions and offer solutions to a specific problem within the global climate crisis.

Once the class has thoroughly accessed their prior knowledge concerning research questions, Ms. M. can move the class to step three, *brainstorming*. She asks the next question in the problem-solving process, "How might I complete this task? What are some possible ways?" Students think about some strategies they have in mind for how to draft a research question that offers solutions to a problem within the global climate crisis. While eliciting student strategies, Ms. M. offers some of her own:

> *You've already come up with a narrower idea under the broad topic of the global climate crisis, and you've already asked ten questions about that topic. Some of you have questions about rising sea levels and some about mosquito-borne diseases. So, one of my strategies is to use those questions to draft a research question.*

> *What do I mean by use? Well, we could take two of our most interesting questions and try to combine them. As we take a look at the sample questions I provided, look for important ideas, and try to also combine them. Let's remember that we are regulating our thinking in this step. Again, we are planning the best way to tackle this challenge.*

Once Ms. M. elicits strategies from the class and provides one or two of her own, she lets the students try it on, guiding them to the next step in the process, *evaluation*. She says, "So, what is the best way to complete this task? You and your partner will need to decide."

Ms. M. then lets students work together for about ten minutes. At the end of the time, she says:

> *Now that you've decided the best strategy, you can move to the next step of our problem-solving process, planning and acting. As you do, ask yourself, "What will I do first, second, and so on?" And, while you're writing your research question, I'd like you to monitor your thinking along the way. Ask yourself how it's going. Ask yourself why you are making a particular choice, such as including an idea in your research question.*

After the students write their research questions, Ms. M. asks for a written reflection on the process students used. Using the questions in the science SELf-question set—Did it work? How do I know? Do I need to go back and try again?—she also revises the specific wording of these questions to further assess students' metacognition. For example, because she wants to focus on metacognitive knowledge, particularly how previous experiences with research questions impact a student's choices in this context, she asks students, "Did any strategies that you used when creating a research question for a different project work here? Please explain how they did or did not."

According to researchers Marcel V. J. Veenman, Bernadette H. A. M. van Hout-Wolters, and Peter Afflerbach (2006):

> Three fundamental principles are known from the literature for successful meta-cognitive instruction: a) embedding metacognitive instruction in the content matter to ensure connectivity, b) informing learners about the usefulness of meta-cognitive activities to make them exert the initial extra effort, and c) prolonged training to guarantee the smooth and maintained application of metacogni-tive activity. (p. 9)

In the context of this section's example, our hypothetical instructor is using academic SELf-questions to both teach a standard from NGSS while at the same time covering two of the three fundamental principles of successful metacognitive instruction. For the moment, think of these three principles as *embedding* (*a*), *informing* (*b*), and *training* (*c*). This example covered embedding and informing, but we advise teachers not to stop there. Use the SELf-questioning problem-solving process to ensure that you cover training throughout a semester or school year. While doing so, be explicit about each metacognitive step. For example, in one assignment, you could focus on the importance of planning; in another, the importance of evaluating; and so on until the students have gained an understanding of all the components and how they appear in each step of the problem-solving process. This way, teachers are less overwhelmed and don't feel the need to teach all the components and subcomponents of metacognition or have students thoroughly understand the importance of each problem-solving step in one lesson. Instead, just like teaching the SELf-question set steps, teachers can scaffold the components and subcomponents throughout a unit, semester, and year.

Now, let's take a look at some other specific grade-band scenarios that illustrate how teachers can use the academic SELf-question set in the science classroom.

Scenario: Grades K–2

Class: First-grade classroom (Mr. L.; teacher)

Objective:

- Determine what is needed to see a picture in the dark.

Standards:

- Make observations to construct an evidence-based account that objects in darkness can be seen only when illuminated. (1-PS4-2; NGSS Lead States, 2013)
  - Science and engineering practice—constructing explanations and designing solutions

continued ▶

> ◆ Disciplinary core idea—electromagnetic radiation
>
> ◆ Crosscutting concept—cause and effect
>
> • With guidance and support from adults, recall information from experiences or gather information from provided sources to answer a question. (W.1.8; NGA & CCSSO, 2010a)

Imagine that a first-grade science class in the middle of a unit on light and sound waves is presented with a shoebox. Inside the shoebox, a photograph of an apple is taped to one side. On the opposite end of the box is a hole. Mr. L. asks students to come up to the box, look in the hole, and report what they see.

The following sections explain how he uses SELf-questioning with the class. Note that Mr. L. talks about metacognition throughout and differentiates between metacognitive knowledge and metacognitive regulation (planning, monitoring, and evaluating) in an age-appropriate way. For example, although he has discussed the word *metacognition* with his class before, he prefers to use phrases like *awareness of our own thinking*. For the components and subcomponents, he uses *knowledge*, *planning*, *monitoring*, and *evaluating* with the idea that this is not the first time students will hear these terms, nor will it be the last.

SELECT A FOCUS

Questions: What is the problem? What is the question? What is the task?

Mr. L. begins by saying:

Today we are going to try to answer the question, What does it take for us to be able to see something? I'd like you to notice that before we get started on answering a question or solving any problem, it's a good idea to say what the question or problem is. This is a type of planning, as you've heard me say before. Now, as we try to answer this question, we're going to use both what we think we know about seeing and a little experiment with this shoebox. Inside this shoebox is a picture. I'd like you to come up in pairs and take a look inside. What do you see?

Student responses range from "Nothing" to "Black" to "It's all dark."

He continues, as he looks for opportunities to use age-appropriate language to indicate the components and subcomponents of metacognition:

Right. It's all dark. Before we get started on the shoebox experiment, let's think a little bit about what we know about seeing. Remember, whenever we try to answer a question or solve a problem, we always want to think about the knowledge we already have that could help us. If we think about these things, we'll have a better chance of success.

GATHER INFORMATION

Questions: What do I know? What do I need to know? What is similar, and what is different?

With a focus established, Mr. L. shifts toward teaching students how to gather information:

> So, What do we know so far? We know that it's dark and that we can't see the picture on the back of the box. What else do we know? We know we need to find a way to see it. But before we hear your ideas about what we should do so that we can see the picture, ask yourself, Is this experiment similar to anything you've done before? For example, are there any times at home when you can't see something that you want to see? Before you answer, I'd like you to notice that asking this question is another way that we can demonstrate awareness of our own thinking. This time, we're remembering what we know about other experiences to see if they can help us here.
>
> OK, so what do you think? Have you done something like this before?

Students begin to offer answers. One student says, "Yes, when it's dark, or when the lights are out." Mr. L. answers, "Right. So, when it's dark at night, what do you do if you want to see?"

Again students begin to think about answers, and one says, "Turn on the lights," while another offers, "Use a flashlight." Mr. L. replies, "These are good ideas. Now let's think about how this situation is different. Are there lights in this shoebox that we could turn on?" The students acknowledge there are not.

BRAINSTORM

Question: How can I solve this problem or complete this task?

Mr. L. continues, "Right. So now that we've thought about what we already know, how could we solve this problem? How could we make it so we could see what's in the box? Would a flashlight work here?" A student affirms that it could, and Mr. L. asks how. The student answers, "We could shine it in the hole." Mr. L. answers, "Nice. As we brainstorm some different strategies, we're planning again. I like it!"

Mr. L. pushes them to think of other options: "What else could we do so that we could be able to see the picture?" A student suggests taking off the lid. When Mr. L. answers, "What else?" another student notes they could cut holes in the top. At this point, there are a variety of approaches they could take.

EVALUATE

Questions: What is the best way to solve this problem? Does this make sense?

Mr. L. says, "OK, I think we have some good suggestions about how to see the picture. We have the flashlight idea, taking the lid off, or cutting holes. Which one do you think is the best? Let's take a vote."

Ultimately, the class decides that cutting holes in the top of the box is the best way to see the picture. Students reach this conclusion after a discussion reveals that there isn't a flashlight in the classroom and because taking the lid off would be, in the words of one student, "cheating." Mr. L. praises the class for this discussion and explains that what they're doing as they decide the best strategy is called "monitoring their thinking." "In other words," he adds, "as you choose the best strategy, you're taking the time to look at why each strategy may or may not work."

PLAN AND ACT

Questions: What do I do first? Second? Is this working?

Mr. L. cuts two holes in the top of the box and invites students to come up and take a look through the view hole again. He gives them a moment to consider what they see before continuing. "Let's monitor our thinking again," he says. "Is it working?" The two students looking into the box answer, "Yes!"

REFLECT

Questions: Did it work? How do I know? Do I need to go back and try again?

After every student has had a chace to look in the shoebox, they return to their seats. Mr. L. says, "Now, let's evaluate our thinking. This is really important to do after we complete something, so we can make sure we've understood, or we might notice if we still have a question or a problem to solve." He asks, "Did it work? Could we see the picture?"

The students agree that they could, but Mr. L. asks some questions to further their thinking. He says, "Great! What is it a picture of?" The students respond that they saw an apple, so he then asks, "So, why were we able to see it all of a sudden when we couldn't before?" The students reply that it's because they cut holes in the box. To confirm students understand the connections, he finally asks, "Yes, and what did the holes allow to come in?" The students correctly answer, "Light."

As a way of wrapping up this lesson and making sure students meet the standards, a teacher might ask students to engage in an additional task, such as drawing a picture of the experiment they conducted and then answer a question, such as, What do you need to be able to see the apple?

You may have noticed in this scenario that Mr. L. tries to accomplish at least two goals at once. He'd like his students to meet NGSS standard 1-PS4-2, and he'd like them to learn about metacognition as they use structured SELf-questioning. He knows that these goals in tandem will entail slowing his lesson down a little as he becomes as explicit as possible with his students about the type of metacognition they are engaged in. But he believes his deliberateness is worth it; if done throughout the school year, it will set his students up for success in the present while also preparing them for deeper metacognitive instruction in the upper grades.

Scenario: Grades 3–5

Class: Fifth-grade classroom (Mr. K.; teacher)

Objective:

- Use a computer application (Bloxels) to create a game that demonstrates how the energy in plants and animals derives from the sun.

Standards:

- Use models to describe that energy in animals' food (used for body repair, growth, and motion, and to maintain body warmth) was once energy from the sun. (5-PS3-1; NGSS Lead States, 2013)

  - Science and engineering practice—developing and using models

  - Disciplinary core idea—energy in chemical processes and everyday life; interdependent relationships in ecosystems

  - Crosscutting concept—energy and matter

- Include multimedia components (e.g., graphics, sound) and visual displays in presentations when appropriate to enhance the development of main ideas or themes. (SL.5.5; NGA & CCSSO, 2010a)

Mr. K.'s class has already spent a few weeks learning about the food chain and the interconnectedness of ecosystems. He introduces this unit with a video called "Why Would a Hawk Move to New York City?" (Mystery Science, n.d.). After watching the video, students gather in small-group teams to play a food chain card game that helps them begin to understand relationships between predators and prey. Beyond terms directly related to this topic, Mr. K. introduces students to other terms such as *producer, consumer, herbivore, carnivore,* and *decomposer.* Next, Mr. K. tells the students that they will use a computer application called Bloxels to create a game that demonstrates how the energy in plants and animals derives from the sun. In terms of metacognition, he wants to focus students on metacognitive regulation, specifically the subcomponent of planning.

SELECT A FOCUS

Questions: What is the problem? What is the question? What is the task?

To begin the lesson, Mr. K. says:

Let's begin this activity the way we begin all of our class assignments—with some metacognitive questions. As you know, asking ourselves these questions can help us understand the ideas that we are learning more thoroughly. First, we want to focus on understanding the assignment. Remember, when we focus on understanding the assignment, we're regulating our thinking. This type of regulation is called planning.

As Mr. K. explains this type of metacognitive regulation, he uses a chart he's hung in the classroom that has both the steps of structured SELf-questioning and the metacognitive components and subcomponents that align with each step. He continues, "So, let me first ask you, What is the task? What are we trying to do with our game? At your tables, get together and talk about this for a minute or two."

After student teams discuss their thoughts, Mr. K. brings the whole class back together and elicits some responses from each group table. One student says that they are trying to build a game with Bloxels. Although this is accurate, it shows only a surface-level understanding of the task; so, Mr. K. follows this up by asking, "What do we want this game to show that we understand?" Another student answers, "Relationships between animals," while another adds, "Relationships between the sun and living things."

Mr. K. acknowledges these answers and further clarifies, "To tap into our metacognitive knowledge about this task, let's ask ourselves, "Do you think creating this game will be easy or hard? What will be hard about it? What will be easy?"

Some of the students' answers include the following.

- "This game will be easy because I love to play video games."

- "Easy, because I like to create characters on the computer."

- "Hard, because it might not look the same on the computer as when I drew it."

- "It will be hard, because it might not work."

- "Hard, because I don't know what I want my game to be like."

GATHER INFORMATION

Questions: What do I know? What do I need to know? What is similar, and what is different?

For the next step in the problem-solving process, Mr. K. asks students to answer questions at their group tables. He moves between the tables and solicits answers from students as they work.

- "What do we know about how energy from the sun becomes energy for animals?" A student answers, "We know that plants get energy from the sun."

- "What examples can we think of that show how energy is transferred from the sun to producers to herbivores or omnivores?" A student answers, "Energy goes from the sun to an oak tree, to an acorn, to a squirrel."

- "What other information do we need to know to make our game?" A student answers, "We need to figure out which organism will be our main character. We need to know how we will show the relationship in the game."

- "How is making this game similar to other things we have done in this class?" A student answers, "We created a game in Bloxel before. We designed a game where we explored a particular planet that we had researched."

- "How is making this game different from other things we have done in class?" A student answers, "Our game was about space. This is about animals and takes place on earth."

BRAINSTORM

Questions: How can I solve this problem or complete this task?

Mr. K. recognizes that, although many students seem to understand that the energy organisms use was once the sun's, they are struggling with how to represent that relationship in their game. So, for the third step in the problem-solving process, he focuses the class on this specific challenge. He asks them to think of as many strategies as they can for depicting that relationship. He says:

> *As you know from using this problem-solving process in the past, planning is an important step. At the beginning of class, we used planning to understand the larger task. But now planning can help us in another way—we can use planning to define the specific problem we're facing. In this case, many of us are not sure how to build our game to show that the energy organisms use comes from the sun. As we try to solve this problem, let's brainstorm all the possible options. At your tables, you will use the thirteen-by-thirteen grid planning sheet to draw and design your game.*

As students work through this activity, Mr. K. walks around and talks with students about their ideas. It's important to remember that Mr. K.'s goal is to model metacognitive problem solving but not to provide answers for the students. He doesn't want everyone's game to look the same or like a game he would design.

As he wraps up this step of the problem-solving process, he reminds students that what they've been doing is once again regulating their thinking with planning. He tells them that they've now used planning for the first three steps of the problem-solving process and that planning is one of the many tools they can use when they encounter a task or a problem in science.

EVALUATE

Questions: What is the best way to solve this problem or complete this task? Does this make sense?

Once students brainstorm and share ideas at their tables, Mr. K. instructs each student to choose a strategy that will work best. He asks, "As an individual, which idea about how to represent energy transfer do you like the best?" For example, we'll focus on one student, Anna, who chooses the black bear as her main character. She decides the black bear will wander around a forest on a sunny day looking for berries to eat.

PLAN AND ACT

Questions: What do I do first, second, and so on? Is this working?

Mr. K. continues:

Now that you've picked a food chain that makes sense, you can start to design the characters and the game using your grid planning sheet. Then you can create your game using your tablets. Before you do, think for a moment and ask yourself, What will you do first? Second? As you are working, please monitor the choices you make along the way. Remember, you can always press the Test button as you're creating the game to see how your characters work or how the game plays.

Anna starts by creating her chosen environment, the forest. Using the planning sheet, she draws trees, grass, and the sun. Next, she adds the bear on the left and a few berry bushes on the right.

REFLECT

Questions: Did it work? How do I know? Do I need to go back and try again?

Mr. K. concludes this portion of the unit with a peer review in which students review each other's grid planning sheets and fill out a rubric in which they evaluate each other's work. Mr. K.'s rubric directs them to answer the following questions.

1. Does your peer's game show the relationship between the sun and the other characters?

2. How do you know?

This scenario demonstrates how Mr. K. has used the social and academic question set in science to guide students through one part of a unit on the food chain. Along the way, he also explicitly reminded students why they are using SELf-questioning and how some of the SELf-questions align with the practice of metacognitive planning. As students finish their peer reviews and begin to work within Bloxels, other tasks, questions, and problems will inevitably arise. When they do, Mr. K. can use the question sets again from the beginning to help students work through the assignment. As they do, he can remind them about the various ways they are using planning to regulate their thinking.

Scenario: Grades 6–8

Class: Sixth-grade STEM class (Ms. D.; teacher)

Objective:

- Design a model that identifies the most earthquake-resistant foundation.

Standards:

- Develop a model to describe the cycling of Earth's materials and the flow of energy that drives this process. (MS-ESS2-1; NGSS Lead States, 2013)
  - Science and engineering practice—developing and using models
  - Disciplinary core idea—Earth's materials and systems
  - Crosscutting concept—stability and change

- Integrate multimedia and visual displays into presentations to clarify information, strengthen claims and evidence, and add interest. (SL.8.5; NGA & CCSSO, 2010a)

- Conduct short research projects to answer a question (including a self-generated question), drawing on several sources and generating additional related, focused questions that allow for multiple avenues of exploration. (WHST.6-8.7; NGSS Lead States, 2013)

Some communities located in areas where earthquakes frequently occur need to plan and prepare for potential disaster. For this experiment, Ms. D. tasks student groups with researching, planning, and creating an earthquake-resistant house. Ms. D. provides each group of students with three different foundations they could use to create their structure: (1) sand, (2) plaster, and (3) sand mixed with glue. The goal is for students to build the highest earthquake-resistant structure they can place atop the foundation of their choice, utilizing a limited number of toothpicks and marshmallows. Ms. D. also provides students with a documentation log for the experiment, which you can see in figure 11.2 (page 188). Note that the original iteration of this log came from science teachers at both Edgar Middle School and Metuchen High School, with guidance from the district science supervisor Kathleen Henn. We've adjusted the original log to align with metacognitive components and SELf-questions, as we find that using a log such as this is useful for engaging students in independent practice. At the same time, this log is supplemental to other direct instruction and discussion pertaining to the components and subcomponents of metacognition.

Unlike the previous scenarios in this chapter, which focus on how teachers guide students through the questioning process, in this scenario, Ms. D. chooses to challenge her students to work through the entire process without instruction or prompting. Therefore, the following sections in the SELf-question set each list a written student response derived from the documentation logs they used to guide their collaborative work through the scientific problem-solving process.

SELECT A FOCUS

Questions: What is the problem? What is the question? What is the task?

The following are some sample student responses to the focus questions.

- How do we create a house that can successfully withstand earthquakes?

- Can small houses survive an earthquake?

- Can I create a house that will be able to withstand most earthquakes?

After the students write their answers to this first step, Ms. D. asks a few students to read their answers aloud. This way, she is able to verify that student groups understand the question or task before students begin to conduct research on building earthquake resistant structures.

Name: _____

Lab partners: _____

Graphic	Steps	Date	Log
	1. Select a focus. Make sure you understand the situation and clarify the specific problem. When you do so, you are using both your metacognitive knowledge and metacognitive regulation.		What are we trying to do or find out? What problem are we trying to solve?
	2. Gather information. As you gather information, you are using your metacognitive knowledge about yourself, about the task or problem you are facing, and possibly your knowledge about strategy.		What information is important? What do we already know What is similar or different? (Include sources.)
	3. Brainstorm (for ideas). Generate lots of ideas using your creativity. Not all of your ideas will work, and that's OK. Here, you are just getting your ideas down. Note that as you do, you're using both your metacognitive knowledge about strategy and your regulation of your thinking by planning. So, you're using both components of metacognition at the same time.		How can we solve this problem or complete this task? What are the pros and cons of each idea?
	4. Evaluate (make a choice). As you answer these questions, you're using your knowledge about strategies in general while you engage in planning which one will work best in this situation.		Which is the best option? Why have we chosen this one?
	5. Plan and act (and observe). In this step, you're adding monitoring to the other types of metacognition that you've already engaged in. You're monitoring your own thinking processes as you carry out your plan. You're deciding whether or not your plan is working.		What steps will we take? Is it working? How do we know?
	6. Reflect. If it worked, great! Think of ways to improve it further. If it did not work, that's great too! Brainstorm again and pick another solution. In this step, we're regulating our thinking again. The difference is that this time we're doing so after the process is complete. Notice how we both monitor our thinking while we're carrying out our plan. When we're finished, we evaluate and reflect on what we've done.		What worked well or didn't work? Do we need to go back and try again? What might we do differently?

Figure 11.2: Path to problem solving documentation log.

*Visit **go.SolutionTree.com/instruction** for a free reproducible version of this figure.*

GATHER INFORMATION

Questions: What do I know? What information is important? What is similar, and what is different?

The following are some sample student responses to the gather-information questions.

- Important characteristics of an earthquake-resistant house are good soil quality, a strong foundation, proper building height, suitable distribution of the load over the foundation, structural design, and quality building materials.

- Earthquake proof houses are built to support vertical weight. Houses fall over because earthquakes move side to side, so people build pillars into the ground for stability.

- The Writers Hive [source identified by students] lists important characteristics of earthquake-resistant houses, including good soil, a strong foundation, proper height, suitable distribution of load over the foundation, structural design, and quality building materials.

Having students conduct research toward the question prior to building their models was a choice Ms. D. made since students had very limited background knowledge when they began. If students were to ask themselves what they know about designing earthquake-resistant structures prior to conducting research, the written responses here would have been very limited. In situations when students have more background knowledge or more experience with metacognition and structured SELf questioning, less or no research may be needed for this step. As a result of conducting some research, all students have information they can utilize for their model designs in the brainstorming step.

BRAINSTORM

Question: How can I solve this problem?

The following are some sample student responses to the brainstorm questions.

- Use underground pillars, a raised foundation, dampeners with beams, and braces for the building.

- Use a box or triangle shaped structure, make walls thick so they are braced and can withstand shaking, and make the building tall enough to flow with the movement.

- From our research, we decided to do an Eifel Tower design, a strong base with walls that are diagonal from the top to the ground like a pyramid.

EVALUATE

Questions: What is the best way to solve this problem? Does this make sense?

The following are some sample student responses to the evaluate questions.

- Use underground pillars.

- Use raised foundations.

- Use dampeners with beams.

- Use braces for the buildings.

PLAN AND ACT

Questions: What do I do first, second, and so on? Is this working?

The following are some sample student responses to the plan and act questions.

- We put our ideas together after having done a lot of research, careful planning, and choosing specific ideas that we knew would help our structure. We just followed our plan.

- The reason we spent so much time choosing what shape we would use was so we could hopefully stick with our plan and that our plan would work.

- We didn't have an idea because we couldn't think of anything that would work. When we started to think, we wanted to just build the sticks straight up with marshmallows. It didn't work.

Here we can see a wide range of performance. By having students write about their process and submit these logs at the end of the lesson, Ms. D. is able to identify students or student groups who are struggling with various steps in the problem-solving process. This enables her to immediately intervene and model as needed. As she does, she offers further details about the metacognitive components involved and the reasons they're important to understand. For example, for the third group of students in this plan and act list, she might offer some positive feedback about the fact that they realized their strategy wasn't working. She could say, "I like that you monitored your thinking here by documenting what didn't work. Believe it or not, this is an important step. When this happens to me, I usually like to go back a step or two and see if I can't brainstorm some more ideas."

REFLECT

Questions: Did it work? How do I know? Do I need to go back and try again?

The following are some sample student responses to the reflect questions.

- Our project worked really well. When we shook it on the earthquake table, the only thing that fell was the one toothpick on top, and that was only because we shook it really hard.

- The only thing I feel we could've improved on was preventing the structure from leaning. Maybe if we balanced and distributed the weight better, we could've avoided it leaning the way it did.

- This taught us that a lot of careful research and planning will pay off in our final project!

- Our group first started out with our original plan, making the structure very sturdy and tall so it could reach the height requirement (one foot). That didn't work because we used all of the toothpicks at the bottom to make it sturdy, but then we didn't have enough toothpicks to meet the height requirement. Then the same thing happened multiple times after the original try, but with marshmallows. We didn't have enough marshmallows to meet the height requirement, so we tried to mush the marshmallows together to make a marshmallow glue that would make it sturdy. This actually made it fall because the marshmallow mush hadn't dried. After those failed tries, we tried again by making it sturdy at the bottom while having enough toothpicks and marshmallows for the top, and it worked! Even though it twisted a little, the structure stood on its own.

These responses demonstrate how, after teacher modeling early in the year and consistent use of SELf-questions, students now have more to write in their conclusions and do a great deal more reflection. Typical labs without explicit instruction on metacognitive components and practice with problem solving are often limited to student conclusions about the outcomes. However, here you can see that students are not only making scientific conclusions about content (how structures withstand earthquakes), but also how students are drawing conclusions about their own metacognition: reflecting on their inquiry process, recognizing the need for adaptive thinking, and building knowledge collaboratively.

Scenario: Grades 9–12

Class: Tenth-grade chemistry class (Ms. L.; teacher)

Objective:

- Determine the melting and boiling points of various elements.

Standards:

- HS-PS1-3: Plan and conduct an investigation to gather evidence to compare the structure of substances at the bulk scale to infer the strength of electrical forces between particles. (HS-PS1-3; NGSS Lead States, 2013)

  - Science and engineering practice—planning and carrying out investigations

  - Disciplinary core idea—structure and properties of matter

  - Crosscutting concept—patterns

- WHST.9-12.9: Draw evidence from informational texts to support analysis, reflection, and research. (WHST.9-12.9; NGA & CCSSO, 2010a)

Using the NGSS Lead States (2013) standard HS-PS1-3, students select five elements within a group to research each element's bulk properties. Prior to this exercise, the students are generally unfamiliar with the elements; however, Ms. L. asks students to group the elements based on trends from data they notice during their research and to justify their reasoning for their groupings.

To help students set their focus and engage in the SELf-question set, Ms. L. provides students with a documentation log, similar to the one we described for this chapter's grades 6–8 scenario (refer to figure 11.1, page 172). Also similar to the grades 6–8 scenario, the following sections focus on select students' written answers to the SELf-questions. We'd like to note here that this lesson occurs toward the beginning of the year in a college-preparatory science course. Ms. L. understands her students may not have an affinity for science and that they may not expect to enjoy the class. For these reasons, she gets them to engage in scientific inquiry using a relatively straightforward and solvable problem. Although this may seem overly simple for high school students, this lesson serves as a jumping-off point to more complex problem solving. The key is that the students have engaged in inquiry using the steps and questions, and they've begun to notice some of the specific ways their metacognition is functioning as they work.

SELECT A FOCUS

Questions: What is the problem? What is the question? What is the task?

The following are some sample student responses to the focus questions.

- We are trying to find trends within the properties.
- Finding trends and patterns.

Note that students are using the word *trend* in this step and in some other student writing you will see in this scenario to refer to commonalities among the elements. Notice from these responses that the students are engaging in the metacognitive subcomponent of regulation (more specifically, planning) as they define the task. Ms. L. can provide further instruction on the subcomponent *knowledge of task* by asking students verbally whether they think the task will be easy or hard and why.

GATHER INFORMATION

Questions: What do I know? What information is important? What is similar, and what is different?

The following are some sample student responses (after conducting research) to the gather information questions.

- We discovered several trends within the different substances.
- We found similarities between the melting points.
- We found similarities between boiling points.
- We found similarities between atomic masses.

BRAINSTORM

Questions: How can I solve this problem?

The following are some sample student responses brainstorming what they could gather data about.

- Melting points
- Boiling points
- Atomic mass points
- Density

- Thermal conductivity
- Properties (metal versus nonmetal)

EVALUATE

Questions: What is the best way to solve this problem? Does this make sense?

The following are some sample student responses to evaluate questions.

- Determine melting and boiling points to find trends because there will be more consistency between those two points.
- Determine atomic mass, because it is fast and organized.
- Determine average atomic mass points.

Here, as students evaluate their options for grouping the elements, they're engaging in the two components of metacognition: (1) knowledge about strategy and (2) planning. In other words, they're accessing their general strategic knowledge concerned with grouping based on similarities while simultaneously planning the strategy that will work best for this particular task.

PLAN AND ACT

Questions: What do I do first? Second? Is this working?

The following are some sample student responses to plan and act questions after conducting multiple tests.

- We went to a website for the periodic table.
- We categorized the metals by specific properties.
- We made a bar graph of the information.

REFLECT

Questions: Did it work? How do I know? Do I need to go back and try again?

The following are some sample student responses to reflect questions.

- Organizing the data by melting and boiling point was the most efficient and simple way to sort every substance.
- Excluding hydrogen worked. Before doing this, we found no pattern.
- Organizing the elements by their physical properties alone didn't work, so we added boiling points and melting points to the way we organized the data.

Although the documentation log does remind students about the metacognitive components and subcomponents the students are engaging in throughout the problem-solving process, after further practice, Ms. L. enhances the development of the metacognitive components here by gradually removing explanations of the metacognitive components from the log. Instead, she provides students with the definitions of these components on a separate sheet of paper. On the log, teachers ask students to identify, in writing, the type of metacognition they are engaging in during or after each step. For example, in step one, as each student selects a focus and responds to a question such as "What is the task?" a follow-up question might read, "What type of metacognition did you use when answering this question? Please explain." This extra self-reflective measure helps students take a step back to engage in inquiry, accelerates their learning about the metacognitive components, and provides a quality assessment of student learning of these components.

Character Corner: Adaptivity

Given the increasing rate at which the world is changing, teachers need to develop students' ability to think adaptively to new and different situations. Adi Ben-David and Anat Zohar (2008) conducted a study on the metacognitive subcomponent *meta-strategic knowledge* (MSK), which is closely aligned with knowledge of task and strategy outlined in this chapter and with scientific inquiry (Ben-David & Zohar, 2009). In the study, a mix of over one hundred high- and low-achieving eighth graders participated in twelve science lessons during a unit on reproduction. The experimental group was also taught explicitly about MKS, including naming a strategy and knowing when to use it, while the control group was not. First, the authors found that explicit teaching of this metacognitive subcomponent significantly improved student outcomes for both high-achieving and low-achieving students. Second, they found that students who were taught knowledge of task and strategy were better equipped to transfer (adapt) their learning to a different task three months later. This finding supports the idea that the explicit teaching of the components and subcomponents can help low-achieving students or those who may not express an interest in science in general to perform more adaptive thinking toward scientific inquiry and transfer that thinking to new situations in life in general.

This meets with our own experience in which students who don't express an interest in science still find connection to science-based curricula through structured SELf-questioning. By focusing students on problem-solving steps, SELf-questions, and the metacognitive components and subcomponents aligned with them, science teachers can show students how the knowledge and regulation they are learning through SELf-questioning serves to enhance their adaptive thinking and how to apply adaptive thinking to different forms of scientific inquiry. The metacognitive components and subcomponents of structured SELf-questioning that support greater adaptive thinking are not only applicable to scientific inquiries that students may encounter in science courses but may also apply as enhancements to students' adaptive thinking for any inquiries they will encounter throughout school and in life.

Autonomous Use of SELf-Questioning and Metacognition

> *"The greatest sign of success for a teacher is to be able to say, "The children are now working as if I did not exist."*
>
> —Maria Montessori

In SELf-questioning, we, as teachers, are concerned with both student autonomy and teacher autonomy. *Autonomy*, Lexico (n.d.b) tells us, is "the right or condition of self-government" and "freedom from external control or influence; independence." Of course, all educators want students to become independent and not be teacher dependent. The goal, as with any approach to gradual release of responsibility, is to do away with the mediator. To do this, teachers begin the process by helping students to use external mediators (the specific SELf-question sets, visuals, step names, and other prompts teachers might provide) and end it with students no longer needing mediators to autonomously demonstrate self-awareness and self-managment, social awareness, and responsible decision making, as envisioned in the this book's introduction. Let's first take a look at how SELf-questioning develops student autonomy, initially, through the strategic use of external mediators.

To begin, let's clarify the distinction between external and internal mediators. Think of *external mediators* as supports and scaffolds to guide self-talk that can be made available to students from external stimuli, such as teacher or student modeling, visual poster charts or graphic organizers, apps, and so on. *Internal mediators* are when an individual creates for oneself a way to support inner dialogue or self-talk to achieve an individual goal, like recognizing and managing one's own stress or generating one's own solution to a problem. This is the ultimate goal. Since life's stressors and day-to-day problems and challenges are so personal, following others' leads and using prompts from external sources, no matter how open-ended the models and prompts may be, is a short-term goal. The long-term vision is for students to be able to do away with external mediators and be able to think flexibly and adaptively, utilizing independently and strategically their own learned skills and strategies as well as their own learned thinking skills, thereby tapping into their inherent and enhanced academic, social, and emotional intelligence.

Paul Tough (2012), an author and journalist specializing in education topics, discusses the idea of mediators to guide students' self-talk in his seminal book, *How Children Succeed*. In it, he writes about a model of teaching that he observed during a visit to a preK classroom in Red Bank Primary School in New Jersey (where Rick was principal at the time). Tough came to Rick's school to observe and write a *New York Times Magazine* article about the implementation of an innovative early childhood curriculum (Tools of the Mind; https://toolsofthemind.org) designed to teach the youngest of school-aged children the executive function skills inherent in self-regulation. Tough (2012) writes the following about what he saw during his visit and what he learned about teaching children to succeed in guiding their self-talk:

> Tools of the Mind students are taught a variety of strategies, tricks, and habits that they can deploy to keep their minds on track. They learn to use "private speech": talking to themselves as they do a difficult task (like say forming the letter *W*), to help them remember what steps come next (*down, up, down, up*). They use "mediators": physical objects to remind them how to complete a particular activity. (p. xii)

Until students are ready to develop their own self-created questions, the SELf-questions in our strategy, the step names, and the visuals we recommend in this book serve as external mediators that help students "keep their minds on track . . . help them remember what steps come next . . . and remind them how to complete a particular activity" (Tough, 2012, p. xii).

For students to achieve autonomy in their SELf-questioning, teachers utilize the gradual release of responsibility model we introduced in chapter 1 (page 26). They introduce students to the step names, SELf-questions, and the visuals icons along with teacher modeling. Once students have internalized the steps and SELf-questions, our metacognitive strategy does away with the need for teacher prompting and has students use the question prompts, or visual icons as mediators, by themselves. After all, students won't always have a teacher on the side to pose or prompt SELf-questions. Eventually, even the external mediators should become unnecessary.

The visual icons provided in this book will end up guiding a student's self-talk through a specified set or sequence; however, doing away with external mediators is necessary given the variability of the problems students will face. Sometimes problems can be extremely simple, meaning not all the steps are needed to be followed from start to finish. Sometimes we need to go back a step or two. And sometimes problems are not isolated to just an academic, social, or emotional problem. Therefore, it is in the best interests of all students to develop the ability to think adaptively, by developing and customizing their own SELf-question sets to fit their situation, task, challenge, or problem in any context. Significant teacher modeling of adaptive thinking is necessary for students to truly become adaptive, intelligent, and autonomous critical thinkers and problem solvers. This chapter explains how to model adaptive thinking and empower students to become so.

In this chapter, we look at the importance of adaptive metacognition as a necessary foundation for achieving autonomy. This is important not just for students but for teachers as well. To that end, we explore how teachers achieve autonomy by adapting and personalizing our SELf-question sets. We also provide the information you need to teach students how to develop their own SELf-questions. We close with a rumination on balance and our firm belief that a society that can engage in autonomous SELf-questioning can achieve anything.

The Importance of Adaptive Metacognition for Autonomy

When it comes to structured SELf-questioning, the process of getting to autonomy is the same for teachers as it is for students. This is why teacher autonomy plays a major role in achieving the ultimate goal of student autonomy. As adults, once you have developed autonomy and are free from the use of external mediators, you are empowered to define for students what autonomy means and demonstrate what autonomy looks and sounds like.

We believe that autonomy, with regard to structured SELf-questioning, is best defined as internalization of the habit of mind of taking a step back and having a think by guiding self-talk with SELf-questions that you design and refine to fit the situation at hand. Another way to look at metacognitive autonomy is to say that it is achieved when one becomes totally free of external mediators and has the ability to design one's own internal mediators that help guide thinking through stressors and challenges. In other words, we believe that meta-cognitive autonomy is equivalent to becoming a coder of our own brains.

We say that designing your own SELf-questions is like coding your brain in part because SELf-questioning can have the effect of sending your thinking directly to an area of your brain called the *anterior cingulate cortex* (ACC). According to the Neuroscientifically Challenged (2015) website, this part of the brain is "thought to be involved with a number of functions related to emotion including the regulation of overall affect, assigning emotions to internal and external stimuli." The site goes on to explain, "there are other areas of the ACC that are involved in various aspects of cognition ranging from decision-making to the manage-ment of social behavior" (Neuroscientifically Challenged, 2015).

SELf-questioning provides just the right amount of internal mediators (introspective questioning to guide self-talk) along with supports and scaffolds from external stimuli (step names, visual icons, technology tools, posters, worksheets, and so on) for anyone to become a coder of his or her own brain, capable of managing his or her cognitive and metacognitive functioning. With the metacognitive strategy of structured SELf-questioning internalized and made a habit, anyone can be empowered to decide for him- or herself which questions to ask and eventually adapt SELf-questions to fit the nature of the stressor, problem, or emotions at hand. It is this type of emotional and cognitive control your students need in order to develop true coping skills.

In addition to the research supporting guiding self-talk (Butler et al., 2011, Fisher et al., 2016, Shure, 2001, and more), there is an abundance of anecdotal evidence of the success of SELf-questioning as a strategy that uses external mediators for students to learn to guide their self-talk. We cite further ELA and mathematics test results in the book introduction (see Reflect, page 13) that are similarly encouraging because they indicate structured SELf-questioning may lead to dramatic increases in academic achievement and growth.

Grant Wiggins was also a big believer and had begun venturing into the world of meta-cognition and literacy, blogging about the benefits of metacognition on curriculum and instruction of reading. Wiggins (2015a) lists recommendations for what he believed vari-ous avenues of research coalesce around. One such recommendation regards metacognition, reading, transfer, and autonomy:

Do students understand that the aim of instruction is transfer of learning? Make this year-long goal crystal-clear all year. Design instruction backward from autonomous transfer of a repertoire of meta-cognition and comprehension strategies. Vary the tasks, contexts, and texts to ensure that students learn to self-prompt and transfer, regardless of prompt or task specifics; decrease prompts and reminders over time, sometimes suddenly, to see what learners do when unprompted. (Wiggins, 2015a)

After reading this entry, and overjoyed with the parallel thinking, Rick and Sue reached out to Grant and were fortunate to engage him in an in-depth discussion about the potential efficacy of structured SELf-questioning. On June 2, 2015, Grant agreed to come to Metuchen to conduct the first-ever training on the new strategy. Eight days prior to the training, he passed away, and Rick and Sue had to cancel the training. We share this because we believe SELf-questioning fits into the effort to continue Grant's brilliant work and his legacy as a reformer of and champion for whole child education.

Finally, the belief that structured SELf-question sets serve as mediators you can use to learn to code your own brain is consistent with psychologist Reuven Feuerstein's "The Theory of Structural Cognitive Modifiability" on adaptive thinking and how to modify intelligence (Presseisen, Sternberg, Fischer, Knight, & Feuerstein, 1990). In her book about her application of Feuerstein's theory, *Pedagogy of Confidence*, Jackson (2011) says:

For Feuerstein, intelligence (or adaptability) depend on three different phases of cognitive behavior: (a) taking in information (input phase), (b) reasoning about or thoughtfully operating on information that has been taken in (elaboration phase), and (c) effectively communicating the results of this reasoning (output phase) (Narrol & Giblon, 1984/2001, p. 10). (Jackson, 2011, p. 59)

Feuerstein's Theory of Structural Cognitive Modifiability is built on two important constructs: (1) intelligence is dependent on a basic structure of three steps or phases, and (2) the ability of students to think flexibly or adaptively within the structure and apply cognitive skills and strategies within each phase of the structure to align with the nature or condition of the problem. Jackson (2001) further states:

The structure of these cognitive functions can be changed or modified positively or negatively in response to both external stimuli and internal conditions throughout life—which means that intelligence itself is modifiable. (p. 59)

In other words, there is freedom within the structure, but the structure is just as vital to success as the choices made within each phase of that structure.

Here again, we see that developing autonomy and control of one's thinking involves structuring cognitive functioning with the support of both internal and external stimuli each step of the way. Through the use of external mediators, such as names of steps, visual icons, and graphic organizers, anyone can internalize the structure of adaptable, intelligent thinking and learn to self-prompt and transfer the cognitive skills and strategies that hold up that structure. Think of it this way, the steps of structured SELf-questioning are a framework for adaptive thinking, and cognitive skills and coping strategies are the building blocks that individuals place brick by brick and step by step as they work through the framework.

We've aligned the structure of SELf-questioning to Feuerstein's three phases of cognitive behavior that lead to adaptive, intelligent thinking. Table 12.1 shows how the structure, steps, names, visuals, and SELf-questions support users structuring and prompting the cognitive functioning of each of the three phases of intelligence.

Table 12.1: SELf-Question External Mediators to Support the Cognitive Phases of Intelligence

Phases of Cognitive Behavior	Self-Question Visuals	Self-Question Step Names	Academic and Social SELf-Question Set	Emotional SELf-Question Set
Input		Select a focus or self-empathy	What is the problem? What is the question? What is the task?	What am I feeling? How do I feel?
Input		Gather information	What do I know? What do I need to know? What is similar, and what is different?	What is causing this feeling?
Elaboration		Brainstorm	How can I solve this problem? What are possible solutions? What can I do?	What strategies can I use to make myself feel better?
Elaboration		Evaluate	What is the best way to solve this problem? Does this make sense?	Has this strategy helped me in the past? How did it help? How did I feel after?
Output		Plan and act	What do I do first, second, and so on? Does this work? Is this working?	What do I do first, second, and so on? Does this work? Is this working?
Output		Reflect	Did it work? How do I know? Do I need to go back and try again?	Did it work? How do I know? Do I need to go back and try again?

Remember from this book's introduction that, according to Feuerstein, introspective questioning is very effective intervention (as cited in Jackson, 2011). *Introspective questioning* is an intervention "that specifically elicits cognitive functions or mental tools that helps individuals create meaning in, adapt to, or control their environment" (Jackson, 2011, p. 59). You may have guessed from that that we designed our SELf-question sets to serve as external mediators each step of the way to elicit specific cognitive functions that are carefully and thoughtfully aligned to the three phases of adaptive, intelligent thinking. Jackson (2011) summarizes Feuerstein's observations of the impact of such an approach by teachers on students by stating that "when the students were guided through introspective questioning and bridging to familiar experiences, processes indicative of intellectual behavior . . . were strengthened" (p. 58).

Teacher Autonomy and Personalized SELf-Question Sets

Earlier in this book, we made the point that SELf-questioning is not a script, and we've provided many examples and scenarios regarding how teachers have used SELf-question sets as a baseline tool to create their own SELf-questions that still align with the core concept. As a new example, consider figure 12.1, which shows a chart Sue created with a group of kindergarten teachers at Moss School. They used this to increase the consistency of the language, visuals, and application of strategies when using the SELf-question sets.

This umbrella chart reflects utilizing SELf-questioning in an add-as-you-go format. It starts with just the base SELf-question set (light-gray cards), and teachers add the dark-gray cards to the chart in a vertical list as they introduce specific strategies. The strategy cards at the top of a column have to do with decoding, and the strategy cards on the bottom have to do with comprehension. By the end of the year, the kindergarteners could utilize all the reading strategies on this chart with some level of independence and autonomy. The teachers evaluated their students' application of these metacognitive strategies while using the SELf-question sets during reading conferences.

We have a couple of additional tools that might help you apply SELf-questioning with students in your classroom, school, or school district. Figure 12.2 (page 202) offers an overview of the general categories in metacognitive SELf-questioning. This chart may give you some ideas on what questions or categories of questions would help a particular student or help you determine which would make a more effective SELf-question tailored for your classroom. For example, perhaps a student has a tendency to procrastinate. A teacher might encourage the student to choose some questions from the Plan category to focus his or her planning.

Before we settled on only two SELf-question sets (the academic and social set and the emotional set), we had domain-specific question sets, as shown in table 12.2 (page 203). As we moved along in our work, we felt the chances of retention and transfer increased if students only had two slightly different question sets to work with. However, you may want to have domain-specific question sets that simply share the same categories. In that case, table 12.2 may give you some ideas toward that end.

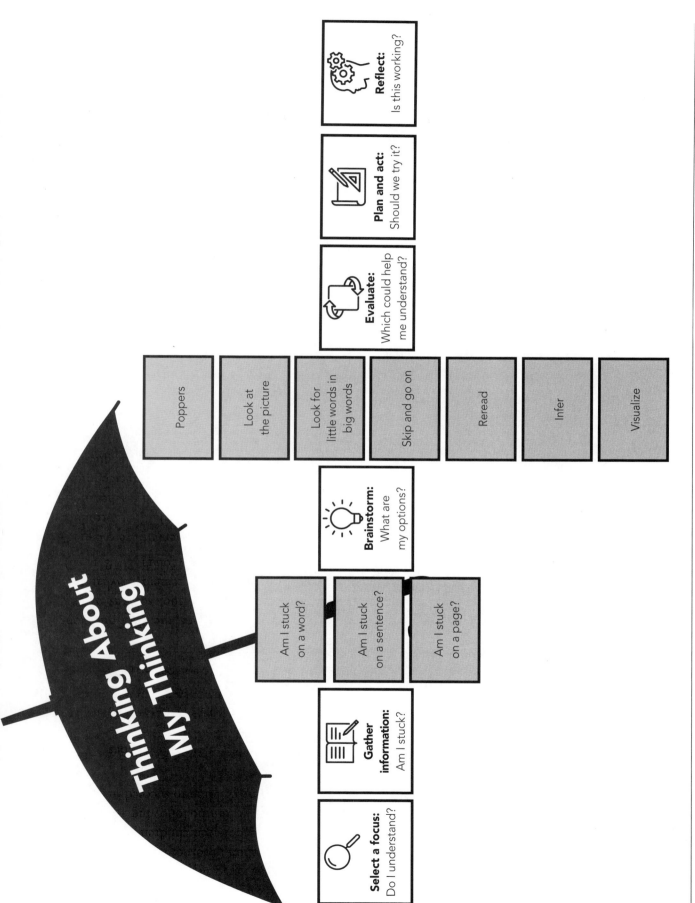

Figure 12.1: SELf-question chart.

Metacognition

Metacognitive Knowledge

Meta-Comprehension	Know Person Variables	Know Task Variables	Know Strategy Variables
Do I know it? Do I understand it?	How do people learn?	**What do I know about this task?**	**How can I solve this problem?**
What is the problem, question, or task?	How do I learn?	**What do I need to know about this task?**	**What are possible solutions?**
	What is my mindset?	What will this task demand?	What cognitive strategies might help?
	What are my strengths and weaknesses?	How can I scaffold this task?	What metacognitive strategies might help?
	What is my personality type?	**What is similar and what is different to other tasks?**	When should I use these strategies?
	What is my learning style?		
	How am I feeling? Is it affecting me?		

Metacognitive Regulation

Plan	Monitor	Evaluate	Reflect	Revise
What is the best way to solve this problem?	Does this work? Is it working?	**Did it work? How do I know?**	Create: What should I do next?	How can I use what I have discovered to make this better?
What do I do first, second, and so on?	**Does this make sense?**	What works and what could I improve?	Evaluate: How well have I done?	
How will I approach this task?	Am I doing my best work?	What would I do differently next time?	Analyze: Do I see any patterns in what I've done?	
How much effort will this take?	Am I in an optimal environment?	How can I scaffold this task to begin work again?	Apply: Where can I use this again?	
How much memory will this take?	Does this feel familiar or difficult?	Am I finished?	Understand: What was important?	
How should I allocate my time?	Am I focused? Do I need a break?		Remember: What did I do?	
Am I working alone or with others?				

Source: Adapted from Stevens, 2017.

Figure 12.2: Overview of metacognition with SELF-questions emphasized.

Table 12.2: Domain-Specific SELf-Question Sets

SELf-Question	Mathematics	Science	Writing and Research	Reading	Social	Emotional
Select a Focus	What is the problem asking me to solve?	What are my questions? Which question is most relevant?	How do I select a topic or focus? What questions do I have about my topic or focus? What are my best questions?	Do I understand what I'm reading? Does what I'm reading make sense?	Empathy: What happened?	Empathy: What am I feeling?
Gather Information	What do I know? What do I need to know?	How will I gather information? What is my hypothesis?	How will I gather information on some or all of my questions?	What do I understand? What do I need to understand?	Who? What? When? Where? Why? How?	What is causing this feeling?
Brainstorm	What are ways I can solve this problem?	How will I design an experiment? How is this similar to previous experiments?	How could I organize and present my information?	What strategies could help me understand?	What am I willing to do? What have I tried? What might work?	What strategies can I use to make myself feel better?
Evaluate	What is the best way to solve this problem?	What is the best choice?	What is the best choice? Why?	What is the best choice? Why?	What are the pros and cons? Which option is the best choice?	Has this helped me in the past? How did it help? How did I feel after?
Plan and Act	Can I make a model?	What do I do first, second, and so on? Is this working?	What do I do first, second, and so on? Is this working?	What do I do first, second, and so on?	What are my next steps? How can I do it?	How can I use this strategy?
Reflect	Did it work? How do I know?	What did I learn? How do I know?	What was surprising about my research? What did I do well, and how can I improve?	Is this working? Do I understand now?	Did it work? How do I know? Do I need to go back and try again to solve this?	Did it work? How do I know? Do I need to go back and try again to solve this?

How to Design Your Own SELf-Questions

If you want to create your own SELf-questions, here is a simple, four-step formula we recommend to get started.

1. **Link thinking skills:** In 2020, CASEL (n.d.) revised their SEL framework, including the core competency for self-awareness, which added the language for linking feelings, values, and thoughts. One way to link thinking skills is to identify two specific actions.

    a. Identify the critical-thinking skill within an academic learning standard for the content and grade level you teach.

    b. Identify the same critical-thinking skill found within a social and emotional learning standard from CASEL's (n.d.) list of SEL skills (visit https://casel.org/sel-framework).

    Typically, this step means looking for the active verb or verbs found in both the academic standard and the language for an SEL skill or competency. To check, ask yourself if both the academic standard and SEL skill ask students to perform the same cognitive action. For example, determine if they each use one or more of the following verbs: *identify, analyze, evaluate, generate, reflect,* or so on. Perfect matches between standard and skill language are great but not absolutely necessary. If you don't see obvious matches, look for synonyms. For example, many academic standards include the verb *identify*, while many SEL skills use the word *recognize*. For the purposes of linking thinking skills, these are equivalent.

2. **Identify and link academic content:** Within the state or provincial standard, determine the academic content, which typically consists of identifying the nouns in the standard connected with the verbs. Then, do the same for the SEL skill, looking for potential alignment. For example, you might identify teaching the noun-diverse perspective in social studies and align that to the teaching of diverse perspectives common to SEL skill sets. While helpful, linking content is never necessary and should only occur after you've first linked thinking skills (step 1). From our experience, if the goal is to teach students ways to guide their self-talk flexibly and across contexts, you can meet that goal by focusing on common thinking skills, which consistently overlap academic content areas and social and emotional contexts.

3. **Develop an open-ended and self-directed SELf-question:** At this point, the question you develop entirely depends on the context of your linked thinking skills and linked content. Focus your development of the question on the academic content, but be sure the SELf-question asks students to conduct the type of thinking you have selected. Ensure the question has more than one right academic answer and that it challenges students to think for themselves about the content you have selected.

4. **Test the SELf-question for transfer:** To test your SELf-question, ask yourself, "Can I ask myself this very same question without modifying any of the wording to help me think about either a social or emotional situation?" If the answer to this question is *yes*, congratulations! You have done it. If not, ask yourself, "How can I make my academic-focused question more open ended, so it doesn't fit only this specific content or context?"

Once you've designed a new SELf-question, we encourage you to associate it with a named problem-solving step. You can always apply our names, of course, but if you prefer your own name for problem-solving steps, go ahead and create them. In any case, always keep clear in your mind that the skill you are targeting for your lesson is to engage students in a very specific type of critical thinking or behavior (select, evaluate, reflect, and so on).

Let's take a quick look at three example scenarios of teacher-designed SELf-questions. The first is an example of a true SELf-question, the second is an example that does not align to the academic content of the targeted academic standard, and the third is a modified version of the questions an early childhood teacher of special needs students designed so they would be more developmentally appropriate for her students. The examples derive from participants in trainings we host on how teachers teach, model, and facilitate structured SELf-questioning. The last component of the workshop trained teachers on how they can design their own SELf-questions to best fit their class and personal style. Because these scenarios are based on teacher designs, they do not follow the grade-band differentiation we used for scenarios in previous chapters.

Scenario: A True SELf-Question

Ms. F. is a special education ELA teacher. She wants her students to demonstrate the New Jersey State Board of Education (2017) reading standard NJSLSA.R3: "Analyze how and why individuals, events and ideas develop and interact over the course of a text." She identifies the critical-thinking skill *analyze*, she wants to link to an SEL competency of responsible decision making. Specifically, she decides to connect to the SEL skill, "Learning to make a reasoned judgment after *analyzing* information, data, facts" (CASEL, 2020). Notice how both skills use the *analyze* skill.

In reviewing the language of both academic and SEL skills, she identifies there is also a strong correlation between content—the academic standard covers events, and the SEL skills broadly refer to information and facts. She develops two open-ended questions for students to use while reading and for note-taking.

1. What happened?

2. How can I organize this information?

Ms. F. then asks herself if she could use these same questions in her own life outside of reading and work. She is confident she can. Notice how they meet all four of the recommended steps we listed at the start of How to Design Your Own SELf-Questions. Asking students to find facts and analyze ways to categorize the facts, such as events or things characters said challenges them to collect and analyze information from a text. Students can then use this same critical-thinking skill of analyzing information and these same SELf-questions when trying to resolve social conflicts or more personal inquiries.

Next comes applying it to a step in the SELf-questioning process. Ms. F. decides that her questions already align well with the *gather information* step in the SELf-questioning process, and she decides to present the new questions to the students in her reading class when that academic standard comes up in the curriculum.

Scenario: A Missing Link

During SELf-question design training, Ms. Y., a second-grade science teacher, asks for feedback on a SELf-question she wants to use to combine SEL with the disciplinary core idea LS2.A ("Plants depend on water and light to grow"), which is part of the overall science standard 2-LS2-1 ("Plan and conduct an investigation to determine if plants need sunlight and water to grow"; NGSS Lead States, 2013). She posits two questions.

1. What do I need to live and grow?
2. How do I get what I need to live and grow?

Can you spot the issue with these questions? If you determined that they were not directly aligned with the academic content from the science standards, you are correct. This science standard focuses on plants, while these SELf-questions focus on the needs of human beings. Although step 2 for designing your own SELf-questions does state academic and SEL content do not have to match, the SELf-question you design should still lead students to think about your designed or intended academic content. We also see in this example that the SELf-question was not one that transferred across content effectively.

With this feedback, Ms. y. decides to go back and try again. She further opens the question to cover both plants and human beings by asking, "What do all living things need to live and grow?"

Scenario: An Adaptation for Special Circumstances

Mrs. P. is a speech-language pathologist for students ages three to five who qualify for preschool programming due to having special needs. In the following example, you can see her redesign of three SELf-questions. These changes involve modifying the questions and providing stems for student responses to make them more developmentally appropriate for her specific students.

Self-empathy: How do I feel?
Stem: "I feel . . . ."

Brainstorm: What can I do?
Stem: "I can . . . ."

Evaluate: Did that tool work last time?
Stem: "Last time, ..."

How to Teach Students to Design SELf-Questions

As you build experience developing new SELf-questions, we recommend giving them some thought, trying them out, and reflecting and revising them to suit your specific classroom and students. Use figure 12.3 to help you develop your SELf-questions.

Phase of Cognitive Behavior	SELf-Question Visual	SELf-Question Step Names	Academic and Social SELf-Question Set	Emotional SELf-Question Set	Your SELf-Question Set
Input		Select a focus or empathy	What is the problem?	What am I feeling?	
Input		Gather information	What do I know?	What could be causing this feeling?	
Elaboration		Brainstorm	What are possible solutions?	What strategies can I use to make myself feel better?	
Elaboration		Evaluate	What is the best way to solve this problem?	Has this helped me in the past?	
Output		Plan and act	What do I do first, second, and so on?	How can I use this strategy?	
Output		Reflect	Did it work? How do I know?	Did it work? How do I know?	

Figure 12.3: Developing your own SELf-questions.

*Visit **go.SolutionTree.com/instruction** for a free reproducible version of this figure.*

Once you have developed the ability to design your own SELf-questions and are confident using them for classroom instruction, we recommend teaching students how they can design their own SELf-questions. Simply guide them through the following.

1. Acting on the four simple steps for designing one's own SELf-questions, which we listed earlier in this chapter (page 204); depending on your students' background knowledge and understanding, you may want to conduct a

minilesson on the difference between open and closed questions, as well as nouns and verbs, depending on the age group.

2. Providing examples and feedback

3. Providing the opportunity to practice writing and using SELf-questions in class

While there is no consensus on exactly how many hours it takes to master a new strategy—and even the definition of *mastery*, in this context, is fluid—author Malcolm Gladwell (2008) states it can take as many as ten thousand hours. However, were we to consider this the definitive time frame necessary for moving from practice to mastery of any skill or strategy, no matter how complex, that translates into nine years. That may seem hopelessly implausible at first glance, but consider that by teaching SELf-questioning in grades K–8 and across academic content areas, school districts can say with confidence that their students will master their ability to design their own SELf-questions and guide their self-talk with full autonomy by the time they reach high school. In so doing, all students are ready to independently and creatively solve complex, real-world problems across all academic content areas as they begin their final push toward being college and career ready.

That said, having students come up with their own SELf-questions is not something your entire district, school, or even your whole department or grade level must do to have a positive impact. An important goal for any individual teacher is to teach students the habits of mind we dreamed of in the introduction to this book. The goal of having your students try to design just one SELf-question in your classroom will serve well to implement evidence-based pedagogy from Butler and colleagues (2011) when they say to "introduce an overall strategy for guided self-talk" (pg. 4). It is our hope that you think it is much easier, after having read this book, to introduce an overall strategy for guided self-talk than when you first read that evidence-based recommendation in the introduction.

There are also numerous benefits for your classroom environment and your own well-being when students are challenged to develop their own SELf-questions. First, when students develop their own SELf-questions, there are fewer questions for teachers to design. Second, when students design and use their own SELf-questions, they are often more motivated to try them. Third, student-driven SELf-questioning means more freedom for teachers to focus on those few students who do require direct, hands-on supports. You will see fewer hands raised with questions about something you just went over, more students comfortable with collaborative problem solving and group work (as well as with their own thinking), and more opportunities for students to extend their interests and learning.

To further students' practice toward this goal of student-developed SELf-questions, you can utilize some additional effective practice opportunities or activities, which are well suited for student-designed SELf-questions at school. Options include the following.

- **Make it a homework assignment:** Have students make their own SELf-questions for homework by assigning an article for them to read (the article could be student or teacher selected). Instruct them to develop their own SELf-question that covers the content from the text but challenges them to think adaptively and flexibly about the connections the article could have to real life.

Then, ask them to independently try linking the feelings, values, and thoughts within the text to their own feelings or the feelings of others.

- **Use learning stations for open-ended reading-response questions:** Have students generate their own SELf-questions for books they read at a literacy station. Students can then use the questions to generate written responses. SELf-questions you find particularly strong, you can pose to other students reading the same content at the station.

- **Create new SELf-questions for classroom peer mediation and conflict-resolution:** Many teachers engage students in developing class rules. We recommend also engaging students in developing the SELf-questions that students can use for resolving social conflicts that occur within the classroom. If students are new to developing SELf-questions, we recommend conducting this activity later in the semester or school year, after they've built up experience with them.

- **Create personalized think sheets:** Just as you can engage students in making SELf-questions for academic and social problem solving, you can also engage them in creating their own whole-class or individual think sheets. In particular, have students develop think sheets that will help them self-calm or develop coping flexibility.

Beyond these suggestions, using role play, skits, readers' theatre, video productions, and peer tutoring also provides ample opportunities to engage students in SELf-questioning.

Finally, we recommend that students redesign the SELf-questions you use in your classroom for academic problem solving, research, and inquiry so that they may apply them outside the classroom for social and emotional problem solving and decision making. As students gain confidence in their own SELf-question set designs, they are ready to attempt to teach and model the strategy for others, especially younger students. Encouraging students to autonomously adapt SELf-questions to their needs is the most effective way to get true buy-in from them (as is often the case with teachers as well).

Character Corner: Balance

Through SELf-questioning, you have a strategy and the time to teach all students four of the five SEL competencies we list in this book's introduction (page 1), as well as the coping mechanisms students need to better deal with the academic, social, and emotional stressors of life in and out of school. This alone should offer you a greater sense of peace because you now have the tools to strike a better balance between academic instruction and SEL instruction.

Students are exposed to incredible volumes of external stimulation and mediators. By teaching them to develop their own SELf-questions, teachers can help students strike a healthier balance between the amount of external mediators and internal mediators they rely on. Further, students also endure exposure to a great deal of negativity in the news, in social media, and in the world. Teaching them to develop their own SELf-questions also helps create more balance between negative and positive thoughts, since the act of SELf-questioning promotes positive self-talk.

Last but not least, we believe the more balance (socially, emotionally, and academically) all educators promote within the next generation, the greater all our hopes for the future. As a worldwide community of educators, our current students will someday lead our world. By teaching future leaders they can solve even the most complex problems and challenges by staying calm, taking a step back, and having a think about their thinking and feelings, those leaders will have the skills they need to respond more peacefully to stressors, problems, and conflicts. This approach will also pay forward when they pass on to others that same sense of confidence gained through a more balanced approach to challenges. With the help of SELf-questioning, generations of children can grow up in a world full of greater self-awareness, self-management, empathy, intelligence, character, peace, and balance.

Epilogue

I realized that becoming a master of karate was not about learning 4,000
moves but about doing just a handful of moves 4,000 times.

—Chet Holmes, (2007)

We wrote this book because we believe wholeheartedly and have seen firsthand how transformative structured SELf-questioning is for both students and teachers. As educators, administrators, professional development providers, and counselors with collectively more than one hundred years of experience serving thousands of students and educators, we know all too well what the data say about the overwhelming challenges students and teachers face. The effects of these negative stressors cause high teacher burnout and turnover rates, which result in further decreases to student performance (Greenberg et al., 2016). Further, when teacher turnover increases, costs for retraining of new teachers go up. With increases in student stress and mental health concerns, schools require more in-school therapists to manage that need, which also escalates costs. In short, increasing levels of student and teacher stress and mental health concerns lead the United States to pay more for lower levels of student performance and well-being.

To be clear, we know that in-school therapeutic programs are effective in addressing students with mental health disorders and are a great source of support for teachers of students with mental health disorders. However, this support alone is insufficient in addressing an issue that is rising to crisis levels. These programs are expensive and must focus a very high percentage of their services on individual students with the most severe needs. And what if a school or district does not have the funds to provide in-school therapeutic services? Will under-resourced school systems have more students falling further behind, even greater teacher burnout, and increased teacher turnover? Are mental health crises increasing the student achievement gap—academically, socially, and emotionally?

As educators, we all need to be part of breaking the cycle and reversing the downward spiral in ways that are cost effective, restore teacher health, and increase student academic achievement and their social and emotional well-being. But if providing the help and support that so many students and teachers need seems unlikely, maybe impossible, the big SELf-question we are left asking ourselves is, "How can we solve this problem for all?" Perhaps, when the challenge appears too big, and there is no one best solution, the best pathway forward is to empower everyone with the capacity and competencies they need to come up with their own best solutions and to make their own best decisions. It is our hope that with the widespread application of SELf-questioning, we can not only improve students' and teachers' success in their classrooms and schools, in their homes, in their workplaces, and in their lives, but also have a broad and enduring societal impact in a way that is practical, scalable, and affordable.

To that end, we encourage you to move into the application stage of what you have read in this book. When teachers read educational books, they usually come away from them focusing on one thing that they will apply in their classrooms immediately. The one thing we would like you to hold onto from this book is using our problem-solving strategy in your teaching, regardless of content area, as a way of deeply internalizing a critical-thinking and problem-solving matrix that will equip you and your students for life.

When we look at the continuum of teachers, at one end, we see new teachers, straight out of college—excited and nervous—who are applying their learned skills in their own classrooms. These teachers are often in survival mode. The main thing they can take from this book is a metacognitive strategy that can help them not only survive but thrive by enriching their teaching quickly and easily. On the other end of the continuum, we see teachers who continue to learn and apply their learning deeply throughout their careers. These teachers have teaching toolboxes worthy of a hardware superstore, and the main thing they can take from this book is this same, simple strategy that can deepen and focus their teaching quickly and easily.

You may decide to dip your toes in the water and start with one question in one area. Or you may want to jump in the deep end and introduce the questions into all content areas at one time. We have experienced ourselves and seen teachers experience personal and professional success with both approaches. No matter which approach you take to initiate the use of structured SELf-questioning in your classroom, you will reap the benefits we have discussed throughout this book.

The following statements are testimony from just a few teachers who have found great success using SELf-questioning to teach SEL, metacognition, and critical-thinking and problem-solving skills without requiring significant additional time or planning:

> Structured SELf-questioning allows students to ask themselves specific questions and brainstorm better solutions that work for them. It's so encouraging when you see a student who has been struggling socially or emotionally suddenly experience their *ah-ha* moment and then watch them continue to make better choices that work for them because they are able to use the structured SELf-questioning model.
>
> —*Erica Hsu, school counselor*
> *(personal communication, April 15, 2020)*

I was hesitant at best to try structured SELf-questioning as my students' self-awareness is still emerging. However, I have been amazed at the way my modeling of this strategy has allowed my students the opportunity to develop not only stronger self-awareness but also the ability to take control over what they can do for themselves under certain stressors. Behaviors have decreased, and boy has feelings language increased! Modeling structured SELf-questioning has changed my classroom, made me a better teacher for my students, and has allowed my students to take control over what they can do when their body is feeling a certain way, instead of an adult dictating that for them.

—*Katie McKenna, preschool special education teacher*
(personal communication, April 14, 2020)

It's truly a win-win situation! I find that it gives structure to learning while allowing freedom of thought and accountability on the part of the students.

—*Julie Anderson, elementary special education teacher*
(personal communication, April 9, 2020)

By using the same question set for solving problems, students have been able to keep our routine of problem solving. This shows how repeating the SELf-questions eventually ingrains them in students' minds, and they begin to solve problems (academically or socially) independently.

—*Danielle Movsessian, second-grade teacher*
(personal communication, April 17, 2020)

Structured SELf-questioning helps both the teacher and student because it sets up a common language that can fluidly be used in a classroom setting, transfers from year to year, and is useable across subjects as well as in social situations.

—*Sofia Lopes, fourth-grade teacher*
(personal communication, April 8, 2020)

I have witnessed students using this structured approach to problem solving display more focus to work through and solve problems that they may have originally abandoned. As a result, collaborative workgroups became more inclusive and productive.

—*Rachel DiVanno, middle school mathematics and science teacher*
(personal communication, April 13, 2020)

> SELf-questioning provides the framework that individuals can internalize and then recall for use in solving both academic and social problems.
>
> —*Vincent Caputo, superintendent*
> *(personal communication, April 19, 2020)*

We share these messages of testimony and hope to let you know the excitement and transformative power that not only we but so many others have found in this simple strategy of cross-domain problem solving. When we get together to talk about using SELf-questions, we rhapsodize about the effect this could have on our communities and even the world. We believe this approach can not only help current and future generations increase their academic, social, and emotional intelligence, but also their ability to empathize, show grit, maintain self-control, demonstrate responsibility, and achieve inner peace.

We agree with what Martin Luther King Jr. (1947) wrote in the Morehouse school newspaper, "The function of education is to teach one to think intensively and to think critically. Intelligence plus character—that is the goal of true education." Together, let's develop the next generation as masters of great thought, intelligence, and character.

Appendix

This appendix offers reproducible resources we've referenced throughout the book. These include a series of problem-solving posters and think sheets that utilize our academic and social and emotional SELf-question sets.

Academic and Social Problem-Solving Poster

	Action Step	SELf-Questions
	1. Select a Focus	What is the problem? What is the question? What is the task?
	2. Gather Information	What do I know? What do I need to know? What is similar, and what is different?
	3. Brainstorm	How can I solve this problem? What are possible solutions? What can I do?
	4. Evaluate	What is the best way to solve this problem? Does this make sense?
	5. Plan and Act	What do I do first, second, and so on? Does this work? Is this working?
	6. Reflect	Did it work? How do I know? Do I need to go back and try again?

The Metacognitive Student © 2021 Richard K. Cohen, Deanne Kildare Opatosky, James Savage, Susan Olsen Stevens, and Edward P. Darrah • SolutionTree.com
Visit **go.SolutionTree.com/instruction** to download this free reproducible.

Emotional Problem-Solving Poster

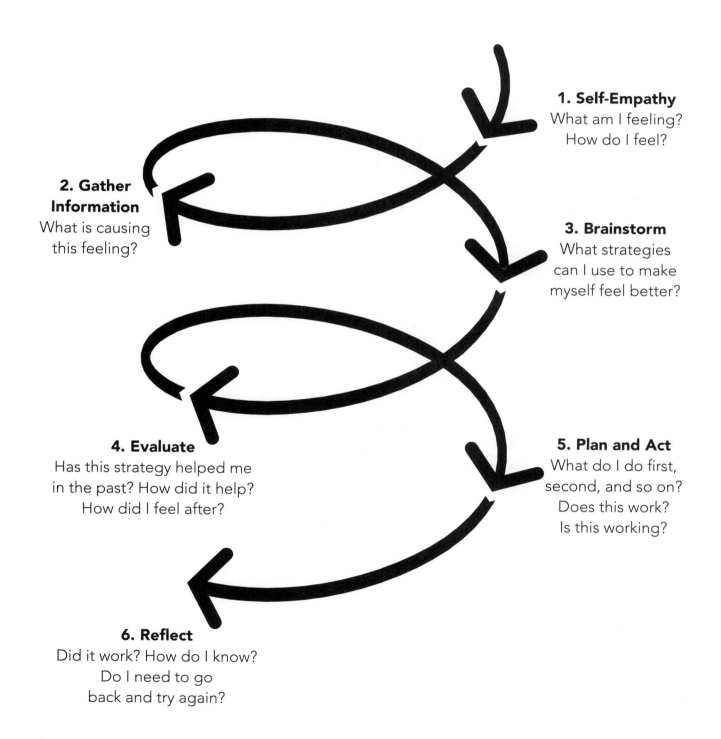

1. Self-Empathy
What am I feeling?
How do I feel?

2. Gather Information
What is causing
this feeling?

3. Brainstorm
What strategies
can I use to make
myself feel better?

4. Evaluate
Has this strategy helped me
in the past? How did it help?
How did I feel after?

5. Plan and Act
What do I do first,
second, and so on?
Does this work?
Is this working?

6. Reflect
Did it work? How do I know?
Do I need to go
back and try again?

Academic and Social Problem-Solving Think Sheet: Design 1

Steps and SELf-Questions	Your Thinking
Select a Focus What is the problem? What is the question? What is the task?	
Gather Information What do I know? What do I need to know? What is similar, and what is different?	
Brainstorm How can I solve this problem? What are possible solutions? What can I do?	
Evaluate What is the best way to solve this problem? Does this make sense?	
Plan and Act What do I do first, second, and so on? Does this work? Is this working?	
Reflect Did it work? How do I know? Do I need to go back and try again?	

The Metacognitive Student © 2021 Richard K. Cohen, Deanne Kildare Opatosky, James Savage, Susan Olsen Stevens, and Edward P. Darrah • SolutionTree.com
 Visit **go.SolutionTree.com/instruction** to download this free reproducible.

Emotional Problem-Solving Think Sheet: Design 1

Steps and SELf-Questions	Your Thinking
Self-Empathy What am I feeling? How do I feel?	
Gather Information What is causing this feeling?	
Brainstorm What strategies can I use to make myself feel better?	
Evaluate Has this strategy helped me in the past? How did it help? How did I feel after?	
Plan and Act What do I do first, second, and so on? Does this work? Is this working?	
Reflect Did it work? How do I know? Do I need to go back and try again?	

Academic and Social Problem-Solving Think Sheet: Design 2

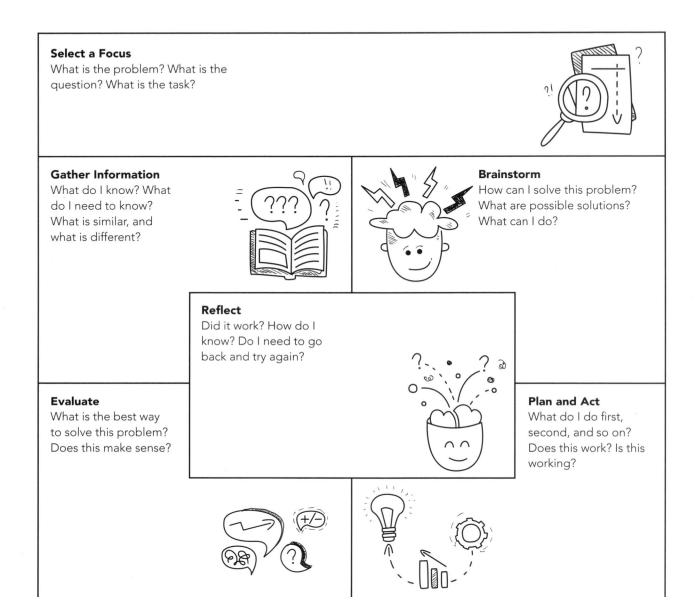

Select a Focus
What is the problem? What is the question? What is the task?

Gather Information
What do I know? What do I need to know? What is similar, and what is different?

Brainstorm
How can I solve this problem? What are possible solutions? What can I do?

Reflect
Did it work? How do I know? Do I need to go back and try again?

Evaluate
What is the best way to solve this problem? Does this make sense?

Plan and Act
What do I do first, second, and so on? Does this work? Is this working?

Emotional Problem-Solving Think Sheet: Design 2

Self-Empathy
What am I feeling? How do I feel?

Gather Information
What is causing
this feeling?

Brainstorm
What strategies can I use to
make myself feel better?

Reflect
Did it work? How do I
know? Do I need to go
back and try again?

Evaluate
Has this strategy
helped me in the past?
How did it help? How
did I feel after?

Plan and Act
What do I do first,
second, and so on?
Does this work? Is
this working?

The Metacognitive Student © 2021 Richard K. Cohen, Deanne Kildare Opatosky, James Savage,
Susan Olsen Stevens, and Edward P. Darrah • SolutionTree.com
Visit **go.SolutionTree.com/instruction** to download this free reproducible.

Linking Cognitive Verbs in CCSS and SELf-Questions

Cognitive Verbs Found in CCSS (and the number of times they appear in K–12 standards)	Structured SELf-Question Set for Solving Academic and Social Problems
Identify (35)	What is the problem?
Determine (80) Analyze (86)	What do I know? What do I need to know?
Create (41) Develop (71)	How can I solve this problem? What are some possible solutions?
Evaluate (36)	Which is the best choice?
Solve (111)	What do I do first, second, and so on?
Interpret (78) Reflect (26)	Did it work? How do I know? Do I need to try again?

Source: National Governors Association Center for Best Practices & Council of Chief State School Officers. (2010a). Common Core State Standards for English language arts and literacy in history/social studies, science, and technical subjects. *Washington, DC: Authors. Accessed at www.corestandards.org/assets/CCSSI_ELA%20Standards.pdf on October 16, 2020.*

References and Resources

Allington, R. L. (2012), *What really matters for struggling readers: Designing research-based programs* (3rd ed.). Boston: Pearson.

Anderson, L. H. (2008). *Chains*. New York: Atheneum Books.

Anderson, M., & Jiang, J. (2018). *Teens, social media & technology 2018*. Accessed at www.pewresearch.org/internet/2018/05/31/teens-social-media-technology-2018 on August 21, 2020.

Anxiety and Depression Association of America. (n.d.). *Understand the facts: Stress*. Accessed at https://adaa.org/understanding-anxiety/related-illnesses/stress on August 13, 2020.

Archambeau, K., & Gevers, W. (2018). (How) are executive functions actually related to arithmetic abilities? In A. Henik & W. Fias (Eds.), *Heterogeneity of function in numerical cognition*. London: Academic Press.

Avargil, S., Lavi, R., & Dori, Y. J. (2018). Students' metacognition and metacognitive strategies in science education. In Y. J. Dori, Z. R. Mevarech, & D. R. Baker (Eds.), *Cognition, metacognition, and culture in STEM education* (pp. 33–64). Cham, Switzerland: Springer.

Bandura, A. (1977). Self-efficacy: Toward a unifying theory of behavioral change. *Psychological Review, 84*(2), 191–215.

Bandura, A. (1986). *Social foundations of thought and action: A social cognitive theory*. Englewood Cliffs, NJ: Prentice Hall.

Bandura, A. (1997). *Self-efficacy: The exercise of control*. New York: W. H. Freeman.

Barrett, L. F. (2018). *Try these two smart techniques to help you master your emotions*. Accessed at https://ideas.ted.com/try-these-two-smart-techniques-to-help-you-master-your-emotions on December 17, 2020.

Bed-David, A., & Zohar, A. (2008). Explicit teaching of meta-strategic knowledge in authentic classroom situations. *Metacognition and Learning, 3*, 59–82.

Ben-David, A., & Zohar, A. (2009). Contribution of meta-strategic knowledge to scientific inquiry learning. *International Journal of Science Education, 31*(12), 1657–1682.

Benedictine University. (2017, May 9). *What is appreciative inquiry? A short guide to the appreciative inquiry model and process* [Blog post]. Accessed at https://cvdl.ben.edu/blog/what-is-appreciative-inquiry on November 9, 2019.

Berrett, D. (2014). *Students can transfer knowledge if taught how*. Accessed at www.chronicle.com/article/students-can-transfer-knowledge-if-taught-how/?bc_nonce=g9cakblw4jdqotqi8z5dv&cid=reg_wall_signup on September 3, 2020.

Blad, E. (2019, March 14). *Schools grapple with student depression as data show problem worsening*. Accessed at www.edweek.org/ew/articles/2019/03/14/schools-grapple-with-student-depression-as-data.html on August 10, 2019.

Boaler, J., & Zoido, P. (2016, November 1). *Why math education in the U.S. doesn't add up*. Accessed at www.scientificamerican.com/article/why-math-education-in-the-u-s-doesn-t-add-up on October 7, 2019.

Boulware-Gooden, R., Carrker, S., Thornhill, A., & Malatesha, J. R. (2007, September). Instruction of metacognitive strategies enhances reading comprehension and vocabulary achievement of third-grade students. *Reading Teacher, 61*(1), 70–77.

Brendtro, L. K., Brokenleg, M., & VanBockern, S. (2019). *Reclaiming youth at risk: Futures of promise* (3rd ed.). Bloomington, IN: Solution Tree Press.

Brentar, J. T. (2018). *Student stress and anxiety: Is the American educational system at fault?* Accessed at http://www.morrissey -compton.org/articles/Student_Stress_Anxiety.pdf on August 13, 2020.

Bridgeland, J., Bruce, M., & Hariharan, A. (n.d.). *The missing piece: A national teacher survey on how social and emotional learning can empower children and transform schools.* Accessed at www.casel.org/wp-content/uploads/2016/01/the-missing-piece.pdf on August 6, 2020.

Bridges, L. (2018). All children deserve access to authentic text [Blog post]. Accessed at https://edublog.scholastic.com/post/all -children-deserve-access-authentic-text on December 16, 2020.

Bronte, C. (2014). *Jayne Eyre.* New York: Black & White Classics.

Building Learning Power. (n.d.). Sorting out resilience, perseverance, and grit [Blog post]. Accessed at www.buildinglearning power.com/2015/11/sorting-out-resilience-perseverance-and-grit on December 16, 2020.

Burke, K. (2009). *How to assess authentic learning* (5th ed.). Thousand Oaks, CA: Corwin.

Butler, L. B., Romasz-McDonald, T., & Elias, M. J. (2011). *Social decision making / social problem solving: A curriculum for academic, social, and emotional learning—Grades K–1.* Champaign, IL: Research Press.

Calkins, L. (2013). *A guide to the Common Core writing workshop: Primary grades.* Portsmouth, NH: Heinemann.

Calkins, L. (2015). *Units of study for teaching reading, grade K: A workshop curriculum.* Portsmouth, NH: Heinemann.

Carey, M. P., & Forsyth, A. D. (2009). *Teaching tip sheet: Self-efficacy.* Accessed at www.apa.org/pi/aids/resources/education/self -efficacy on November 29, 2020.

Castles, A., Rastle, K., & Nation, K. (2018, June 11). Ending the reading wars: Reading acquisition from novice to expert. *Psychological Science in the Public Interest, 19*(1), 5–51.

Centers for Disease Control and Prevention. (2019). *Standard 5: Students will demonstrate the ability to use decision-making skills to enhance health.* Accessed at www.cdc.gov/healthyschools/sher/standards/5.htm on December 3, 2019.

Character.org. (2018). *11 principles framework for schools: A guide to cultivating a culture of character.* Washington, D.C.: Character.org.

Chmielewski, A. K. (2019). The global increase in the socioeconomic achievement gap, 1964 to 2015. *American Sociological Review, 84*(3), 517–544.

Cody, A. (2011). *Interview: How much does stress affect learning?* [Blog post]. Accessed at http://blogs.edweek.org/teachers/living -in-dialogue/2011/06/interview_how_does_classroom_s.html on December 7, 2020.

Cohen, R. (2019). *SGP results 2019.* Accessed at https://core-docs.s3.amazonaws.com/documents/asset/uploaded_file/1026323 /Final_2019_SGP_Test_Results_presentation.pdf on December 20, 2020.

Cohen, R., Peragallo, B., McPeek, K., Porowski, E., Evans, N., & Khoudja, D. (2019). *2019 statewide assessment results: Measuring college and career readiness.* Accessed at https://core-docs.s3.amazonaws.com/documents/asset/uploaded_file/1067355/ Final_2019_NJSLA_Results_Presentation_3_2020.pdf. on December 20, 2020.

Cohen, R., Savage, J., Opatosky, D., Darrah, E., & Stevens S. (2018). SELf-Q (Beta) [Mobile application software]. Accessed at https://selfq.org.

Colburn, L., & Beggs, L. (2021). *The wraparound guide: How to gather student voice, build community partnerships, and cultivate hope.* Bloomington, IN: Solution Tree Press.

Collaborative for Academic, Social, and Emotional Learning. (n.d.). *SEL: What are the core competence areas and where are they promoted?* Accessed at https://casel.org/sel-framework on December 20, 2020.

Collins, J. (2018, February 21). *45% of teens say they're stressed "all the time," turn to online resources and apps for help says poll on stress and mental health* [News release]. Accessed at www.globenewswire.com/news-release/2018/02/21/1372739/0/en/45-of- Teens-Say-They-re-Stressed-All-the-Time-Turn-to-Online-Resources-and-Apps-for-Help-Says-Poll-on-Stress-and-Mental -Health.html on July 9, 2019.

Collins, R., & Legg, T. (2017). *Exercise, depression, and the brain*. Accessed at www.healthline.com/health/depression/exercise on November 29, 2020.

Cooperrider, D. L., & Whitney, D. (1999). Appreciative inquiry: A positive revolution in change. In P. Holman & T. Devane (Eds.), *The change handbook: Group methods for shaping the future* (pp. 245–262). San Francisco: Berrett-Koehler. Accessed at www.wrha.mb.ca/professionals/collaborativecare/files/AppreciativeInquiry2013.pdf on December 19, 2012.

Costa, A. L., & Garmston, R. J. (2016). *Cognitive coaching: Developing self-directed leaders and learners*. Lanham, MD: Rowman & Littlefield.

Council of Chief States School Officers. (2014). *English language proficiency (ELP) standards with correspondences to K–12 English language arts (ELA), mathematics, and science practices, K–12 ELA standards, and 6–12 literacy standards*. Accessed at https://ccsso.org/sites/default/files/2017-11/Final%204_30%20ELPA21%20Standards%281%29.pdf on September 4, 2020.

Coutinho, S. (2008). Self-efficacy, metacognition, and performance. *North American Journal of Psychology, 10*(1), 165.

Cuncic, A. (2020, January 20). *How to develop and practice self-regulation*. Accessed at www.verywellmind.com/how-you-can-practice-self-regulation-4163536 on August 7, 2020.

Curry, D. L. (2002). *I can, we can*. New York: Scholastic.

Daniels, H. (2017). *The curious classroom: Ten structures for teaching with student-directed inquiry*. Portsmouth, NH: Heinemann.

Desilver, D. (2017). *U.S. students' academic achievement still lags that of their peers in many other countries*. Accessed at www.pewresearch.org/fact-tank/2017/02/15/u-s-students-internationally-math-science on December 18, 2020.

@DreamBox_Learn. (2013, June 24). *Explaining CCSS standards for mathematical practice* [Blog post]. Accessed at www.dreambox.com/blog/explaining-ccss-standards-for-mathematical-practice on August 5, 2019.

Dr. Seuss. (1957). *The cat in the hat*. Boston: Houghton Mifflin.

Duckworth, A. (2016). *Grit: The power of passion and perseverance*. New York: Scribner.

Durlak, J. A., Weissberg, R. P., Dymnicki, A. B., Taylor, R. D., & Schellinger, K. B. (2011) The impact of enhancing students' social and emotional learning: A meta-analysis of school-based universal interventions. *Child Development, 82*(1), 405–432.

Dweck, C. (2016). *Mindset: The new psychology of success* (Updated ed.). New York: Ballantine Books.

Education Corner. (n.d.). *The learning pyramid*. Accessed at www.educationcorner.com/the-learning-pyramid.html on September 15, 2020.

Education Week. (2017, April 19). *What is 'transfer of learning' and how does it help students?* [Video file]. Accessed at www.youtube.com/watch?time_continue=189&v=N8QfkT8L9lo&feature=emb_title on August 7, 2020.

Elias, M. J., & Arnold, H. (Eds.). (2006). *The educator's guide to emotional intelligence and academic achievement: Social-emotional learning in the classroom*. Thousand Oaks, CA: Corwin.

Elias, M. J., Ferrito, J. J., & Moceri, D. C. (2016). *The other side of the report card: Assessing students' social, emotional, and character development*. Thousand Oaks, CA: Corwin.

Endres, G., & Gething, M. J. (2007). *Jane's aircraft recognition guide* (5th ed.). London: Collins.

Fadel, C., Bialik, M., & Trilling, B. (2015). *Found-dimensional education: The competencies learners need to succeed*. Boston: Center for Curriculum Redesign.

Farris, C. K. (2006). *My brother Martin: A sister remembers growing up with the Rev. Dr. Martin Luther King Jr*. New York: Simon & Schuster.

Ferlazzo, L. (2017, May 6). *Response: Learning 'transfer is our collective goal'* [Blog post]. Accessed at http://blogs.edweek.org/teachers/classroom_qa_with_larry_ferlazzo/2017/05/response_learning_transfer_is_our_collective_goal.html on August 6, 2020.

Ferlazzo, L. (2018, March 20). *'Learning follows a spiral': Doug Fisher & Nancy Frey on learning transfer* [Blog post]. Accessed at https://blogs.edweek.org/teachers/classroom_qa_with_larry_ferlazzo/2018/03/learning_follows_a_spiral_doug_fisher_nancy_frey_on_learning_transfer.html on November 29, 2020.

Fisher, D., Frey, N., & Hattie, J. (2016). *Visible learning for literacy, grades K–12: Implementing the practices that work best to accelerate student learning.* Thousand Oaks, CA: Corwin.

Fitzhugh, L. (2016). *Harriett the spy.* New York: HarperCollins.

Florida Department of Education. (2010). *Classroom cognitive and metacognitive strategies for teachers: Research-based strategies for problem-solving in mathematics K–12.* Accessed at http://floridarti.usf.edu/resources/topic/academic_support/kops/class_strategies.pdf on September 15, 2020.

Flowers, P., Theopold, K., Langley, R., & Robinson, W. R. (2019). *Chemistry* (2nd ed.). Houston, TX: Rice University Press. Accessed at https://open.bccampus.ca/browse-our-collection/find-open-textbooks/?uuid=cfcf2c49-fbed-4945-9ccb-914d48ea145f&contributor=&keyword=&subject= on August 26, 2020.

Fountas, I. C., & Pinnell, G. S. (2001) *Guiding readers and writers, grades 3–6: Teaching comprehension, genre, and content literacy.* Portsmouth, NH: Heinemann.

Fountas, I. C., & Pinnell, G. S. (2017). *Guided reading: Responsive teaching across the grades* (2nd ed.). Portsmouth, NH: Heinemann.

Freeman, M. S. (2000). *Non-fiction writing strategies: Using Science Big Books as models.* Gainesville, FL: Maupin House.

Freire, P. (1970). *Pedagogy of the oppressed* (M. B. Ramos, Trans.). New York: Herder and Herder.

Funke, C. (2000). *The thief lord.* New York: Scholastic.

Gallagher, K. (2003). *Reading reasons: Motivational mini-lessons for middle and high school.* Portland, ME: Stenhouse.

Gallup. (2014). *State of America's schools report.* Accessed at www.gallup.com/services/178709/state-america-schools-report.aspx on August 6, 2020.

Gardiner, J. R. (2010). *Stone fox.* New York: Harper Collins.

Geiger, A. W., & Davis, L. (2019). *A growing number of American teenagers—particularly girls—are facing depression.* Accessed at www.pewresearch.org/fact-tank/2019/07/12/a-growing-number-of-american-teenagers-particularly-girls-are-facing-depression on November 29, 2020.

Gladwell, M. (2008). *Outliers: The story of success.* New York: Little, Brown.

Golding, W. (1954). *Lord of the flies.* New York: Perigree.

Goldstein, D. (2019, December 3). *'It just isn't working': PISA test scores cast doubt on U.S. education efforts.* Accessed at www.nytimes.com/2019/12/03/us/us-students-international-test-scores.html on December 4, 2019.

Goleman, D. (2006). *Emotional intelligence: Why it can matter more than IQ.* New York: Bantam Books.

GoodTherapy. (2019). *Insecurity.* Accessed at www.goodtherapy.org/blog/psychpedia/insecurity on November 29, 2020.

Gotter, A., & Weatherspoon, D. (2020). *Box breathing.* Accessed at www.healthline.com/health/box-breathing#slowly-inhale on August 6, 2020.

Gray, A. (2016, January 19). *The 10 skills you need to thrive in the Fourth Industrial Revolution.* Accessed at www.weforum.org/agenda/2016/01/the-10-skills-you-need-to-thrive-in-the-fourth-industrial-revolution/ on September 20, 2019.

Greenberg, M. T., Brown J. L., & Abenavoli, R. M. (2016). *Teacher stress and health: Effects on teachers, students, and schools.* Accessed at www.rwjf.org/en/library/research/2016/07/teacher-stress-and-health.html on September 29, 2020.

Hall, G. (2016, May 22). *Mathematics problem solving strategies* [Blog post]. Accessed at https://garyhall.org.uk/maths-problem-solving-strategies.html on August 3, 2019.

Harvard Health Publishing. (2020, July 7). *Blue light has a dark side.* Accessed at www.health.harvard.edu/staying-healthy/blue-light-has-a-dark-side on August 6, 2020.

The Hechinger Report. (2017, November 27). *U.S. ranks no. 13 in international collaborative problem-solving test.* Accessed at www.usnews.com/news/best-countries/articles/2017-11-27/us-ranks-no-13-in-new-pisa-collaborative-problem-solving-test on October 28, 2019.

Henry, M. (1948). *King of the wind.* Chicago: Rand McNally.

Hill, H. N. (2016). Tutoring for transfer: The benefits of teaching writing center tutors about transfer theory. *The Writing Center Journal, 35*(3), 77–102.

Holmes, C. (2007). *The ultimate sales machine: Turbocharge your business with relentless focus on 12 key strategies.* New York: Portfolio.

Horowitz, J. M., & Graf, N. (2019, February 20). *Most U.S. teens see anxiety and depression as a major problem among their peers.* Accessed at www.pewsocialtrends.org/2019/02/20/most-u-s-teens-see-anxiety-and-depression-as-a-major-problem-among-their-peers/ on July 25, 2019.

InnerDrive. (n.d.). *How to improve metacognition in the classroom.* Accessed at www.innerdrive.co.uk/improve-metacognition/ on July 18, 2017.

Jackson, Y. (2011). *The pedagogy of confidence: Inspiring high intellectual performance in urban schools.* New York: Teachers College Press.

James, M. A. (2008). The influence of perceptions of task similarity/difference on learning transfer in second language writing. *Written Communication, 25*(1), 76–103.

Jensen, E. (2019). *Poor students, rich teaching: Seven high-impact mindsets for students from poverty* (Rev. ed.). Bloomington, IN: Solution Tree Press.

Kato, T. (2012, April). Development of the Coping Flexibility Scale: Evidence for the coping flexibility hypothetis. *Journal of Counseling Psychology, 59–273.*

Keene, E. O. (2008). *To understand: New horizons in reading comprehension.* Portsmouth, NH: Heinemann.

Keene, E. O., & Zimmermann, S. (2007). *Mosaic of thought: The power of comprehension strategy instruction* (2nd ed.). Portsmouth, NH: Heinemann.

King Jr., M. L. (1947). *The purpose of education.* Accessed at http://okra.stanford.edu/transcription/document_images/Vol01Scans/123_Jan-Feb1947_The%20Purpose%20of%20Education.pdf on January 11, 2020.

Kolencik, P. L., & Hillwig, S. A. (2011). *Encouraging metacognition: Supporting learners through metacognitive teaching strategies.* New York: Peter Lang.

Konigsburg, E. L. (2007). *From the mixed-up files of Mrs. Basil E. Frankweiler* (3rd ed.). New York: Simon and Schuster.

Kuhn, D., & Dean, D., Jr. (2004). Metacognition: A bridge between cognitive psychology and educational practice. *Theory Into Practice, 43*(4), 268–273.

Kuypers, L. M. (2011). *The zones of regulation: A curriculum designed to foster self-regulation and emotional control.* Santa Clara, CA: Think Social Publishing.

Lai, E. R. (2011). *Metacognition: A literature review.* Accessed at http://images.pearsonassessments.com/images/tmrs/Metacognition_Literature_Review_Final.pdf on February 7, 2021.

Leaf, C. (2013). *Switch on your brain: The key to peak happiness, thinking, and health.* Grand Rapids, MI: Baker Books.

Levine, G. C. (1997). *Ella enchanted.* New York: HarperCollins.

Lexico. (n.d.a). *Anxiety.* Accessed at www.lexico.com/definition/anxiety on August 6, 2020.

Lexico. (n.d.b). *Autonomy.* Accessed at www.lexico.com/definition/autonomy on August 6, 2020.

Lexico. (n.d.c). *Cognition.* Accessed at www.lexico.com/definition/cognition on August 6, 2020.

Louisiana Department of Education. (2018). *Leap 2025 mathematics: 2018 practice test—Grade 4.* Accessed at www.louisianabelieves.com/docs/default-source/assessment/leap-2025-grade-4-math-paper-practice-test.pdf?sfvrsn=3 on August 6, 2020.

Mackenzie, A. (n.d.). *Your reading comprehension tootlkit: Determining importance* [Blog post]. Accessed at https://bookpagez.com/blog/reading-comprehension-toolkit-determining-importance/ on August 6, 2020.

Marzano, R. J., Pickering, D. J., & Pollock, J. E. (2001). *Classroom instruction that works: Research-based strategies for increasing student achievement.* Alexandria, VA: Association for Supervision and Curriculum Development.

McGraw-Hill Education. (2018). *2018 social and emotional learning report.* Accessed at www.mheducation.com/prek-12/explore/sel-survey.html on March 7, 2020.

Miller, A. (1976). *Death of a salesman.* New York: Penguin.

Miller, D. (2002). *Reading with meaning: Teaching comprehension in the primary grades* (1st ed.). Portland, ME: Stenhouse.

Miracle Math Coaching. (2017, August 28). *Importance of kids learning to explain their math thinking.* Accessed at https://miracle mathcoaching.com/importance-kids-learning-explain-math-thinking on December 19, 2020.

Moats, L. C. (1998). Teaching decoding. *American Educator, 22*(1–2), 42–49, 95–96. Accessed at www.aft.org/sites/default/files /periodicals/moats.pdf on October 6, 2020.

Morin, A. (2017, November 3). *10 reasons teens have so much anxiety today* [Blog post]. Accessed at www.psychologytoday.com/us /blog/what-mentally-strong-people-dont-do/201711/10-reasons-teens-have-so-much-anxiety-today?page=1 on July 10, 2019.

Montessori, M. (1995). *The absorbent mind.* New York: Holt Paperbacks.

Morrow, L. M., & Gambrell, L. B [Eds.]. (2019). *Best practices in literacy instruction* (6th ed.) New York: The Guilford Press.

Mystery Science. (n.d.). *Why would a hawk move to New York city?* [Video file]. Accessed at https://mysteryscience.com/ecosystems /mystery-1/food-chains-predators-herbivores-carnivores/119 on September 14, 2020.

Narrol, H. G., & Giblon, S. T. (1984). *The fourth "R": Uncovering hidden learning potential.* Baltimore: University Park Press.

National Alliance on Mental Illness. (n.d.). *Mental health in schools.* Accessed at www.nami.org/Learn-More/Public-Policy/Mental -Health-in-Schools on August 10, 2019.

National Cancer Institute. (n.d.). *NCI dictionary of cancer terms.* Accessed at www.cancer.gov/publications/dictionaries/cancer -terms/expand/C on August 13, 2020.

National Council for the Social Studies. (n.d.). *National curriculum standards for social studies: Introduction.* Accessed at www.social studies.org/standards/introduction on January 18, 2020.

National Council of Teachers of Mathematics. (n.d.). *Algebra: Understand patterns, relations, and functions.* Accessed at www.nctm .org/Standards-and-Positions/Principles-and-Standards/Algebra on September 18, 2020.

National Governors Association Center for Best Practices & Council of Chief State School Officers. (2010a). *Common Core State Standards for English language arts and literacy in history/social studies, science, and technical subjects.* Washington, DC: Authors. Accessed at www.corestandards.org/assets/CCSSI_ELA%20Standards.pdf on October 16, 2020.

National Governors Association Center for Best Practices & Council of Chief State School Officers. (2010b). *Common Core State Standards for mathematics.* Washington, DC: Authors. Accessed at www.corestandards.org/assets/CCSSI_Math%20Standards .pdf on August 6, 2020.

National Reading Panel. (2000). *Teaching children to read: An evidence-based assessment of the scientific research literature on reading and its implications for reading instruction.* Washington, D.C.: National Institute of Child Health and Human Development.

National Research Council. (2000). *How people learn: Brain, mind, experience, and school* (Expanded ed.). Washington, DC: National Academy Press.

Neuroscientifically Challenged. (2015, September 1). *Know your brain: Cingulate cortex* [Blog post]. Accessed at www.neuroscientifically challenged.com/blog//know-your-brain-cingulate-cortex on February 16, 2020.

New Jersey Department of Education. (2014). *New Jersey student learning standards for social studies.* Accessed at www.state.nj.us /education/cccs/2014/ss/standards.pdf on September 3, 2020.

New Jersey Department of Education. (2020). *New Jersey student learning standards for social studies: Introduction.* Accessed at www.state.nj.us/education/cccs/2020/2020 NJSLS-SS.pdf on September 3, 2020.

New Jersey State Board of Education. (2017). *New Jersey social and emotional learning competencies and sub-competencies.* Accessed at www.nj.gov/education/students/safety/sandp/sel/SELCompetencies.pdf on September 3, 2020.

NGSS Lead States. (2013). *Next Generation Science Standards: For states, by states.* Washington, DC: National Academies Press.

Niemi, K. (2020). *Niemi: CASEL is updating the most widely recognized definition of social-emotional learning. Here's why.* Accessed at www.the74million.org/article/niemi-casel-is-updating-the-most-widely-recognized-definition-of-social-emotional-learning -heres-why on December 20, 2020.

Niezink, L., & Train, K. (2020). *The self in empathy: Self-empathy* [Blog post]. Accessed at www.psychologytoday.com/us/blog /empathic-intervision/202007/the-self-in-empathy-self-empathy on December 10, 2020.

Okon-Singer, H., Hendler, T., Pessoa, L., & Shackman, A. J. (2015). *The neurobiology of emotion-cognition interactions: Fundamental questions and strategies for future research.* Accessed at www.frontiersin.org/articles/10.3389/fnhum.2015.00058/full on September 15, 2020.

Organisation for Economic Co-operation and Development. (2018). *PISA 2015 results in focus.* Accessed at www.oecd.org/pisa/pisa-2015-results-in-focus.pdf on August 6, 2020.

Organisation for Economic Co-operation and Development. (2019). *Programme for International Student Assessment (PISA) results from PISA 2018.* Accessed at www.oecd.org/pisa/publications/PISA2018_CN_USA.pdf on August 6, 2020.

Palincsar, A. S., & Brown, A. L. (1984). Reciprocal teaching of comprehension-fostering and comprehension-monitoring activities. *Cognition and Instruction, 1*(2), 117–175.

Park, B. (2001). *Junie B. Jones, first grader (at last!).* New York: Random House.

Peak, C. S. (2015). *Linking mindset to metacognition.* Accessed at www.improvewithmetacognition.com/linking-mindset-metacognition on February 9, 2021.

Pearson, P. D., & Gallagher, G. (1983). The gradual release of responsibility model of instruction. *Contemporary Educational Psychology, 8*, 112–123.

Perkins, D. (1992). *Smart schools: Better thinking and learning for every child.* New York: Free Press.

Perkins, D. N., & Salomon, G. (1992a). *The science and art of transfer.* In A. L. Costa, J. Bellanca, & R. Fogarty (Eds.), If minds matter: A forward to the future (Vol. 1) (pp. 201–210). Palatine, IL: Skylight Publishing.

Perkins, D. N., & Salomon, G. (1992b). Transfer of Learning. *Contribution to the International Encyclopedia of Education*, Second Edition. Oxford, England: Pergamon Press.

Pintrich, P. R. (2002). The role of metacognitive knowledge in learning, teaching, and assessing. *Theory Into Practice, 41*(4), 219–225.

Polacco, P. (1998). *Thank you, Mr. Falker.* New York: Philomel Books.

Polaris Teen Center. (2018). *Important teen mental health statistics for parents.* Accessed at https://polaristeen.com/articles/teen-mental-health-stats on July 27, 2019.

Presseisen, B. Z., Sternberg, R. J., Fischer, K. W., Knight, C. C., & Feuerstein, R. (1990). *Learning and thinking styles: Classroom interaction.* Washington D.C.: National Education Association.

Price-Mitchell, M. (2015, April 7). *Metacognition: Nurturing self-awareness in the classroom* [Blog post]. Accessed at www.edutopia.org/blog/8-pathways-metacognition-in-classroom-marilyn-price-mitchell on July 18, 2017.

Programme for International Student Assessment. (2018). *Country overview: United States.* Accessed at www.compareyourcountry.org/pisa/country/usa?lg=en on December 14, 2020.

Pugalee, D. K. (2001). Writing, mathematics, and metacognition: Looking for connections through students' work in mathematical problem solving. *School Science and Mathematics, 101*(5). Accessed at http://link.galegroup.com/apps/doc/A76927405/PROF?u=23414_sjcpl&sid=PROF&xid=f178003c on August 25, 2018.

Purdue Online Writing Lab. (n.d.). *Aristotle's rhetorical situation.* Accessed at https://owl.purdue.edu/owl/general_writing/academic_writing/rhetorical_situation/aristotles_rhetorical_situation.html on September 3, 2020.

Reading Rockets. (n.d.). *Comprehension.* Accessed at www.readingrockets.org/helping/target/comprehension on August 7, 2020.

Reilly, N. N. (2017/2018). The bonds of social-emotional learning. *Educational Leadership, 75*(4), 56–60. Accessed at www.ascd.org/publications/educational_leadership/dec17/vol75/num04/The_Bonds_of_Social-Emotional_Learning.aspx on August 7, 2020.

Rhodes, S. (2019). How did you solve it? Metacognition in mathematics. *Teaching Students to Think About Thinking, 15*(7). Accessed at www.ascd.org/ascd-express/vol15/num07/how-did-you-solve-it-metacognition-in-mathematics.aspx on February 17, 2021.

Richmond, E. (2016, December 7). *How do American students compare to their international peers?* Accessed at www.theatlantic.com/education/archive/2016/12/how-do-american-students-compare-to-their-international-peers/509834/ on September 12, 2019.

Rose, R. (1955). *Twelve angry men*. New York: Bloomsbury.

Rutgers Social-Emotional and Character Development Lab. (n.d.). *STAT overview*. Accessed at www.secdlab.org/about-stat on March 17, 2020.

Schleicher, A. (2019). *PISA 2018: Insights and interpretations*. Accessed at www.oecd.org/pisa/PISA%202018%20Insights%20 and%20Interpretations%20FINAL%20PDF.pdf on August 21, 2020.

Scott, B. M., & Levy, M. G. (2013). Metacognition: Examining the components of a fuzzy concept. *Educational Research eJournal, 2*(2), 120–131. DOI: 10.5838/erej.2013.22.04

Shakespeare, W. (1994). *King Lear*. Mineola, NY: Dover. (Original work published 1608)

Shure, M. B. (2001). *I can problem solve: An interpersonal cognitive problem-solving program, preschool* (2nd ed.). Champaign, IL: Research Press.

Sipos, R. (2016). *Character and academics—how to integrate*. Accessed at https://exchange.character.org/character-and-academics -how-to-integrate on September 15, 2020.

Siwa, J. (2017). *JoJo's guide to the sweet life: #PeaceOutHaterz*. New York: Abrams.

Smith, S. (2018). *5-4-3-2-1 coping technique for anxiety* [Blog post]. Accessed at www.urmc.rochester.edu/behavioral-health -partners/bhp-blog/april-2018/5-4-3-2-1-coping-technique-for-anxiety.aspx on September 9, 2020.

Social and Character Development Research Consortium. (2010). *Efficacy of schoolwide programs to promote social and character development and reduce problem behavior in elementary school children (NCER 2011–2001)*. Washington, DC: National Center for Education Research. Accessed at https://ies.ed.gov/ncer/pubs/20112001 on October 16, 2020.

Sousa, D. A. (2001). *How the brain learns: A classroom teacher's guide* (2nd ed.). Thousand Oaks, CA: Corwin.

Stavros, J. M., Godwin, L. N., & Cooperrider, D. L. (2016). Appreciative inquiry: Organization development and the strengths revolution. In W. J. Rothwell, J. M. Stavros, & R. L. Sullivan (Eds.), *Practicing organization development: Leading transformation and change* (4th ed., pp. 96–116). Hoboken, NJ: Wiley.

Sterner, T. M. (2012). *The practicing mind: Developing focus and discipline in your life—Master any skill or challenge by learning to love the process*. Novato, CA: New World Library.

Stevens, S. O. (2012). *Dr. Goodreader: Teaching students to read metacognitively*. Scotts Valley, CA: CreateSpace.

Stevens, S. O. (2017). *The little golden book of metacognition*. Scotts Valley, CA: CreateSpace.

The Story of Mathematics. (n.d.). *Egyptian mathematics—Numbers & numerals*. Accessed at www.storyofmathematics.com /egyptian.html on August 6, 2020.

Suni, E. (2020). *Teens and sleep*. Accessed at www.sleepfoundation.org/articles/teens-and-sleep on August 7, 2020.

SUNY Empire State College. (n.d.). *Ethical responsibility*. Accessed at www.esc.edu/global-learning-qualifications-framework /learning-domains/ethical-responsibility on January 23, 2020.

Tanap, R. (2018, March 28). *Mental health conditions are legitimate health conditions* [Blog post]. Accessed at www.nami.org /Blogs/NAMI-Blog/March-2018/Mental-Health-Conditions-are-Legitimate-Health-Con on July 10, 2019.

Taylor, R. D., Oberle, E., Durlak, J. A., & Weissberg, R. P. (July/August 2017). Promoting positive youth development through school-based social and emotional learning interventions: A meta-analysis of follow-up effects. *Child Development, 88*(4), 1156–1171.

Tough, P. (2012). *How children succeed: Grit, curiosity and the hidden power of character*. New York: Houghton Mifflin Harcourt.

Twenge, J. M. (2017, September). *Have smartphones destroyed a generation?* Accessed at www.theatlantic.com/magazine/archive /2017/09/has-the-smartphone-destroyed-a-generation/534198/ on September 12, 2019.

The Understood Team. (n.d.). *What is executive function?* Accessed at www.understood.org/en/learning-attention-issues/child -learning-disabilities/executive-functioning-issues/understanding-executive-functioning-issues on August 7, 2020.

Veenman, M. V. J., van Hout-Wolters, B. H. A. M., & Afflerbach, P. (2006). Metacognition and learning: Conceptual and methodological considerations. *Metacognition and Learning, 1*(1), 3–14.

Verhoeven, C., Maes, S., Kraaij, V., & Joekes, K. (2003). The job demand-control-social support model and wellness/health outcomes: A European study. *Psychology & Health, 18*(4), 421–440.

Walker, M. (2019, April). *Sleep is your superpower* [Video file]. Accessed at www.ted.com/talks/matt_walker_sleep_is_your _superpower?language=en on August 7, 2020.

Wallace, J. B. (2019, September 26). *Students in high-achieving schools are now named an 'at-risk' group, study says.* Accessed at www.washingtonpost.com/lifestyle/2019/09/26/students-high-achieving-schools-are-now-named-an-at-risk-group/ on October 11, 2019.

Wells, D., & Legg, T. (2020). *Anxiety: Breathing problems and exercises.* Accessed at www.healthline.com/health/anxiety /anxiety-breathing on November 29, 2020.

White, E. B. (2014). *Charlotte's web.* New York: Penguin Random House. (Original work published 1958)

White, T. H. (2016). *The once and future king.* New York: Penguin Books.

Wiggins, G. (2012a, January 16). *The research on transfer and some practical implications (transfer, part 2)* [Blog post]. Accessed at grantwiggins.wordpress.com/2012/01/16/the-research-on-transfer-and-some-practical-implications-transfer-part-2 on July 18, 2017.

Wiggins, G. (2012b, January 11). *Transfer as the point of education* [Blog post]. Accessed at grantwiggins.wordpress.com/2012 /01/11/transfer-as-the-point-of-education/ on January 19, 2019.

Wiggins, G. (2015a, March 31). *On literacy and strategy, part 6: My first cut at recommendations* [Blog post]. Accessed at grantwiggins.wordpress.com/2015/03/31/on-literacy-and-strategy-part-6-my-first-cut-at-recommendations/ on August 7, 2020.

Wiggins, G. (2015b, April 20). *On transfer as the goal in literacy (7th in a series)* [Blog post]. Accessed at grantwiggins.wordpress.com /2015/04/20/on-transfer-as-the-goal-in-literacy-7th-in-a-series/ on December 23, 2019.

Wilson, D., & Conyers, M. (2016). *Teaching students to drive their brains: Metacognitive strategies, activities, and lesson ideas.* Alexandria, VA: Association for Supervision and Curriculum Development.

WISE Channel. (2013, October 25). *Stop teaching calculating, start learning maths!—Conrad Wolfram* [Video file]. Accessed at www.youtube.com/watch?v=xYONRn3EbYY on July 18, 2019.

Yancey, K. B. (1998). *Reflection in the writing classroom.* Logan, UT: Utah State University Press.

Yancey, K. B., Robertson, L., & Taczak. K. (2014). *Writing across contexts: Transfer, composition, and sites of writing.* Boulder, CO: University Press of Colorado.

youcubed. (n.d.) *Painted cube.* Accessed at www.youcubed.org/tasks/painted-cube on October 22, 2020.

youcubed. (2018). *Squares & more squares: Grades 6–8.* Accessed at www.youcubed.org/wp-content/uploads/2019/08/WIM -Squares-and-More-Squares-Grades-6-8.pdf on December 14, 2020.

Yousafzai, M. (2013). *I am Malala: The girl who stood up for education and was shot by the Taliban.* London: Weidenfeld & Nicolson.

Yousafzai, M. (2014). *Malala Yousafzai—Nobel lecture.* Accessed at www.nobelprize.org/prizes/peace/2014/yousafzai/26074 -malala-yousafzai-nobel-lecture-2014 on September 3, 2020.

Zhang, J. (2018, February). The metacognitive strategy in English listening comprehension. *Theory and Practice in Language Studies, 8*(2), 226–231.

Zohar, A., & Barzilai, S. (2013). A review of research on metacognition in science education: Current and future directions. *Studies in Science Education, 49*(2), 121–169.

Index

Mindfulness Practices
Christine Mason, Michele M. Rivers Murphy, and Yvette Jackson
Build compassionate school communities that prioritize high levels of learning and high levels of well-being. Based on the latest neuroscience research, *Mindfulness Practices* details how to use mindfulness to transform the way educators teach and students learn in prekindergarten through high school.
BKF833

Transformative Teaching
Kathleen Kryza, MaryAnn Brittingham, and Alicia Duncan
Examine the most effective strategies for leading diverse students to develop the skills they need inside and outside the classroom. By understanding and exploring students' emotional, cultural, and academic needs, educators will be better prepared to help *all* students become lifelong learners.
BKF623

Two-for-One Teaching
Lauren Porosoff and Jonathan Weinstein
In *Two-for-One Teaching*, authors Lauren Porosoff and Jonathan Weinstein outline how to seamlessly incorporate social-emotional learning into academic classrooms. Empower students to discover what matters to them using research-based strategies that foster agency, community, self-reflection, and vitality in the classroom.
BKF923

The Wraparound Guide
Leigh Colburn and Linda Beggs
Your school has the power to help students overcome barriers to well-being and achievement—from mental health issues to substance abuse to trauma. With this timely guide, discover actionable steps for launching and sustaining wraparound services embedded within your school that support the whole child.
BKF956

Behavior Solutions
John Hannigan, Jessica Djabrayan Hannigan, Mike Mattos, and Austin Buffum
Take strategic action to close the systemic behavior gap with *Behavior Solutions*. This user-friendly resource outlines how to utilize the PLC at Work® and RTI at Work™ processes to create a three-tiered system of supports that is collaborative, research-based, and practical.
BKF891

Solution Tree | Press · a division of · Solution Tree

Visit SolutionTree.com or call 800.733.6786 to order.

Wait! Your professional development journey doesn't have to end with the last pages of this book.

We realize improving student learning doesn't happen overnight. And your school or district shouldn't be left to puzzle out all the details of this process alone.

No matter where you are on the journey, we're committed to helping you get to the next stage.

Take advantage of everything from **custom workshops** to **keynote presentations** and **interactive web and video conferencing**. We can even help you develop an action plan tailored to fit your specific needs.

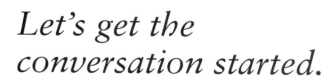

Let's get the conversation started.

Call 888.763.9045 today.

 SolutionTree.com